THE POLITICAL ECONOMY OF MIDDLE EAST PEACE

Discussions of the Middle East peace process have tended to focus narrowly on political-diplomatic preconditions for conflict resolution. This collection, based on new empirical research, is unique in examining the Arab and Israeli negotiations process through an analysis of the political economy of regional trade.

The contributors investigate the ways in which trade regimes have developed in the region as a result of agreements reached between the Arab states and Israel and of the direction of labor and import–export flows between the Levant and the Gulf States. Subjects discussed include:

- economic diplomacy in the region;
- the influence of core conglomerates on Israeli elections;
- economic discrimination in Israel;
- the economics of human rights abuses in Palestine;
- economic reconstruction in Lebanon;
- regional patterns after the cold war.

Based on the controversial view that trade relations rather than politics are driving events related to the Middle East peace process, the authors argue that the failure to consider conflicting trade agendas has led to stagnation in the peace process and has reinforced rather than reduced diplomatic barriers to security in the region. This volume will be of interest to students and researchers in international economics, Middle East studies and political economy, as well as officials working on international commercial and government policy.

J. W. Wright, Jr. is a Diplomacy Fellow for the American Association for the Advancement of Science and an Advisor to the Rule of Law Team at the United States Agency for International Development's Centre for Democracy and Governance. Before that he was a Business Development Specialist at the Dubai Chamber of Commerce and Industry, as well as a Fulbright Scholar in Jordan and the United Arab Emirates. He is the author of *Business Development in Saudi Arabia* (Macmillan, 1996) and the editor of *Saudi Arabia: Tradition and Transition* (Hayden-McNeil, 1993).

ROUTLEDGE FRONTIERS OF POLITICAL ECONOMY

THE POLITICAL ECONOMY OF MIDDLE EAST PEACE

The impact of competing trade agendas

Edited by
J. W. Wright, Jr.

London and New York

First published 1999
by Routledge
11 New Fetter Lane, London EC4P 4EE

Simultaneously published in the USA and Canada
by Routledge
29 West 35th Street, New York, NY 10001

Selection and editorial matter © 1999 J. W. Wright, Jr.
Individual chapters © 1999 individual contributors
Technical assistance provided by Joann Shams

Typeset in Baskerville by Routledge
Printed and bound in Great Britain by TJ International Ltd, Padstow, Cornwall

British Library Cataloguing in Publication Data
A catalogue record for this book is available from the British Library

Library of Congress Cataloging in Publication Data
A catalogue record for this book has been requested.

ISBN 0–415–18395–2

DEDICATION

On maps that mattered, there were – and always would be – borders
between countries. The precise line of demarcation might shift with
events, but the fact that such lines existed would not. Of this,
government leaders were quietly and confidently aware. But they
were wrong. In some companies – and in most governments – there
is a gap of more than a century between the cross-border realities of
the external world and the framework of ideas and principles used to
make sense of them. Old ideas, old expressions die hard. And the
more obvious and matter of fact they seem, the harder they die. The
century-long gap between intention and result cannot be closed by
better execution or implementation. Nothing can close it. The principles themselves have to change.

Kenichi Ohmae, *The End of the Nation State:*
The Rise of Regional Economies

And so it is in the Middle East, a region where borders were never
what they seemed, and where the principles that demarcated nation-
states were based on very old ideas and expressions. This book is
dedicated to those who are trying to change these ancient and prejudicial principles so that peace can be secured.

J. W. Wright, Jr.

CONTENTS

ILLUSTRATIONS

Tables

Figures

CONTRIBUTORS

Shimshon Bichler is a Lecturer in Political Science at the Yezreel Academic College, Israel. His recent work focuses on the political implications of resource transfers made during the Arab–Israeli peace process, with special attention given to the ways voters' perceptions about economic issues affect the outcomes of Israeli elections. He has published widely on related topics in Israel and in the West in both Hebrew and English.

Laura Drake is a Middle East academic and consultant specializing in the region's political-military and strategic affairs. At present she teaches international relations and Middle East politics at the American University in Washington, DC. Her recent research includes analyses of the military and political aspects of the Arab–Israeli conflict, the results of the United States containment strategies against Iraq and Iran, and the issue of unconventional weapons proliferation in the Middle East region.

Shaul M. Gabbay is a Lecturer at the William Davidson Faculty of Industrial Engineering and Management, Technion – Israel Institute of Technology. He formerly taught sociology at the University of Illinois in Chicago. He has authored *Social Capital in the Creation of Financial Capital* (1997) and co-edited *Corporate Social Capital: Networks for Strategy, Marketing, Human Resources, and Entrepreneurship* (forthcoming).

Imad Harb teaches in the Department of Political Science at the University of Utah, where he specializes in Middle East Studies and where his research focuses on the political economy of Lebanon's relationship with Syria and Israel. Before this he taught at San Francisco State University. Harb is currently writing a book on the Lebanese political system's reaction to reconstruction in the face of aggression from its neighbors.

Noah Lewin-Epstein is a Professor of Sociology and Director of the Institute for Social Research at Tel Aviv University. He, along with Moshe Semoyanov, has authored *Hewers of Wood and Drawers of Water*, a study of Arabs in the occupied territories, and *The Arab Minority in Israel's*

Economy: Patterns of Ethnic Inequality, a study of the economic, occupational and socio-political positions of Arab Israeli citizens living in Israel.

Robert E. Looney is a Professor of National Security Affairs at the Naval Postgraduate School in Monterey, California. He has also served as a Development Economist at the Stanford Research Institute and taught at the University of California at Davis. He has also been an advisor to several governments, including Iran and Saudi Arabia. He has a forth-coming book on *Saudi Arabia's Economic Challenge* (Edward Elgar, 1999).

Davy H. McCall is currently the Chair of the Department of Economics at Washington College in Chertertown, Maryland. Dr. McCall has spent the majority of his career directing economic development projects in the Middle East. He was the U.S. Agency for International Development's (USAID) Capital Development Officer in Syria, and has worked on economic development projects and served in various capacities for World Bank programs in Jordan, Israel, Lebanon, and North Africa.

Jonathan Nitzan is both a scholar and a commercial analyst. He is Assistant Professor of International Political Economy at York University, Canada. He is a writer for the publication *Emerging Market Analyst*, and works with the Montreal-based Bank Analyst Research Group, a financial services and investment firm. His publications in academic journals focus on the changing structures of trade in developing countries. He has been a particularly prolific writer on Israeli industrial change in the 1990s.

Moshe Semoyanov is the Chair of the Sociology Department at Tel Aviv University and Professor of Sociology at the University of Illinois in Chicago. He, along with Noah Lewin-Epstein, has authored *Hewers of Wood and Drawers of Water*, a study of Arabs in the occupied territories, and *The Arab Minority in Israel's Economy: Patterns of Ethnic Inequality*, a study of the economic and occupational positions of Arab Israeli citizens.

Amy J. Stein is currently a consultant at Hewitt Associates, Lincolnshire, Illinois, where she specializes in conflict resolution, change management, and organizational development. She holds both a Masters in Arts in Middle Eastern Studies and a Masters of Business Administration from the University of Chicago.

George Wilson received his doctorate from Cornell University in 1955, and has since served as an economics advisor during the administrations of Presidents Kennedy, Johnson, Nixon, and Ford. Wilson has 145 publications to his credit, including several books and over 100 articles, predominantly on transportation systems and more recently on global business patterns. He is currently a Distinguished Emeritus Professor of Business Economics and Public Policy at Indiana University.

J. W. Wright, Jr. specializes in Arab regional economic relations and inter-regional commercial diplomacy. He is a member of the Committee for Rule of Law at the United States Agency for International Development (USAID) and a Diplomacy Fellow for the American Association for the Advancement of Science. This project was completed while working as a Fulbright Regional Research Scholar at the United States Information Service (USIS) in Abu Dhabi and the Juma Al Majid Centre for Culture and Heritage on Dubai.

Fatemeh Ziai wrote her contribution to this volume while she was Counsel at the Human Rights Watch/Middle East, where she covered Israel, the West Bank, and the Gaza Strip. A graduate of the Harvard Law School, she has recently joined the United Nations, where she also works with human rights issues. Ms. Ziai is currently on assignment in Bosnia, working with the United Nations' efforts to bring peace to that region.

PROLOGUE

I have been involved with the economic aid and development process in the Middle East for over thirty years, at some points working for the U.S. Agency for International Development (USAID), at other times for the World Bank, and on other occasions as an academic or a consultant. Before that, I studied economic development in John Kenneth Galbraith's first class on that subject. It was there that I realized how important trade relations were to diplomacy.

Shortly after that I went to South Asia, then to the Middle East, and saw that his words rang true in both of these troubled regions. What has always struck me about the Middle East is the people's tenacity for trading, as well as the goodwill that commercial relationships develop between groups living throughout the region. For example, the most successful tourist souvenir/antique shop in Damascus is a partnership owned by an Iranian-Jewish family and a family of Palestinian-Muslim refugees. In Arabia the prospects of good business can bring together members of hostile nations, patrons of rival tribes, and people espousing variant religious beliefs.

Unfortunately, while trading partnerships may have survived over the centuries, prosperity has floundered under the hostile regimes that have characterized recent decades. As we look toward a new century, in which we hope Arab and Jewish governments function in peace, we must hope that business people can reopen contacts between Israel and its Arab neighbors; merchants in both areas are actively prospecting for commercial opportunities with each other. Assuming that Middle East peace becomes more firmly established, with the passage of time strong trading ties can be redeveloped. A successful record of mutually beneficial commercial trading will be essential for regional economic integration, and for the wounds of war to heal.

Thus, in addition to overcoming deep political and religious hostilities, as well as significant mutual distrust among the people living in the region, major economic obstacles must also be overcome in order for the peace process to survive. Some of these obstacles include rivalries over the region's scarce resources, huge disparities in earnings capacities, and the achievement of cooperation on technological advancement. Nevertheless, with mutual economic motivation, time, and historic relationships to support new commercial ties, there are enough Israelis and Arabs with enterprising minds, perseverance, and imagination to create trading ties of mutual benefit. As these new opportunities are opened through the continuing process of peace-building, the importance of the politics of trade will become increasingly evident to everyone.

Davy H. McCall

ACKNOWLEDGMENTS

Many people have helped me throughout the process of developing and editing this collection. Most recently, Joann Shams has spent many hours reading the chapters, commenting on their content, and helping me edit the text. The authors of the individual chapters, of course, have not only made significant contributions to the book, but have also been helpful and patient through the production process. Among this group, Laura Drake has provided particularly strong support for my work. Alison Kirk and her staff at Routledge have also been very good people to work with.

Much of the work on the collection was done while I was living in Dubai and working as a J. William Fulbright Research Scholar and a United States Information Service (USIS–Abu Dhabi) Visiting Scholar. The staff of the Council for the International Exchange of Scholars (CIES) deserve acknowledgment for helping me to get the most out of the Fulbright experience. In the region, special notes of thanks need to be made to Jonathan Rice, Nadia Ibrahim, Margaret Hamood, and Attullah Hooshang in Abu Dhabi; Aida Dabass in Amman; and Gary Garrison and David Adams in Washington, DC. During my Fulbright year I was assigned to the Juma Al Majid Centre for Culture and Heritage. Dr. Obaid Bin Butti, Fawzi Khoury, and their staffs were not only helpful, but also gracious and supportive throughout.

Several other people have given general support to me while I was working on this project. In Dubai, Willie Fainsan helped me gather research material at the Al Majid Centre, and helped me to organize this work at various stages in the process. Mr. Mohammed Abdulrahman Clyde Leamaster read several drafts of my chapter, and it is stronger because of his thoughts and comments. Nahla Kasrawi at the Dubai Chamber of Commerce and Industry also provided (and provides) significant support for my research efforts. While I was in Jordan, Jaraolav Stetkevych and Suzanne Pinckney Stetkevych helped to keep me sane during a period when I was keeping a less-than-sane writing, research, and travel schedule. I also appreciate Alan Douglas and Fedwa Malti-Douglas's early support for this project. John Presley and Rodney Wilson also deserve thanks for their ongoing support of my academic interests, as do Allen Omoto, Mary Schmidt,

Michael Stevenson, Mary Willis, and J. Wayne Wright, all of whom visited me in Dubai in order to help me organize programs so that we could present our research. M. Diane Wright and the rest of my family deserve thanks for supporting my work.

A final note of thanks goes to Dr. John Kenneth Galbraith, who supported the project through his correspondence. Unfortunately, he had fallen ill by the time of this writing. All contributors to this work hope he enjoys the final product and wish him a speedy recovery.

INTRODUCTION[1]

J. W. Wright, Jr.

On October 24, 1998 the *Washington Post* reported on a "Netanyahu, Arafat Accord." It called the accord "a remarkable chapter of personal diplomacy" for Bill Clinton. President Clinton himself said that brokering the agreement was party of "my job as president, my mission as a Christian, and my personal journey of atonement." On *Face the Nation*, Secretary of State Madeleine Albright and the commentators around her called this a "personal political victory" for the key negotiators. Patrick Buchanan offered similar commentary on *The McGlaughlin Group*.

The important linkages here are that the spectacles through which the peace process is being viewed are only personal and political, and not pragmatic and practical. Few new accords were reached – most of what was agreed to had already been recorded in other pacts or protocols, and no steps toward implementation were guaranteed; to talk more was about all the agreement really required. "Personal agendas" aside, the sustainability of the accord quickly founders because it fails to address economic realities that plague the peace process. It is very likely that, on the ground, this agreement will expedite rather than slow the rise of tempers between Israelis and Palestinians. Thus, while rhetoric alone may save the day – or at least serve to avert attention away from the day's other problems – it will not create peace. Both politicians and pundits seem to have, once again, missed the point: peace is unsustainable as long as issues related to commerce and corruption are continually side-stepped in negotiations or in the implementation of plans.

The purpose of this book is to reveal the relationships between politics and competing trade agendas with direct reference to the Arab–Israeli peace process. The relationships between trade and political processes have not been adequately considered in literature about Middle East diplomacy, or writing on regional economic integration. The result has been that far too often negotiators and others in the region have allowed rhetoric rather than reality to control their actions and perceptions. The further result is that progress in the peace process has been impeded by peoples and polities wanting to avoid discussions of real issues. In the process, scantly qualified

1

individuals, political alliances, and even radical fundamentalist forces have been able to assert themselves as being more important than they should be. In some places they have even taken control, which has admittedly made them important, but it did not have to be this way.

A personal experience I had in mid-1997 may be illustrative. A few months before the 1997 Economic Summit I gave a series of lectures in Doha, Qatar on economic barriers to peace. Before I arrived, my sponsor received a request from the Israeli trade representative to meet me. I agreed and a dinner party was arranged. In addition to the two of us, a Qatari government official was also invited. Before accepting, he felt he needed to get permission from his director, who felt he needed to consult the minister, who felt permission needed to be taken from the Emir, who gave his permission on the proviso that one of his leading advisors, a relative, attend the dinner. Hearing this, an ambassador invited himself to the dinner.

To place this event in better context, and in contrast, I was also asked to come to the Japanese Embassy to meet with their commercial attaché. He wanted to know how Japanese corporations could best position themselves at the Doha Summit. He noted that if one looks at Qatar's import/export figures one sees that trade relations with Japan and other Asian states are major concerns. We needed no chaperones and even decided to have lunch the next day. In both instances, we had productive conversations even though no ambassadors attended or gave us permission to talk.

My dinner party had became a diplomatic event, even though I personally have no influence in regional diplomacy or politics. More importantly, neither does the Israeli trade representative. He seemed nice, intelligent, and interesting, but in the end he is only an upscaled salesman – a trade representative trying to push Israeli products. Given the topic of my lecture, he probably wanted to see if I was pro- or anti-Israeli, full stop. My guess is that he did not have to ask permission from anyone before initiating the dinner because doing this sort of thing was part of his job as a salesman. Rather, he was made important by the Arab side's assumption that he had state-level influence. This assumption and the approval process that came with it gave the man a much higher profile than he needed to be given.

The point of this symposium had been missed; the pragmatics lost. Or had it? Is it valid to assume that the Israeli trade delegate lacks real influence? Maybe not. But if he has influence it is commercial and not political. Thus I thought a turnabout in thinking needed to take place when the Arab Gulf Cooperation Council (GCC) states were determining whether or not they should boycott the Doha Economic Summit. To do so was a mistake. For one thing, political dialogues are much more easily broken than are trade regimes. Missing the summit was therefore a less than casual walk into the Israeli trap. Israel wanted to meet the GCC states on an individual basis rather than at the summit because to meet them en masse would have meant losing control of the agenda. By arranging it so that they could meet Arab business leaders on an individual basis, Israeli representatives were able to talk trade and not politics, and they could more firmly develop contracts with merchants who have influence on government leaders. Such a web of commercial ties would not so easily be broken. All the while, the Israeli government could avoid dialogue on inflammatory issues. *Ergo*, to miss the summit played directly into Israel's divide-and-conquer strategy.

Moreover, "Israel itself has little strategic interest in promoting a form of inter-Arab cooperation that does not center around itself, for it would then run the risk of inadvertently providing the catalyst for a new pan-Arabism" (Chapter 1). Thus it becomes strategically important for Israel to intervene in (or stop) economic negotiations that might allow the Arab states to reach cooperative agreements which could strengthen the intra-Arab position and/or exclude Israel from both commercially profitable and politically beneficial patterns of trade. Of course there is little threat that Egypt, Jordan, and Lebanon (even Syria) could form trade alliances that could negate an Israeli presence in the region. These states have neither the power, the funds, nor the geostrategic positions to make such a system work. However, the GCC states have all the above, and *could* therefore build strong cooperative commercial and corporate networks. This made breaking up the only economic summit to be held in the Gulf as part of the regional peace process a crucial part of the Israeli trade agenda.

The road to Middle East peace has been plagued by dinner parties like the one held for me in Doha. The political spectrum has identified people as influential who need not be made important. Practicality and reality seem to have eluded the diplomatic realm in the peace process. For example, was it such a coincidence that the Dubai air show, the second largest aerospace show in the world, finished the day before the Doha Summit began? Probably not, in a region that spends four times the per-capita average on military hardware (see Chapter 8). Few people benefit from these arms sales. It will be a shame if the arms dealers and rhetoricians continue to dominate negotiations. This will help neither the Palestinians nor most Israelis.

John Kenneth Galbraith warned us nearly thirty years ago about the impact of inequities being developed in the Middle East. He observed, in *Economics, Peace and Laughter*, that "circumstances and politics have given us different and relentlessly hostile friends and clients in the Middle East,"[2] and he asked American diplomats "to distrust the man who blames on revolutionaries what should be attributed to deprivation."[3] Few people would argue that these statements are any less valid today. Indeed, his predictions have come to pass with tragic ends – the intifada (uprising), the Gulf war, and the violence on the ground in Israel are all reflections of frustrated people faced with serious economic deprivation and commercial chaos.

In addition, Galbraith's essay on "Economics and the quality of life" offered crucial insights that could be applied to Arab–Israeli negotiations both then and now. First, they show us that "the test of economic achievement is not how much we produce but what we do to make life tolerable and pleasant."[4] Second, they illustrate how and why, "among the poor, only religion, with its promise of a later munificence for those who endure deprivation with patience, has been competitive with economic circumstances in shaping the general character of the social, political, and spiritual processes of life."[5] Peace and laughter, he claims, are found in economies with relatively equitable distributions of food, water, wealth, and social tolerance. From Galbraith's perspective, sustainable peace is therefore built on complementary trade, and persistent conflict is founded on biased commercial structures that leave standards of living unbearably low. Thus, for peace to be sustained the welfare of the dominating population (or political forces) must be balanced against the misfortune of those left without opportunities.[6]

Unfortunately, the Arab–Israeli conflict has created situations in which economic sources of conflict are endemic to failures in the Middle East peace process; there are few tolerable and pleasant circumstances remaining in the Israeli occupied territories, tiny fragments of which are now administered by the Palestinian Authority (PA). Indeed, diplomats' failures to recognize the destructive nature of the economic inequalities between Arabs and Israelis perpetuate ongoing conflict in the West Bank and Gaza. Similar contentions have been made about legal inequities and their effect on peace.[7] While massive amounts of aid are being sent to the region, observers are compelled to question whether or not these funds are being distributed in ways that will promote peaceful economic integration, and whether or not diplomats are willing to write plans toward changing powerful institutional structures that profit from conflict. Even if they are, will these changes have an impact great enough to overcome the numerous practical issues that impede countries' willingness fully to support the peace process: declining oil revenues, excessive labor-force growth, overburdening civil service payrolls, and budgetary systems dependent on military transfers?

None of the contributors to this collection would dispute the fact that the region's political environment presents an overpowering impediment to achieving regional peace. The positions presented here posit that along with each of the political wars to be won there is a series of economic battles being fought. A "debate" framework encompasses the volume because the contributors do not entirely agree on the strength of, for example, corporate agendas in the peace process. This will become apparent from the positions taken by Laura Drake and myself in the first two chapters, which are continuations of a long-standing debate between the two of us, in public print and in private conversations, about the roles economics and politics play in regional relations. She believes that "political considerations overwhelm economics even when the economic situation is desperate." I

4

tend to believe that people reconcile themselves to oppressive political structures until their economic situation becomes desperate, at which point they have a motive for radical behavior. My chapter asserts that "the remaining obstacles to peace revolve around conflicting budgetary, labor, and social services agendas, which are the real impediments to peace" (Chapter 2).

In all honesty, most of the chapters in this volume support Drake's point more clearly than they support mine. Who wins the debate will be up to the readers. The structural point to be made about the book is that we debate the impact of trade agendas on the peace process, while not necessarily coming to the same conclusions. Our approaches are also heterogeneous. However, when the contributors illustrate what they believe makes the region's diplomatic environment so harsh they each note that negatively constructed and competing trade agendas make the situation worse. We also contest the notion that the writing of purely political solutions will allow sustainable peace to be developed. In each chapter, some written by economists and others written by political scientists and international relations scholars, the conclusion reached is that competing trade agendas greatly affect progress in the Arab–Israeli peace process.

Structurally, the book is divided into three parts. Part 1 sets out the general debate over the greater influence of economics and politics in the peace process. Part 2 includes four chapters which in combination illustrate the impacts of national trade agendas on the peace process. Part 3 draws into the argument two additional factors that have an impact on the peace process's legitimacy: Syria's influence on the fight between Lebanon and Israel, and the detrimental role declining Gulf States' budgets, evidenced most clearly by Saudi Arabia, play in the GCC's support of the peace process. The Epilogue discusses the fall of the Soviet Union and the end of the cold war – without which the peace process would not have been possible.

In Chapter 1 Laura Drake demonstrates how the Israeli vision of "normalization" is seen in terms of "regional cooperation" in the economic realm. This is, she claims, a vision based on a coercive-cooperative process which the Arab regimes cannot embrace without facing unacceptable risk to both their political livelihoods and to their countries' economic structures, which the Israelis clearly want to change and dominate. Thus sustainable progress toward peace is to some extent dependent on certain "economic, cultural, and interpersonal" changes originating in the Arab states. Drake further posits that the dire economic situations which have intensified over the past decade have simply become additional obstacles to ongoing efforts toward political solutions for a long-standing conflict.

My argument is influenced by a heterogeneous set of economic thinkers, ranging from institutionalists like John Kenneth Galbraith to neoclassicists such as Gary Becker and post-Keynesians such as William Darity. In

Chapter 2 my triad of references to this economic literature helps to sustain an argument that there are columns of competing trade agendas which impede peace process negotiations, and rows of political and corporate executives who have significant vested interests in keeping markets in Arab Israeli territories less than fair and less than free. I contend that it is the poor economic conditions of the people and the people who profit from these conditions which are most to blame for failures in the peace process.

Part 2 begins with two articles on the Israeli economic structure. The first (Chapter 3), by Jonathan Nitzan and Shimshon Bichler, presents an argument about the ultimate influence of Israel's core conglomerates on the peace process. This chapter, more academic in style than those in Part 1, is best characterized as a neo-Marxist/post-Keynesian analysis of the industrial regimes which have developed in Israel since the late 1960s. The authors claim that a fundamental transition has taken place in the Israeli economic structure that places it at odds with a peacetime political agenda. They rely on the idea that both "depth" and "breadth" are lacking in Israel"s capital-accumulation markets, which are so heavily tied to "militarized" production cycles that they cannot afford to support the transition into a peacetime economy. They further argue that decision-making in Israel is mired in the subjugation of the private economy to that of a public sector which profits from aid and industrial transfers which might be lost in an era of peace. Thus movements toward "peace and regional integration" are unlikely.

Chapters 4 and 5 deal with issues which arise from severely biased labor-market systems in Israel and the Palestinian territories. Noah Lewin-Epstein, Moshe Semoyanov, and I (Chapter 4) illustrate the ways in which Jewish employers benefit economically from discrimination against Arab workers. We go on to explain that, "while lower income-voters see the most intense threat from Arab workers, it is the elite that gain the most from the status quo." Fatimeh Ziai (Chapter 5) then shows the effect Israeli human rights violations have on Palestinian workers. She also discusses the new problems caused by PA human rights violations. This chapter demonstrates well how collective punishments, such as repeated border closures and the mass detention of suspected political dissidents, have increased an already high unemployment rate and further impoverished people whose sole existence depends on those who have occupied their homeland.

In Chapter 6 Shaul M. Gabbay and Amy J. Stein take us back to the issues of economic relations and the Arab–Israeli conflict. It endeavors to explain why previous attempts at creating common markets in the Middle East have failed. It then attempts to establish a framework within which regional integration can be set in place. The authors show how development of regional infrastructure projects which involve both Arab and Israeli upstream and downstream participation could serve to lessen the distrust that paralyzes the peace process.

Part 3 includes two chapters which might seem to be diversions from the text, except that they provide evaluations of situations peace process nego-tiators must face to the north and south. The fact is that peace in the region is unlikely to be sustained if it is not extended to southern Lebanon. Imad Harb's chapter (Chapter 7) analyzes the current economic situation in Lebanon, and in so doing illustrates how and why the Lebanese position toward peace negotiations is so closely tied to that of Syria. Moreover, he examines the status of Palestinian refugees in southern areas as a means of evaluating the prospects for both economic revival and political stability in Lebanon. In contrast, Robert E. Looney's chapter (Chapter 8) concentrates on the economic problems faced in the Gulf region, with primary attention paid to the budget situations faced by the Saudi regime. He argues that economic growth in Saudi Arabia has diminished greatly since the Gulf war and that this factor threatens to reduce significantly the Kingdom's economic influence in the region; that the Saudi system's "diminishing returns" have led to diminishing power. The implication is simply that Saudi Arabia not only does not want to, but indeed cannot afford to spend additional resources supporting the Arab–Israeli peace process.

The collection is concluded with an Epilogue by George Wilson, one of the world's more prominent economists during the height of the cold war era. His essay reflects this position, and provides a lucid illustration of why the peace process would not have been possible without the demise of the Soviet Union and the subsequent end to the cold war. Now, he claims, we must add to the history of economic ideas the notion that political solutions to ongoing conflicts cannot be sustained unless commercial and monetary morality is in place, as is evidenced by the peace process.

There is significant resistance to the view that negotiators in the Arab–Israeli peace process could be so influenced by mercantilism. By the end of the book we hope you will agree that such naivety is unfortunate, and may not serve anyone's best interests; the failure to see economic decline as an engine for political conflict is akin to blaming revolutionary forces for problems arising from economic deprivation.[8] This perspective does not discount the fact that radical forces are impeding progress toward peace. (The cynic might even claim that radical forces are playing directly into the hands of politicians wanting to use downtime in the peace process to enhance the biased trade regimes they are trying to establish.) Neither does this view negate the opportunities that can be seen for building fairer and freer regional markets. Rather, it sees an equitable distribution of the gains to be made from market development as the real foundation of sustainable peace. Just weeks before this book was published, I attended a briefing at the U.S. State Department where an extremely high level official at USAID stated that "the agency no longer uses aid distributions to promote American security interests." The Middle East specialists in the room were as surprised to hear the admission of the policy as we were to learn is of its demise. We remain dubious. But the briefing leads me to believe that the final question may be as follows: While creating new aid and trade alliances is clearly in the best interests of the stronger nations participating in the process, will these wealthy players share the benefits of increased trade with the region's poor?

By their nature, our chapters may be seen as presenting controversial perspectives on sensitive topics. However, creating controversy for its own sake is not our goal. Rather, we hope to convince readers that the commercial economic side of the region's diplomatic equation has received far too little attention, and that, as a result, inequitable trade regimes have developed and been maintained which significantly impede peace-building. On this final point, all of the contributors agree. Moreover, we hope that our collective efforts on this book will contribute to reversing this trend, and that you will find it informative, interesting, thought-provoking and persuasive.

Notes

1 This introduction was greatly enhanced by the comments of an anonymous reader who reviewed the manuscript. Many of the reader's comments have been directly incorporated into the texts. The editor wishes to thank her/him for this contribution. Alison Kirk, Barbara Duke, Lisa Williams and Andreja also have my appreciation for their work on the book.
2 John Kenneth Galbraith, "Foreign policy: plain lessons of a bad decade," in *Economics, Peace, and Laughter*, Boston, MA: Houghton Mifflin, 1971: 169–70.
3 John Kenneth Galbraith, "Poverty and the way people behave," in *Economics, Peace, and Laughter*: 223.
4 John Kenneth Galbraith, "Economics and the quality of life," in *Economics, Peace, and Laughter*: 4–5.
5 *Ibid.*: 5.
6 *Ibid.*: 4–6.
7 Elia Zureik, Fouad Mougrabi, and Vincent F. Sacco, "Perceptions of legal inequalities in deeply divided societies: the case of Israel," *International Journal of Middle East Studies* 25(3) (1993): 423–42.
8 See also Ahmed S. Khalidi, "Security in a final Middle East settlement: some components of Palestinian national security," *International Affairs* 71(1) (1995): 1–18.

Part I

REGIONAL AGENDAS

1

ARAB–ISRAELI RELATIONS IN A NEW MIDDLE EAST ORDER

The politics of economic cooperation

Laura Drake

> In peaceful conditions we could imagine communications running from Haifa to Beirut and Damascus in the north, to Amman and beyond in the east, and to Cairo in the south....The Middle East, lying athwart three continents, could become a busy centre of air communications, which are now impeded by boycotts and the necessity to take circuitous routes. Radio, telephone and postal communications, which now end abruptly in mid-air, would unite a divided region.
>
> Abba Eban, 1967[1]

Introduction

Although the concept of a "new Middle East" is often portrayed as the personal vision of Israel's elder statesman Shimon Peres,[2] the idea of "Middle Easternism," if not the label he chose for it, precedes him by at least a quarter-century. Indeed, it represents one of the grand objectives that the Israeli state, under Labour and Likud governments alike, has sought and demanded practically since its inception. Israel's kind of peace is a structured peace in that it mandates the initiation of certain irrevocable processes. These include the establishment of normal relations with Arab states and the creation of webs of complex interaction in many different fields among the former enemies. Egypt's commitment fully to normalize relations was a central demand of the Likud government that concluded the Camp David peace treaty. Cairo is often accused of violating the agreement by not living up fully to its normalization stipulations – hence the allegations of "cold peace." Indeed, Tel Aviv has long recognized that a state of war, or even cold war, once terminated by the signing of a treaty, can always be restored as political conditions evolve. The act of signing a piece of paper is a simple event. The signed document can be torn up, ignored, or overtaken by events and rendered obsolete. To avoid that scenario Israel has historically been interested in pursuing a kind of peace that is meant to transcend the particular character of the regime of the day, whether Arab or Israeli, to create a process of peace and not a mere event. An event – the "historic handshake,"[3] the proverbial signing ceremony on the White House lawn – can be overtaken by a rival event that proves to be more salient, such as a revolution or sudden change in regime.

Singular events, in other words, lack structure. While an event is easily overtaken by a rival event, it can be completely dwarfed in significance by a rival process or trend, which does have structure and therefore occurs on an entirely different order of magnitude. The then Israeli prime minister, Shimon Peres, was trying to engineer a process which, had it progressed beyond a particular point, should have reached a degree of structural formidability in which it would no longer be subject to reversal by either the Likud or Arab rejectionists. The Likud, for its part, has been known for its efforts to foreclose the decision of the international consensus – the formula of "land for peace" enshrined in United Nations Security Council Resolution 242 – as a historical option, once and for all. This was to be done through the gradual articulation of its own process, that of "creeping annexation" via the transformation of West Bank settlements into veritable cities.

As Peres was conducting his negotiations with the Palestinians, he was indeed constrained by that process; especially in his negotiations with the Palestinians, he was confronted by the proverbial *fait accompli*, or what the Israelis call the "creation of facts on the ground." Another salient example of a process in the Middle Eastern context is the gradual progress of Islamic fundamentalism. In short, a process, unlike a single event, is not as vulnerable to the shocks of counter-events.[4] Although a process can be overtaken by a more powerful, opposing process, its prior presence in the arena tends to deter the emergence and evolution of rival processes in incremental fashion, thus preventing the counter-trend from making the initial inroads that are prerequisite to eventual success.

In Israeli strategic thought the meaning of the peace process is conceived as the "normalization of relations," achieved through the exchange of embassies, cultural, and interpersonal contacts among the respective populations, "regional cooperation" in the economic realm, and, eventually, a unified regional security regime. The establishment of peace as a process and not merely as an event has the consequence of "concretizing peace,"[5] affording it the attributes of meaning and relevance, and providing it with its own independent historical dynamic. As the scenario of a formal, region-wide peace very recently appeared on the Middle Eastern event horizon, Israeli objectives and strategies regarding the shape of the normalization to come began to appear in detailed fashion. The nature of Arab responses to Israel's specification of its future goals was also beginning to come within the historical line of vision. The insights into the future that have been generated by the developments of that brief period are invaluable. They constitute a precursor of things to come, a veritable storehouse of knowledge as to the concrete intentions of the Israeli establishment regarding normalization and the kind of reaction to be expected from Arab opponents of normalization if and when treaties are concluded between Israel and the remaining Arab states at some future date.[6]

What exactly do the Israelis mean by the concept of regional normalization, and to what extent do Arab states and populations share the Israeli vision? The question goes far beyond the potential economic benefits to this or that Arab state, or the present feasibility of this or that regional cooperation project. Indeed, the concept represents nothing less than an attempt to reconstruct the regional state system, to transform it from a dualistic Arab–Israeli system into a fully integrated system existing under a single "Middle Eastern" umbrella. The systemic character of the change Israel intends is best conveyed in its Arabic form – *al-nizam al-sharq al-awsati al-jadid*, the "new Middle East order,"[7], or *sharq awsatiyya*, "Middle Easternism," for short. These Arabic constructions should not be understood in terms of the Arab conspiracy theory; nor are they acting as a regional parallel to the Western far-right conspiracy theories surrounding the so-called "new world order." Nor should they be understood to be something as extravagant as envisioned by their European predecessors – such as the regional integration on the model of the European Union, or even its precursor, the regional "security community" as envisioned for the "North Atlantic area" by the late international relations theorist Karl Deutsch.[8] Rather, they refer to the restructuring of strategic, political, economic, and cultural relations among existing states to make room for Israeli participation as a major power, but do not portend any kind of chemical fusion among the units themselves.

In the larger theoretical sense, this age-old vision appears to resemble the systematic establishment of regional webs or networks of "complex interdependence"[9] of the kind advocated by neoliberal institutionalists in the global arena. They see the establishment of such linkages as the best guarantee against the reemergence of Arab hostility at some future date. The construction of a new order along these lines involves the quite mundane task of constructing the small individual links which, in their synthesis, are aimed at producing an emergent result at the system level. Here we examine in some detail the main characteristics of the links Israel is seeking to create with Arab states and the likely Arab responses to these efforts in the context of a future regional settlement.[10] Although the phenomenon is regional in scope, a high degree of focus is concentrated on Syria and Lebanon as the last of the Arab confrontation states and the strategic gateway through which Israel must pass to reach the Arab world at large. In the words of George Nader, "A Syrian–Israeli peace will be the underpinning that will reshape a new regional order."[11] The importance of Syria has been conveyed in the same way; the signing of an agreement with Damascus is viewed as the key to peace with the entire Arab world.[12]

At the bilateral level, Israel tends to view economic cooperation with Syria as a necessarily integral component of peace between them, or, as Gideon Fishelson put it, to give Israel's Arab counterparts a "vested interest" in peace.[13] An individual from the government of Shimon Peres (1995–6) described by the Israeli press as a "senior government official" called it "one of the two main pillars of brokering peace between the two countries, alongside security." In contrast to Jordan, with which economic cooperation is described as desirable but not necessary for peace, the lingering Israeli doubts about Syrian intentions have rendered "necessary" that which was previously considered to be theoretical and visionary; in other words, "economic cooperation must stand alongside the security net," so that "close economic links could ensure the continuation of the peace process whether or not the Syrian leaders really want it."[14]

The Syrians, though they reluctantly tolerated the placement of economic cooperation issues on their bilateral negotiating agenda, tend to prefer a more natural, spontaneous form of peace rather than one whose rules are organized in advance. Damascus believes that peace should follow the lines of United Nations Security Council Resolution 242, a resolution ceaselessly advocated by the United States in past years; the Syrians would be liable to consider any further demands on them in the way of peace as an unwarranted moving of the goalposts.[15] This is even more the case with UN Security Council Resolution 425, which calls on the Israelis in unconditional fashion to "withdraw forthwith its forces from all Lebanese territory."[16] Some Lebanese, citing Resolution 425, do not believe the normalization of relations with Israel is incumbent upon them since there is not so much as a hint of it in the resolution. They say, "Leave and we'll decide."[17] Therefore it is unlikely that either Lebanon or Syria will commit itself in irreversible fashion to any blueprint whose key aspects would intrude directly on the future sovereignty of either of them.

Economic cooperation, then, as one aspect of normalization, is primarily a political and not an economic issue. While there are economic ramifications, the question of whether or not this and other aspects of normalization eventually materialize on the ground is an issue of fundamental strategic importance for the future of the Middle East region. Arab fears regarding the potential domination of their economies, or the creation of what Keohane and Nye would call "asymmetrical interdependencies"[18] with Israel (discussed below), should be understood not so much for their strictly economic effects but in terms of strategic repercussions. As Keohane and Nye point out, asymmetrical interdependencies, from an international political point of view, are "sources of power among actors."[19] Any state entering into situations of interdependence wants to be assured that such interdependence cannot someday be used against it, even more so when interdependence is one-sided as it is likely to be in the Arab–Israeli context.

In assessing the prospects for a full-blown Middle Easternism in the context of system change, the focus is on the nature of Arab perceptions and fears regarding the economic cooperation envisaged for a new Middle East order. These fears derive from Israel's economic and political strength, the role of geographical and functional centrality that would be afforded it in the context of economic cooperation, the creation of interdependencies, and the additional strategic leverage all of these would generate for Israel. After identifying and explicating the nature of these fears, we shed light on the dangerous chasm that is growing up in individual Arab states between the official Arab policy of peace with integration on the one hand, and the popular preference for peace with separation on the other.

There are significant sectors in Arab civil society, especially among the professional and highly educated, who deplore the concept of normalization, who do not trust Israel's intentions even in the context of peace. Their opinions are shared by the adherents of Islamist ideology, even in its moderate variation. These elements view Israel's very establishment as evidence of its untrustworthiness and hostility toward them; therefore the passage of time is not seen as relevant. The peacemakers, or at least most of them, once perceived Israel in this same way. However, given Israel's demonstrated superiorities and the proven impossibility of ever confronting it through military means, they have reconciled themselves to forgetting about the past and starting over as if it never happened. This means accepting Israeli definitions of peace, in which Israel is taken on as a key partner by Arab states in a joint effort to build a more stable future for themselves and their peoples. The critical mass of the Arab populace probably lies somewhere between these two poles.[20] Arab populations seem to want prosperity rather than confrontation, but they would rather have invisible peace partners – a Middle East without war, but also without Israelis directly in their midst.

Israel's centrality in a future Middle East

Israel envisions for itself a central role in a future Middle East, a function of its military and economic power and its geographically central location. This centrality forms the basis of much of the official Arab skepticism concerning Israel's intentions. Part of the problem seems to lie in Israel's more or less bilateral approach, which Arabs fear will overtake their connections with one another and impede future cooperation, economic and otherwise, under the strictly "Arab" label. Though proposed under the banner of "regional cooperation," Israel's cooperation proposals are not really "regional," at least not at their core. Rather, they constitute a web of bilateral relations between individual Arab states and Israel, on top of which the multilateral arrangements are built. According to Yossi Beilin, Israel's deputy foreign minister under Shimon Peres:

> We will turn a new page in the economic history of the Middle East. Bilateral [peace] agreements between us will lead to the establishment of bilateral frameworks for economic cooperation .... Beyond the bilateral agreements, we will establish a framework for regional economic cooperation that will guarantee free transfer of goods, persons, and services throughout the Middle East.[21]

While the form of Israel's normalization strategy is often multilateral on the surface, it seems to Arabs to be more bilateral in practice. In place of the concept of the spider's web, in which links are formed spontaneously in many different directions, to understand the nature of Arab fears behold instead the metaphor of multiple spokes on a wheel, all of which come together at a single point.

The concept of Gideon Fishelson, a scholar whose advocacy of regional economic cooperation dates back to the 1970s, epitomizes the Israel-centric vision for the new Middle East. Reminiscent of President Nasser's "three concentric circles"[22] – the Arab, African, and Islamic worlds – converging on Egypt, Fishelson's formulation contains a Middle East divided into "three circles." Fishelson's circles are mutually exclusive, unlike Nasser's, which are overlapping. More importantly, they converge on Israel. Fishelson defines the "inner" circle as inclusive of Israel and the occupied territories, Jordan, Lebanon, and Syria, though he somewhat inexplicably debates whether to include Syria in the central category at all. Egypt, the strongest Arab state, is relegated reluctantly – but relegated nonetheless – to the "median" circle, into the same category as Iraq and Saudi Arabia. Finally, the "outer" circle is comprised of the southern Gulf monarchies, as well as Sudan, Iran, and Turkey.[23]

Israel itself has little strategic interest in promoting a form of inter-Arab cooperation that does not center around itself, for it would then run the risk of inadvertently providing the catalyst for a new pan-Arabism. There is currently little in the way of integration at the inter-Arab level; exclusive of oil, regional trade among Arab states constitutes a mere 4 percent of their total international trade.[24] According to the Israeli normalization strategists, the answer seems to be now, as it was in the 1950s, that Israel should be the agent bridging the Arab states:

> Israel occupies a key position in the peace process [in part] because of its unique geographic location. Under the prevailing state of tension, not only is Israel isolated from its neighbors, but it also separates them from one another. With the establishment of peace, Israel would become a bridge between them. It might become a

center for the supply of services and the transfer of technology, fostering the economic growth and well-being of the entire region.[25]

None of this, however, provides a complete answer to the Arab query. While it may be geographically and economically correct, it serves only to feed Arab suspicions regarding the structure of this integration, especially the repercussions that will be felt at the strategic level. The fear is that Israel may be trying to arrange for a Middle East in which the political and economic roads from Beirut to Cairo, from Cairo to the Gulf, and from the Gulf to the rest of the world must first run through Tel Aviv and Haifa;[26] and that the Arabs, who were previously unable to unite in war against Israel, are now to be united by outside forces for peace – around a new Israeli leadership. As President Mubarak of Egypt told one of his correspondents in a 1995 interview:

> Explain to me, what is a new Middle East? If it's peace and coopera-
> tion, that's OK. But people say Israel wants to be the strongest state
> in the region and control the economy. Talk like this makes all the
> countries in the region afraid.[27]

At the 1994 regional economic summit at Casablanca Israel presented an expansive vision of economic cooperation, though the outlines of such coop-eration were being contemplated by Israeli-oriented scholars and strategists much earlier.[28] However, Israel's overbearing presence at Casablanca – including not only Rabin and Peres, but half the rest of the Israeli cabinet as well, and a business delegation several hundred strong – set off alarm bells all over the Arab world, especially in Cairo, as to what seemed to be the coming hegemony.[29] As Nahum Barnea observed, "The Casablanca confer-ence, which was supposed to mark Israel's entry into the Arab business world, became an Israeli-only presentation. Israel knocked repeatedly and energetically on the doors. The Arabs locked them in a panic."[30] Statements made by Israeli leaders in apparently unguarded moments only fanned the flames. Fawaz Gerges, in an article about what he saw at the time as Israel's strategic competition with Egypt for regional leadership, quotes Peres as saying: "Egypt led the Arabs for 40 years and brought them to the abyss; you will see the region's economic situation improve when Israel takes the reins of leadership in the Middle East."[31]

The Israelis learned from the Casablanca experience and subsequently toned down the manner in which they marketed their message of "coopera-tion." The Israeli deputy foreign minister, Yossi Beilin, in preparation for the follow-up summit in Amman, held in 1995, told Israeli businessmen to "learn the lessons of Casablanca" and tone down their message.[32] Israel sent a much smaller delegation to the Amman summit and proposed projects together with its neighbors instead of unilaterally.[33] Despite the lower profile, the original substance of the proposals did not seem to have changed much. The areas in which Israel has contemplated joint regional efforts have tended to center around the following four spheres: water, transport, tourism, and energy.[34] These are primarily cross-border infrastructure projects (Gabbay provides an example in Chapter 6).[35]

The situation at the Doha was, of course, very different, with the majority of the Gulf States failing to attend. Because they had hoped to submit to the GCC members joint financial and capital accumulations proposals, the Israeli strategy for the summit was significantly weakened. In response, the Israeli's again focused on discussion of regional infrastructure projects between them and the northern Arab states. Even these discussions could not be legitimized because of Egypt's and Syria's absence from the summit.

The most important of Israel's proposed infrastructure projects concerns water.[36] Israel's official and unofficial proposals for water cooperation tend to center around the theme of bringing more water to and/or through Israel. Centering the infrastructure in Israel would do much to ensure that Israel is never without adequate water resources, while at the same time heightening Arab fears of losing control of their resource. Such fears are born of Israel's past practices of forcibly diverting water from occupied areas for its own use: two-thirds of the water Israel is currently using comes from the Golan Heights. Enormous amounts of water have also been diverted for Israeli use from the West Bank and from the aquifers underneath the Gaza Strip.

At the same time, Palestinians have been prohibited from drilling wells for their own use. As a result of heavy Israeli exploitation of their water reserves, Palestinians do not have access to safe drinking water; nor do they have sufficient amounts properly to sustain their agriculture. The Syrians lose much of their other water due to leaky pipes and antiquated irrigation techniques, but they argue that the upgraded technology is currently beyond their financial means. They might also say that it is sovereignty that is at issue, not the level of technological development a given country can afford. The Lebanese would concur. They claim that those portions of their waters that fell under Israeli occupation during the 1978 and 1982 invasions, particularly the Hasbani river, have been subject to diversion.[37]

Israeli water demands are enormous, for two reasons. One is that Israel's industrial facilities require more water than a country of Israel's size and location can sustain alone. Second, Israel pursues a type of agriculture not suited to the region. It has made an ideological tenet of growing water-intensive crops in a quasi-desert climate – that is, "making the desert bloom." The lack of rainfall is compensated for by using intensive irrigation that requires excessive water resources in contrast to the Syrians, who rely primarily on rain-fed agriculture. At least since 1967, Israel has made the desert bloom with Arab water, causing severe shortages to neighboring populations. In the context of peace the Israelis will have to halt this practice and import the water from abroad and/or convince Arab states to engage in cooperative water projects with it to ensure its access to external water supplies.

Some Israeli analysts thought they saw a potential solution to the water problem in the future purchase of Nile waters to irrigate the Negev Desert. This would enable the northern waters originating in Syria and Lebanon, currently transported to the Negev by the Israeli National Water Carrier, to be freed for West Bank consumption. However, thus far such solutions have been anathema to Egyptian public opinion. A second proposition was the diversion of the Litani waters in southern Lebanon to Lake Tiberias, to join southern Lebanon's Hasbani waters that may have already been diverted there, but it is unlikely the Lebanese would agree for reasons of security.[38]

Although Egypt and Lebanon might currently enjoy slight water surpluses, it is improbable that this situation will continue very far into the future.[39] Therefore it may not be wise to create Israeli dependencies on new Arab water sources from which Israel may later be reluctant or even unwilling to disengage peacefully. Patrick Clawson is right to point out the salience of the security aspects surrounding the water resource, and indeed the general precedence of politics over economics in all the regional cooperation issues embodied in the concept of Middle Easternism.[40] The Lebanese, for instance, are interested in harnessing their current water surpluses for export.[41] At the same time, they are worried that if they export to Israel or concede implementation of the diversion proposals they might ultimately lose political control over their resource. Therefore, they are looking for a mechanism by which they can offer the water for sale via a third party, such as an international bank, to avoid entering into a direct legal connection with the importers of the water.[42]

Another alternative was proposed by Turkey: that of the "peace pipeline," in which Ankara would ship waters to several countries in the Middle East from its Seyhan and Ceyhan rivers via a pipeline through Israel and the eastern Arab states and terminating in the Persian Gulf. The U.S. government has been equally engaged in promoting Turkish solutions to the Israeli–Syrian water problem in particular, since a future peace treaty between the two states might otherwise falter on the permanent disposition of the Golan's water resources.[43] This Turkish option, however, is expensive and creates dependencies on Turkey that several Arab states perceive as too dangerous given their already weak strategic positions. The problem has since been compounded by the unexpected emergence of a new Israeli–Turkish military axis. And, after all, as one expert mused, if regional states can cut off oil pipelines for political reasons, then why not water pipelines?[44] Ankara has investigated other ways in which to sell Israel its surplus water,[45] but, as the Israelis themselves recognize, Turkish water surpluses are not likely to last.[46] Desalination, with its interminable supply and absence of at least geographical interdependencies, is coming to be seen as an increasingly attractive option for all the water-starved states in the region.[47] It would, of course, require a major region-wide investment in research and development. This type of project, however, might prepare the ground for a genuine effort toward regional cooperation, one that has the potential to benefit all sides.[48]

The realm of transport and communications is also important for normalizing Israel's status and could reinforce Israel's geographic centrality in the Middle East. However, there is skepticism in some Arab quarters that Israel intends to build infrastructures in the territory of its immediate neighbors primarily to provide itself with a gateway to reach lucrative markets in Europe and the Gulf.[49] The Israelis are particularly interested in connecting their road networks to those of Syria and Lebanon to provide Israel with a direct land route to Europe.[50] While the northern transport routes would provide Israel with overland access to the European marketplace, the eastern routes would open the gates to the future markets of Iraq, Iran, and the southern Gulf, and beyond them to central and south-central Asia. Israel's own road system, particularly the construction of Road no. 90, a complete north–south expanse traversing Israel and the eastern edge of the West Bank, may be linked with existing roads in bordering states and expanded to accommodate international traffic.[51] There have also been proposals to revive old railway systems in disuse since 1948 and to construct new ones; additional proposals concern the rerouting of regional shipping from the eastern Arab world through the Haifa port. In short, most of the functions previously served by Palestine's geographic centrality would be restored through the routing of major regional transport networks through Israel.

Israel also seeks to link its telecommunications networks, including cellular phone systems and data-transmission services, to neighboring Arab states. Israel might seek to have the relevant infrastructure located in its own territory or in that of its ally Jordan. Rendering Israel central in this regard, while it may be a natural outcome resulting from its superior technological sophistication, nonetheless engenders Arab fears of losing control over the information transmissions originating in their own countries.

The tourism sector is universally considered to be the primary beneficiary of any peace, since tourism is particularly sensitive to political instability. Furthermore, in the area of tourism, as Clawson notes, Arab states are on more of an economic par in this field than in any other.[52] Israeli thinkers have envisioned widespread construction of regional tourism infrastructure, putting Israel's own expertise to use inside Arab countries.[53] They are also advocating multiple-destination package tours in which international tourists would cover several Middle Eastern countries in a single visit. Jordan has already been involved in setting up what it hopes will become a regional airline company – "Royal Wings" – for that purpose.[54] There are some fears among Arabs, however, that Israel will be the primary beneficiary of such arrangements, since a large percentage of the profits from tourism are gained by those involved in the service and management aspects. "The fear is that they will be the masters, and we will drive the buses," said one Jordanian observer. He also recalled how Israel sought to monopolize the profits from air travel, according to this individual, it took Jordan more than a year to negotiate a provision allowing package tourists – already entering the Middle East via Tel Aviv – to depart from Amman using the Royal Jordanian airline rather than back through Tel Aviv on El Al.[55] Atif Kubursi cited the additional Arab concern that tourists will base themselves in Israel and venture into Arab states only as day-trippers.[56]

Tourism is considered to be a central component of Arab–Israeli normalization, despite initial problems with Israeli tourists in Jordan.[57] As the Israeli television commentator Ehud Ya'ari explained to the Syrian foreign minister, Farouq Al-Shara, in the first-ever interview of a Syrian official on Israeli television: "The question that many Israelis ask themselves [is]: when will a guy like me be able to take his wife to visit Palmyra?"[58] The Syrians, for their part, are reluctant to commit to such matters in advance in the absence of peace. They see aspects like tourism as more likely to arise gradually, or not, as a result of peace. Informed individuals do not, for instance, envision the Syrians agreeing to an Israeli tourist quota being written into a peace treaty,[59] since this would probably constitute an infringement of their sovereign right to change their mind and revise the number in the future depending on circumstances.

The final major realm slated for regional cooperation is energy (again, as Gabbay shows in Chapter 6). The Israeli proposals in this area contain two main features. One is the interconnection of the region's electricity grids, a multilateral project with large economies of scale. Electricity cooperation also takes advantage of the natural complementarities between the northern and southern parts of the Middle East, whose peak seasons of electricity usage are winter and summer, respectively. The natural partners for such a project, in the Israeli view, are Egypt, Israel, Jordan, Saudi Arabia, Syria, Lebanon, and the occupied territories, with the subsequent inclusion of Iraq and Turkey. However, Egypt has been reluctant to link its grid with Israel's,[60] and a regional plan consisting of Egypt, Iraq, Jordan, Syria, and Turkey already exists; the governments of these states have agreed to link up by the end of the century.[61] Israel has expressed its desire to be included in this plan.[62]

The other feature of energy cooperation involves the reactivation and/or diversion of existing oil and gas pipelines. Cairo is interested in becoming the primary supplier of natural gas to the Middle East and Europe, and wants Israel to become one of its top customers.[63] Israel's ambition, for its part, is to reactivate the Tapline running from Saudi Arabia through Mafraq in Jordan and divert its main terminal from Saida in Lebanon to Haifa, through the construction of an Israeli terminal there.[64] Israel sees itself as the region's natural trans-shipment point for Gulf oil, a less expensive alternative to shipping the crude on tankers from the Persian Gulf to Europe via the Suez Canal. However, existing terminals in Syria and Lebanon – serving the Iraqi pipeline and the Tapline, respectively – could serve the same purpose, the former assuming the full restoration of Iraqi–Syrian ties. This solution might also prove to be more palatable to Arab Gulf states, some of which reportedly harbor serious fears that Israel may ultimately find its way into the decision mechanism for the pricing and production of Gulf oil. This would be accomplished not only through the oil transport proposals but also through the post-boycott participation of the Israeli business community in the global petroleum-related multinationals.[65]

Interdependence or dependence: the question of symmetry

While the post-Second World War European experience served as a major inspiration to the concept of "Middle Easternism," there are strategic and systemic differences, in addition to commercial and corporate ones, between regional economic cooperation in Europe and in the Middle East. There are also differences in the areas of both interactive intensity and cultural affinity. Western Europe, or, if the United States is also included, the "North Atlantic area,"[66] is characterized by a degree of symmetry in levels of development among the countries involved and a corresponding multipolar power structure, at least at the European regional level. This is not so in the Middle East, which, like the African continent, contains a booming first-world island within a sea of declining third-world economies.[67] Geopolitically, the admission of Israel into this pre-industrial region, armed with its vast economic and military superiorities over the combination of its neighbors, threatens to transform the Middle East from a multipolar system into a hegemonic one. As Clawson observed, "In many areas in which functional cooperation has been proposed, Israel is the giant that, no matter how well-intentioned, has the potential to overwhelm its neighbors."[68]

Despite potential efforts by enlightened future peacemakers to create "balanced interdependence," most linkages created among the Israeli economy and its Arab counterparts are likely to result not in interdependence but in dependence. This situation, born of the interaction of advanced economies with undeveloped ones, is likely to give rise to a structure resembling not so much the world of the neoliberal institutionalists, but rather a spatially compressed regional version of Immanuel Wallerstein's global system, in which the "core" enters into a parasitical relationship with the "periphery,"[69] and in which Arab undevelopment is gradually transformed into the more common phenomenon of "underdevelopment." It is difficult at the present time for Arab observers to envision precisely what types of dependencies are likely to emerge from close economic links with Israel. However, they have enough respect for Israel's technological and educational superiority, and enough distrust of what Israel might do to Arab states that might become dependent upon it, to feel threatened by the structural imbalances that would undeniably present themselves. It is in this context that the Palestinian experience with Oslo is seen as a kind of miniaturized model for Israel's future relations with the Arab world at large, with one major difference: thus far, without a nationally independent state, the Palestinians do not have the option of dissociation from Israel, either economically or politically.

The four major areas of proposed cooperation – water, transport and communications, tourism, and energy – lie in the realm of regional infrastructure. In Arab countries the infrastructure networks are controlled by centralized government agencies. Earlier proposals for a Middle East Development Bank, whose purpose would be to finance the infrastructure projects, were greeted with great skepticism in the aftermath of the Casablanca conference. Even if the funds needed to establish the bank could be obtained from reluctant European and Gulf sponsors, it remains unexplained why Arab governments, particularly in the eastern region, would want to borrow additional funds from this or any other bank for cooperative infrastructure projects, given their already high levels of international indebtedness. Damascus owes about $1.4 billion to Western European states, Japan, and the World Bank, not to mention upwards of $15 billion in military debts to the former Soviet Union.[70] With no solution to these outstanding amounts in sight – indeed the Syrians are having trouble meeting the interest payments on the European loans – it might not be feasible for them to borrow billions of dollars from a newly created Middle East Development Bank for a new package of cooperative infrastructure projects. As for Lebanon, its economy will already be accumulating significant debts during the reconstruction of its internal infrastructure after fifteen years of civil war.[71]

Aside from the costs of building the actual infrastructures, it is difficult to estimate what the Arab "costs of dissociation"[72] might be once these are completed. Arab states could become dependent on the high levels of Israeli technological know-how, making it costly and perhaps next to impossible for Arab governments to disengage their economies from Israel's should future political circumstances warrant this. Indeed, this is the major political objective in building these infrastructures.[73] However, as a Syrian observer noted, Arab states of the future might be willing to dissociate whatever the cost, since high-political strategic matters take precedence over economic questions regardless of the degree of economic sacrifice.[74] As Clawson also rightly pointed out, "political considerations overwhelm economics even when the economic situation is desperate"[75] (although this is not in line with Wright's thinking; see Chapter 2).

The problem of dependence, though salient in Israeli-controlled areas, is not likely to manifest itself in regional trade. The Israelis do not envision the emergence of strong and diversified trading patterns between Israel and its Arab peace partners. Nor are Arabs overly worried about Israeli products overwhelming their markets. In the first place, the larger Arab markets in which Israel might be interested – those of Egypt, Iraq, and Syria – are too impoverished to generate much demand for the high-technology merchandise that Israel produces for export. The markets in which there may be demand for such products, primarily the richer Gulf economies, are indeed lucrative, though they are minuscule in comparison to the Western markets to which Israel has become accustomed.[76] The obvious exception is the market for financial investment capital, which the Gulf Arabs could provide (reference the role capital accumulation plays in Chapter 3).

As for the immediate vicinity of Israel, the markets of Lebanon and Jordan are both too small, and the majority of their citizens and institutions too poor, to be able to afford the kinds of items Israel produces for export. There might be a market for Israeli products of lesser significance, such as processed foods and perhaps textiles, but there is also no sound reason why Arab countries could not continue to import such items from Asia and Europe as they have done in the past. Even when Israel forced its products on the Lebanese by dumping them on their markets during its three-year occupation of much of the country, Lebanese citizens did not find themselves overly in need of them. While Israel wants to ensure "free" trade with Arab states as an attribute of "concretized" peace, it is inevitable that its major export markets will remain those of the United States, Europe, and Japan.

Despite this fact, there are other areas in the private sector in which complementarities might threaten to develop in an unbalanced manner in favor of Israel as the only developed country in the region. The most significant of these is the potential exploitation by Israel of complementarities in the factors of production: Israel's provision of capital, technology, and managerial experience in exchange for cheap Arab labor.[77] The relevant workstations would probably not be located in Israel; this would be unacceptable for security and "demographic" reasons. Rather, the pattern would probably resemble more closely that outlined by Sara Roy in the context of Israel's relationship with the Palestinians of the West Bank and particularly Gaza. Roy writes of how Israeli entrepreneurs, in combination with wealthy Palestinian and other Arab expatriates, might jointly invest in certain industries, while Palestinians would continue to act as cheap labor as they have in the past. The only real difference is that these industries, or "industrial parks", would be located near Israel's borders rather than within them, specifically in the occupied territories, thereby alleviating the need for Palestinians to enter Israel to work.[78] If this pattern were to prove successful in the occupied Palestinian territories, it could conceivably be expanded to the larger Arab world, beginning most probably with Jordan.[79] The entrepreneurs might be either Israelis or Jewish individuals based in Western countries, working in joint ventures with Arab counterparts, primarily but not exclusively in the expatriate community. Alternatively, an Israeli firm could open a subsidiary in an Arab country, either openly or through a third-party holding company, so that the company's labor-intensive work could be done in the Arab country while the management decisions were made in Israel.[80]

A "peace of kings and presidents"

Just as a house built on landfill is vulnerable to demolition by earthquakes, a peace treaty built on air is susceptible to being blown away by periodic changes in the winds of Middle East politics. Understanding the peace treaty with Egypt in this way, Israel is interested in anchoring it and any future peace agreements within the solid foundation of a common economic infrastructure. Without some material expression, the device of the Arab–Israeli peace treaty is "little more than a declaration of intent – revocable at will":

> Without the flows of trade in goods and services, of investments, and the movement of people which provide the concrete content of peace, the peace treaty remains, in Israeli eyes, an empty and fragile shell. It is for this reason that Israel has continuously pressed for raising the level of bilateral economic transactions.[81]

Ultimately, however, economic cooperation in and of itself will not be enough to ground the peace: a lasting process of whatever kind, peaceful or otherwise, must involve populations and not only leaders. Just as war cannot be sustained for long without the support of the populace, since it is they who must do the fighting, peace cannot be sustained for long without the involvement of the populace, since it is ultimately they who must live and transact together. Furthermore, it is the politically relevant sections of the populace that will determine the identity and strategic orientation of future leaders. Therefore any peace that is to be lasting must go beyond the concept of bilateralism and even multilateralism, whether political or economic; peace is not a single "lateral" construction among potentially transient governments but rather a series of multiple lateral connections across the many different layers of participating state-societies, from the very bottom all the way up to the level of the ruling regimes. At present, the latter pattern is taking shape in only one area, the business sector. The high levels of attendance at the conferences of Casablanca and Amman, and the ambitious blueprints for private-sector projects and joint ventures that emerged from them are testimony to the interest of Arab commercial sectors in doing business with Israel and Israelis.[82] However, the Arab economies as a whole are ultimately controlled by the governments and not by their populations. Therefore the peace which is grounded in economic cooperation is little more than another form of cooperation among leaders; change the leaders and the businessmen of the future might not find such a hospitable environment for cooperation. In the larger picture, the few successes over the years in what has been known in general terms as the "Middle East peace process" still resemble more an elite accommodation of kings, presidents, and prime ministers than an historic understanding between enemy peoples.

Arab governments, by and large, have committed themselves to putting an end to the confrontation with Israel as the only way to halt the regressive cycle of defeat and occupation in which they have been trapped. However, the populations involved do not seem to savor the idea of close interaction with the Israeli victors. In Jordan, as one Western diplomat said, "He [King Hussein] is frustrated because he wants to make it a warm peace...while his people are not in line and see things differently."[83] Indeed, many of them would seem to prefer the establishment of a peace in which individual Israelis remain invisible to them, as they have been all along, an atmosphere of live and let live, "you don't get in our way, we don't get in yours." This is particularly true of the professional, intellectual, and religious sectors, though it does not seem to be true of the Arab business sector, which is looking forward to an atmosphere of geopolitical stability and openness and the expansive business opportunities these will present.

The reasons for the continuing hostility toward Israel among noncommercial segments of the Arab population are a result of the same perceptions and conditions that generated the conflict in the first place; namely, the widespread belief that Israel's original establishment was an illegitimate and hostile act taken against an important segment of the Arab people and that it is therefore logically impossible that such a state could harbor good intentions toward them. In the eyes of a rational person, historical circumstances such as these are not contingent on the decision of a government to ignore them; such decisions by governments do not affect people's perception that the circumstances are still the same. To these people, a peace treaty is no more than an "intergovernmental political construct," whose fulfillment may be incumbent on their governments but not on them. In short, normalization, in the sense that Israel understands it, cannot be implemented by governments, even authoritarian governments, without the consent of the populations involved.[84] Muhammad Baalbaki, president of the Lebanese Press Association, declared:

> Peace agreements may be signed and [joint] military operations may be held, but there cannot be a cultural peace between the Arabs and Israel. Agreements between governments do not concern us. Nationalism is not so much a government concern as it is a concern of the people.[85]

Such sentiments are still prevalent at the level of populations, especially in the elite sector, despite the accommodations of governments; they continue to form the intellectual rationale that lies behind the popular resistance to full-scale Arab–Israeli normalization. The key concept is the replacement of "Arab" with "Middle Eastern" as a means of collective self-definition, implicit in which is the final extinguishment of "Arabism" and its replacement for all time with the substitute identity of "Middle Easternism" – the regionalized extension of the replacement of Palestine by Israel. And thus the initial existentialism of the Arab–Israeli conflict reappears in the form of its final solution. As one Lebanese observer said of the attitudes prevalent in his country, "Arabs hate two words: one, 'normalization;' and, two, 'Middle Eastern.' They think its purpose is to wipe out the Arab identity."[86] In a recent article a Palestinian sociologist, Samih Farsoun, examines in some depth the rationale underlying this phenomenon:

> In place of an "Arab world" – as it is now – a "Middle East" with new economic, financial, trade, tourism, security, and other institutions will emerge, with Israel as the pivotal state in the Levant while the United States casts its influential hegemony over the whole region. In short, we are now witnessing the Middle Easternization of *Al-Mashreq Al-Arabi* [the eastern part of the Arab world].... Israel will be an integral and advantaged member of this new Middle East.[87]

Lower down the economic scale, at the level of the ordinary Arab citizen, the phenomenon of unfulfilled expectations, generated by an unwarranted *a priori* belief in a Middle Eastern version of the trickle-down theory, provides a second layer of anti-normalization sentiment. Many Arabs, especially Palestinians and Jordanians, resigned themselves to accept the treaty with Israel in the apparently mistaken belief that an end to the hostilities would at least relieve their impoverishment and bring them a degree of economic prosperity. Though such expectations were fueled by leaders in the hope of increasing support for the peace process, it seems many people took them too literally. As one Jordanian observer noted, "People thought the peace process meant a new house, a car, a better living standard. But now they see only that their lives are the same, and in many cases worse."[88]

While an end to the threat of war will gradually free up Arab resources for internal use, this does not translate into a higher standard of living for the average Arab citizen, any more than the end of the cold war brought economic prosperity to most Americans. Indeed, young Americans are probably more economically disaffected now than at any time since the Depression. For in the economic crunch decade of the 1990s a higher rate of growth in the economy at large does not automatically generate a higher standard of living for the middle and lower classes; gains on Wall Street, as the cliché goes, are not always reflected on Main Street. The resentments that are being generated in the Arab populace, as the truth is discovered by the critical mass of popular opinion, have the potential gradually to produce a much larger economic constituency to supplement and provide fuel for the ideological opponents.

To understand how tension between Arab leaders and populations over normalization with Israel is playing itself out among more politically significant sectors of society it is important to remember that it was the Egyptian intelligentsia and their supporters in the elite sections of civil society that led the way to the cold peace of which Israel constantly complains.[89] Egyptians did not seem particularly interested in engaging the Israeli people, culture, or economy in an active way. Some tried to resurrect what was previously an official boycott at the popular level, a pattern which has since been repeated in Jordan. As Amos Perlmutter wrote in 1994:

> Egyptian intellectuals, professionals, journalists and men of letters... as well as clerics and academics, remain adamantly opposed to the peace treaty, to Zionism, and to Israel's sovereignty. This is also true of the Palestinian intellectual and professional classes. They strongly oppose Oslo in the same way that their counterparts in Jordan are against the Jordanian–Israeli peace treaty.[90]

While the Egyptian state could no longer boycott Israel, in line with the terms of the peace agreement it could not hope to stop its population from enacting their own form of boycott without appearing to be a stooge of Israel and thereby incurring unacceptable internal political risks. While Egypt's rulers were compelled by the treaty to fly Israel's flag over Cairo – which is in itself considered highly provocative in Arab countries – they could not force the Egyptian people to change their unfriendly perceptions, or to engage their Israeli counterparts in social, cultural, or economic activities. Furthermore, the leadership was powerless to stop the social and other forms of ostracism threatened against those individual Egyptians who did not share the opinion of the majority, should they decide to conduct dealings with Israel. The government therefore had no choice but to define a happy medium between Israel and its own civil society, to find the middle ground between the largely contradictory demands of its external and internal constituencies, thus bringing about Israeli charges of cold peace. The resulting tug of war with Israel that Fawaz Gerges describes found Israel constantly trying to maximize the degree of normalization and to expand the scope of economic relations, and Egypt primarily interested in minimizing them.[91]

In Jordan the Arab–Israeli fault line, though it has completely disappeared from the common border, has reappeared within the country even more stridently than it did in Egypt, sharply dividing the sentiments of the government from those of its civil society. Jordanian professional associations, representing 80,000 members across the professional spectrum, have followed the lead of their Egyptian counterparts and imposed sanctions, usually expulsion, on any of their members defying the Arab boycott concept and interacting in any fashion with Israel or Israelis.[92] Heading the anti-normalization front in Jordan is Laith Shbeilat, who served a brief prison term in March 1996 on speech charges; this was followed up by a new draconian press law enacted in 1997 and the re-arrest of Shbeilat – all in a country that had not too long before been an open aspirant to democratic status.[93] The government's hard line against internal discontent over the peace treaty is indicative of the urgency of its own commitment to normalization at the foreign-policy level and the major threat presented to that process from deep within its own civil society. Nor was the fact that Shbeilat won reelection from prison to head the Jordanian Engineers' Association by a margin exceeding 80 percent lost on anyone in either Jordan or Israel.[94] The association went so far as to offer a pension to the family of the late Yahya Ayyash, an underground senior military commander in the Izzedin El-Qassam Brigades of Hamas; after all, Ayyash "the Engineer" was a member in good standing of the Engineers' Association.

While it is normal in a democracy for leading figures in civil society to take part in politics outside the formal political party structure and for civil society to shun publicly those individuals with whom it disagrees on fundamental issues of principle, especially political issues, the Jordanian government has decided to step in and draw a line of separation between civil society and politics. Measures to divest the professional associations of their ability to influence political issues of significance, such as the normalization issue, are under strong consideration. The most likely measure will be an end to the requirement of mandatory membership in the professional association of one's field as a condition of working in that profession, thus rendering the threat of expulsion irrelevant at the professional level if not at the larger social level.[95] For this is no ordinary foreign-policy problem; it is a major question of history. The issue at stake is how the Arab–Israeli conflict is to be played out at the popular level within states whose governments are in the process of declaring it settled at the official level.

Early indications from Syria point to a similar posture on the part of Syrian civil society to that of its counterpart in Jordan. One writer phrased the general attitude of most people toward a formal peace with Israel (assuming the return of the Golan) in terms of resignation. While the population understands the need to eliminate the threat of general war, "in most Syrians' minds, the idea of peace with Israel is completely separate from friendly relations with Israel."[96] This reflects the possibility of passive resistance to Israel's efforts to normalize relations below the level of states, although in Syria, unlike Jordan, the opponents of normalization would probably have the tacit support of their government. Egypt is perhaps somewhere inbetween Syria and Jordan in terms of the official attitude toward normalization. As a Western diplomat observed along the same lines, "If the Israelis find their peace with Egypt cold, peace with Syria would be icy."[97]

The negative reaction of Arab civil society so far to full normalization with Israel portends the more general problem of Israel allowing the free movement of people who may still be hostile to its existence. This problem will affect both labor and tourism. While Israel seeks Arab acceptance, and while it believes that interpersonal contact is the only way to secure it over the long run, the Jewish state will have to establish deep controls over which people are allowed to move where and under what conditions. This will involve a major infringement of what would appear to be a major component of normalization at the level of peoples – an infringement required for security and demographic purity, both of which require a degree of separation between the peoples involved.

The experience of Egypt in this regard is again instructive: wary of the risks of allowing Egyptian citizens to visit Israel en masse, Cairo set up a veritable obstacle course to screen and dissuade those of its citizens who wished to make the trip.[98] But in its drive to separate the tourist from the terrorist, Cairo in effect discouraged its citizens from traveling to Israel. If the mountains of red tape were not enough, inquisitions of returning citizens by Egyptian internal security were enough to deter most others from taking the trip. Israel is now considering the potential benefits of requesting an end to the intensive screening net, erected for its own protection, in the hope of recovering a higher degree of normalization at the popular level. While it is not likely that Jordan will repeat the Egyptian tactics, precisely because Israel does not desire it,[99] this continuing necessity to balance normalization against security will pose the most salient dilemma for Israel in its relations with each of its neighbors. Until Arab citizenries at large change their opinion of Israel the latter will not be able to enjoy full normalization and full security at one and the same time, but will find itself constantly in the situation of trading the one off against the other.

The dilemma is acute in the context of Arab–Israeli popular interaction in general, not only tourism. Sustained interaction at the popular level involves the free and spontaneous movement of large numbers of people across frontiers. It requires a minimum of encumbrances of the kind generated by long lines awaiting security clearances at border crossings. Normal relations are of the kind that the United States enjoys with Canada, and that the Europeans share with one another; in both cases, massive numbers of individuals cross each other's borders without so much as a thought. Jordanians, on the other hand, typically wait three hours to cross through Israel's security at the border. Even if personal security fears are eased – which is not likely in the near future – the Jewish state's underlying fears of demographic overload will prevent it from fully opening its frontiers to the free movement of people; a population of 5 million trying to prevent assimilation into a population of 250 million probably does not have that option. Nor are these Israeli fears ungrounded; the demographic dimension of Middle Eastern integration in the conception of some Arabs is exactly thus:

"We should try to dissolve the five million [Israelis] in the Arab World, not the other way around. I think we can occupy Israel economically and cultur- ally because it exists in an Arab environment."[100]

Israel does not take such matters lightly. In the event of normalization, Arabs from surrounding countries will face the problem of residency restric- tions and land-ownership prohibitions against Arabs – especially Palestinians who are of those lands – by an Israel determined to preserve its Jewish char- acter. It is also easy to imagine Arabs from neighboring countries marrying West Bank Palestinians as a result of the new openness, for example, only to find themselves denied by Israeli authorities the papers required to live in the still-occupied Palestinian territories. Even more distressing is the idea that individual non-Palestinian Arabs could be granted residency at Israel's discretion, while at the same time the country's original population – over 4 million Palestinian refugees and expellees from 1948 and thereafter – remains trapped in exile. This kind of imagery is not likely to encourage perceptions at the Arab popular level that the region is really at peace.

There is also the question of Israelis moving freely within Arab countries in which prominent political and civil elements remain hostile to Israel's presence in the Middle East, not to mention the presence of individual Israelis inside their countries. In Syria every Israeli is a potential Elie Cohen; Israel's most successful spy. Intensive surveillance by the internal security is inevitable and will probably not provide the most hospitable atmosphere for Israeli tourists. Many Lebanese, for different reasons, are skeptical that Israeli tourists will be roaming the streets of Beirut anytime soon. Some observers believe this is because Syria will not allow Lebanon to normalize relations with Israel. Not only would Damascus be risking the loss of its position of dominance there, but the consequent power vacuum in Beirut could cause Lebanon and a future government there gradually to fall into a de facto Israeli sphere of influence. Even some Israeli analysts do not see these fears as ungrounded:

[T]he Syrians will not look kindly upon the normalization of Lebanese–Israeli relations. Such normalization will not only sever Lebanon's present dependence on Syria, but it will also redefine Lebanon – as a country looking south to an Israeli economic power, instead of east to its economically fledgling Syrian neighbor.[101]

Internally, the main impediment to economic cooperation and normaliza- tion between Israel and Lebanon (assuming the eventual withdrawal of Israel from the south of the country) will be the expected opposition to any deal- ings with Israel from some of what will become, in the aftermath of peace, former militias – particularly a domesticated Hezbollah. "We cannot now reveal what we will do," said Hassan Nasrallah, Hezbollah's youthful, strate- gically minded secretary-general, "but it is clear that we will struggle against normalization with all the means at our disposal."[102] Although the American State Department's fears for its own citizens seem wildly overblown, apparently hiding a political objective, the same will not hold true for Israeli citizens who might be inclined to venture into Lebanon for business or other purposes in the aftermath of an agreement. For Israeli citizens, personal safety could be a major issue obstructing their ability to travel freely both to Lebanon and within it. If the Palestinian Authority of Yasser Arafat cannot prevent the occasional Hamas attack on Israeli targets in Tel Aviv and West Jerusalem, asked a Lebanese oppositionist sympathetic to the peace process, then what makes anyone think that the Syrian or Lebanese governments could protect individual Israelis in the western part of Beirut, Ba'albek, or southern Lebanon?[103] Certainly the newly reconstructed army of Lebanon, providing internal security for a country fractured by fifteen years of civil war, could not be expected to protect Israeli tourists in the middle of Beirut when Chairman Arafat, and indeed the Israeli government itself, is incapable of protecting its own citizens in the middle of Tel Aviv.

Free movement of goods is more likely to tally with Israel's personal and demographic security requirements than is the free movement of persons. While it is likely that certain kinds of products, especially agriculture, will be protected by state authorities, the end of the Arab boycott will afford Israeli manufactured consumer goods virtually unimpeded entry into Arab markets. It is far from a foregone conclusion, however, that Arab populations will accept Israeli products. Just as the anti-normalization struggle continues in Jordan and Egypt, it is not difficult to imagine its equivalent in Syria and Lebanon taking on much deeper attributes.

In Syria it is easy to imagine individual shop owners refusing to display Israeli goods and the government lending them its tacit support. As for their customers, which Syrian citizen would want to walk around Damascus wearing clothing bearing the label "Made in Israel"? A more likely scenario than the entrance of an undiluted Israeli presence into Syria and other sensitive Arab markets such as those of the Gulf is the establishment of joint ventures between Arab expatriate businessmen and Jewish counterparts living in the West. International conglomerates such as banks and chain hotels already possessing worldwide fame and visibility might simply open branches in the region.[104] Diluting the Israeli label in this fashion may make the Israeli entry into the Arab market more palatable on the one hand, given its Arab component, and more difficult to boycott for the same reason. It is not impossible, however, that someone will think up a way in which informally to impose sanctions on Arab businessmen, expatriate or otherwise, who enter into joint ventures with either Israeli entrepreneurial counterparts or businessmen close to Israel but of Western nationalities.

As for Lebanon, even if Israeli goods begin to enter Lebanese markets en masse a relatively tame Hezbollah may still be capable of organizing the reconstitution of the Arab boycott on Israeli products at the level of the population, at least in the sectors where mostly Muslims live.[105] Though these tactics would be ineffective in stopping individual Lebanese businessmen from cooperating with Israel in the broader international environment, such action within Lebanon itself would probably serve to increase further the general popularity of Hezbollah as a political party competing for seats in parliament and more generalized forms of influence.

Hezbollah is not the only force opposing normalization in Lebanon. Paralleling the Egyptian and Jordanian cases, the secular intelligentsia and professional communities have already stepped into the fray in a preemptive strike against Israel's definition of peace, providing the intellectual and ideological backdrop to the coming anti-normalization drive. According to the resolution of a conference held by these forces in Beirut in 1994, entitled the "Permanent Conference for Combating the Zionist Cultural Invasion," the "principle, details and outcome" of the peace negotiations are to be rejected. Declaring that "the Arab–Zionist conflict is one over existence not borders," conference organizers and their supporters seek the application of the Arab boycott at the popular level: "All Arab individuals, groups, organizations, and institutions that deal or promote dealing with the Zionist entity [Israel] must be condemned and ostracized."[106]

Conclusion: prospects for normalization

Although it is possible for a victorious state to impose normalization terms on its defeated state counterparts, doing the same to the populations involved is quite another matter. Arab state regimes, regardless of how strong or authoritarian, cannot force their populations to interact with Israel "normally" without unacceptable political risks to themselves. King Hussein, advocate of a "warm peace" with Israel, if not outright alliance,[107] is pressing against this limit, while the Egyptian leaders choose not to. Damascus, for its part, is unlikely even to approach it. However, unless the economic, cultural, and interpersonal aspects of a future peace are supported at the level of civil society, particularly among the ranks of the educated and well informed, any Arab–Israeli peace that might be reached will remain a peace of kings and presidents, and it will be vulnerable to the same societal and political shocks as are the rulers holding it in place. The normalization of relations at the level of citizens is not a process that can be forced; rather, it depends on the spontaneous progression of informed opinion within each of the individual countries in that direction. Whether or not it materializes will depend on the perceived fairness of whatever agreements might be reached. It will also depend on the way Israel chooses to deal with the final phase of the Palestinian question, since the Palestinian experience with Israeli peace is widely considered by other Arabs to be a prototypical example of how they can expect to be treated when their time comes.

Notes

1 Abba Eban, "The six days war," United Nations, 1967; reprinted in Walter Laqueur and Barry Rubin (eds.), *The Israel–Arab Reader*, 5th edition, Penguin, New York, 1995, pp. 165–85.
2 Shimon Peres, *The New Middle East*, Henry Holt, New York, 1993.
3 Edward Said, "Oslo I to Oslo II: the mirage of peace," *The Nation*, October 16, 1995, p. 413.
4 A process is actually a chain of events that forms an emergent whole possessing characteristics that cannot be found in its parts taken by themselves, just as chains of molecules combine in unique ways to form realities as complex as the human nervous system.
5 The phrase was used by Uri Savir, head of the Israeli negotiating delegation with Syria, in interview with CNN, 29 December 1995.
6 Some might argue that the current prime minister, Benjamin Netanyahu, has reversed the peace process. What he has done is simply insisted on more time to consolidate the status quo to the point at which it becomes irreversible. At some future point Israel will reemerge with its demands for normalization of relations on the basis of this new *fait accompli*.
7 This term was first encountered by the author during a visit to Iraq and Lebanon in June 1994. The term *"nizam"* is also the generic term used to signify "regime."
8 Karl Deutsch, *Political Community in the North Atlantic Area*, Princeton University Press, Princeton, 1957.
9 Robert O. Keohane and Joseph S. Nye, *Power and Interdependence: World Politics in Transition*, 2nd edition, Scott, Foresman, and Company, London, 1989/77.
10 In addition to published documentation, we rely on personal interviews, which is necessary given the future-oriented character of the subject under review. Interviews were conducted in March 1996 just prior to Netanyahu's election with Arab and Israeli personalities, both official and unofficial, involved in or close to the economic issues of the peace process. Although the views of the Arab and Israeli "man (and woman) on the street" are important, they were not solicited for this study. Severe measures to ensure confidentiality of respondents were necessary due to the high sensitivity of the subject for the participants. Without such assurances no conversations would have been possible. In some cases interviewees requested complete anonymity and no citation of their comments in any form whatsoever. Others agreed to be identified by home town, to signify the nationality of participants and to distinguish them from one another, but without noting in any way their official or institutional affiliations.
11 George A. Nader, "Imagining peace with Syria," *Washington Post*, October 9, 1994.
12 Dan Margalit, "Peace as an incentive to the voter," *Ha'aretz*, January 8, 1996, p. B1.
13 Gideon Fishelson, "Regional economic cooperation in the Middle East," in Steven L. Spiegel (ed.), *The Arab–Israeli Search for Peace*, Lynne Rienner Publishers, Boulder, Colorado, 1992, p. 104.
14 Ora Koren, "Foreign trade at B'not Ya'akov bridge?," *Globes*, December 22, 1995, p. 60.
15 Source must remain anonymous.
16 United Nations Security Council, Resolution 425, March 19, 1978.
17 Interview, Beirut I, March 1996.
18 Keohane and Nye, *Power and Interdependence*, p. 18.

19 *Ibid.*

20 Hilal Khashan, "Partner or pariah: attitudes towards Israel in Syria, Lebanon, and Jordan," Washington Institute Policy Paper no. 41, Washington Institute for Near East Policy, Washington, DC, 1996.

21 Yossi Beilin, Israeli deputy minister of foreign affairs, "Israeli vision of regional peace," presented in his capacity as head of the steering committee of the multilateral peace talks, Tokyo, Japan, December 15, 1993.

22 Gamal Abdel Nasser, *Egypt's Liberation: The Philosophy of the Revolution*, Public Affairs Press, Washington, DC, 1955.

23 Gideon Fishelson, "Regional economic cooperation in the Middle East," pp. 104–7.

24 Atif Kubursi, "The economics of peace: the Arab response," *Regional Economic Development in the Middle East: Opportunities and Risks*, transcript of symposium held by the Center for Policy Analysis on Palestine, Washington, DC, October 6, 1995, p. 39.

25 Meir Merhav, *Economic Cooperation and Middle East Peace*, Weidenfeld & Nicolson, London, 1989, p. 43.

26 This should be taken not only figuratively but also literally. According to Aryeh Mizrahi, director of the Israeli Ministry of Housing, Israel's existing road system would be widened and new sections built to make Israel the main gateway first for the occupied territories and later for Jordan, Saudi Arabia, and Syria, "within 10 to 15 years" of an agreement. (See Ohad Gozani, "Israel aims to become gateway for Arab lands," *Jerusalem Post*, June 12, 1993, p. 16.) Another proposal has an Eilat–Aqaba link serving as the major bridge between Egypt and the Gulf. (See David Horowitz, managing editor of the *Jerusalem Report*, "Enthusiasm hurts Israel: its economic power frightens Arab nations," *World Paper*, September 1995, p. 2.)

27 Reuters, September 1, 1995.

28 See, for example, "The Six Days' War" Eban; Gideon Fishelson, *Economic Cooperation in the Middle East*, Westview Press, Boulder, Colorado, 1989; proceedings of conference held at Tel Aviv University, June 1–3, 1986; and Merhav, *Economic Cooperation and Middle East Peace*. For the recent incarnations, including the Arab component, see Fishelson, "Regional economic cooperation in the Middle East," and Jawad Anani, "Areas of potential economic cooperation in the context of the Middle East peace process," both in Spiegel, *Arab–Israeli Search for Peace*, pp. 103–20 and 121–8, respectively.

29 Horowitz, "Enthusiasm hurts Israel."

30 Nahum Barnea, "Exchange the dream," *Yediot Aharanot*, September 11, 1993, p. B3.

31 Fawaz A. Gerges, "Egyptian–Israeli relations turn sour," *Foreign Affairs* 74(3), May/June 1995, p. 70.

32 Horowitz, "Enthusiasm hurts Israel."

33 Tova Cohen, "Israel sees regional acceptance, trade as reality," Reuters, November 7, 1995.

34 Moshe Ma'oz, "Against most fears," *Yediot Aharanot*, December 17, 1995, p. 5.

35 See Government of Israel proposals, *Development Options for Regional Cooperation*, submitted by the Ministries of Foreign Affairs and Finance to the Middle East and North Africa Economic Summit, Casablanca, Morocco, October, 1994, and widely distributed there to Arab counterparts. It is interesting to note in this connection that almost all the maps in this document, with one or two exceptions, do not contain any trace of the Green Line separating the occupied territories of 1967 from Israel, even though they were formulated by a Labour

government. Indeed, they show the Golan and West Bank as any other part of Israel, without even so much as dotted lines to indicate their unresolved status.

36 Interview, Jerusalem, March, 1996.
37 Interview, Beirut II, March, 1996.
38 These two water-diversion propositions are in Elisha Kally, "The potential for cooperation in water projects in the Middle East at peace," in Fishelson, *Economic Cooperation in the Middle East*, pp. 303–33, and in Merhav, *Economic Cooperation and Middle East Peace*, pp. 60–70.
39 According to one estimate, Egyptian surpluses from the Nile will likely be eliminated, presumably by population growth, by the end of the twentieth century (Merhav, *Economic Cooperation and Middle East peace*, p. 53).
40 Patrick Clawson, "Mideast economies after the Israel–PLO handshake," *Journal of International Affairs* 48(1), summer 1994, p. 155.
41 Interview, Tarrablus, March, 1996.
42 Salim Macksoud, technical consultant, Dar al-Handasah, Beirut, address to the Conference on Lebanon's Reconstruction, Washington, DC, October 6, 1993, cited in American Task Force for Lebanon, *Synopsis of Presentations*, p. 21.
43 Thomas W. Lippman, "End of cold war enhances Turkey's standing in West," *Washington Post*, March 29, 1996, p. A30.
44 John K. Cooley, "Middle East water: power for peace," *Middle East Policy* 1(2), 1992, p. 12.
45 Refet Kaplan, "Water rights divide Syria and Turkey," *Washington Times*, March 20, 1996, p. A12.
46 "Prosperity as peace bait," *Jerusalem Post*, February 9, 1996, p. 6.
47 See, for example, Avishay Braverman, "New water from old sources," *Middle East Insight* 11(1), November/December 1994, p. 36.
48 Its desirability from the Israeli point of view is presaged by its presence in the Oslo Accord. (See the *Israeli–Palestinian Declaration of Principles*, September 13, 1993, Annex IV: "Protocol on Israeli–Palestinian cooperation concerning regional development programs," section B-4: "Regional desalinization and other water development projects.")
49 Suleiman Al-Khalidi, "Israeli integration in Arab world arouses fears," Reuters, November 1, 1995.
50 Koren, "Foreign trade at B'not Ya'acov bridge?"
51 Interview, Tel Aviv, March, 1996; and Government of Israel, *Development Options for Regional Cooperation*, IV-5–1 and IV-5–2.
52 Clawson, "Mideast economies after the Israel–PLO handshake", p. 159.
53 For this aspect, see Merhav, *Economic Cooperation and Middle East Peace*, p. 254.
54 Rana Sabbagh, "Jordan sets up airline for regional tourism," Reuters, February 1, 1996.
55 Interview, As-Salt, March, 1996.
56 Kubursi, "The economics of peace: the Arab response," p. 42.
57 Jordanian nationals and Iraqis passing through Amman report that Israeli tourists do not stay in Jordanian hotels or dine in Jordanian restaurants, that they come to Amman with bag lunches in hand. Some Israelis who have stayed in Jordanian hotels have been accused of removing petty items from the rooms. These types of rumors spread very quickly throughout the Arab countries, poisoning the atmosphere for normalization. There have also been reports of false rumors. One Israeli official interviewed noted the rumor that the walls in Petra had been defaced by Israeli tourists, as evidenced by the Hebrew inscriptions on the rock face, while, according to him, the defacement took place over 150 years ago (Interview, Jerusalem, March, 1996).

58 "Syrian foreign minister addresses Israeli public: Farouk al-Sharaa's unprecedented appearance on ITV," reproduced in *Middle East Insight*, November/December 1994, pp. 18–22.

59 Source must remain anonymous.

60 Steve Rodan, "Energy minister seeks a secure pipeline," *Jerusalem Post*, March 31, 1995, p. 10.

61 Ercan Ersoy, "Turkey to get loan for Middle East power grid," Reuters, February 7, 1996.

62 Government of Israel, *Development Options for Regional Cooperation*, IV-6-2.

63 Steve Rodan, "Energy minister seeks a secure pipeline."

64 Government of Israel, *Development Options for Regional Cooperation*, IV-6-10. The same proposal is also in Merhav, *Economic Cooperation and Middle East Peace*, pp. 111–115.

65 This source requested complete anonymity. Israel's insertion into an annex of the Oslo Accord of a passage concerning "regional cooperation for the transfer, distribution, and industrial exploitation of gas, oil, and other energy resources" is noteworthy in this context. (See the *Israeli–Palestinian Declaration of Principles*, 13 September, 1993, Annex IV: "Protocol on Israeli–Palestinian cooperation concerning regional development programs," section B-7.)

66 Deutsch, *Political Community in the North Atlantic Area*.

67 According to the World Bank, the Middle East is the world's only region where per-capita exports have dropped since the late 1980s. This is attributed to the drop in world oil prices in combination with the failure of regional economies to increase and diversify the non-oil export sector (Suleiman Al-Khalidi, "World bodies say reforms are key to Arab growth," Reuters, January 26, 1996). However, Israel's economy, unlike that of the rest of the region, is booming. Its gross national product (GNP) of more than $70 billion exceeds that of Egypt, Syria, Jordan, and Lebanon *combined*, and is growing at approximately 4–5 percent per year. (See Al-Khalidi, "Israeli integration in Arab world arouses fears.")

68 Clawson, "Mideast economies after the Israel–PLO handshake," p. 159.

69 Immanuel Wallerstein, *The Modern World System*, Academic Press, New York, 1974; Immanuel Wallerstein, *The Capitalist World Economy*, Cambridge University Press, Cambridge, 1979.

70 "Special report Syria," *Middle East Economic Digest*, September 29, 1995, pp. 10–11.

71 Patrick Clawson notes ironically that it is Israel, the state that least needs them, that could make the most efficient use of such borrowing from a Middle East Development Bank. (See Patrick Clawson, "The limited scope for economic cooperation in the contemporary Levant," in Spiegel, *The Arab–Israeli Search for Peace*, p. 96.)

72 Merhav, *Economic Cooperation and Middle East Peace*, p. 11.

73 The Arabs have occasionally flirted with building an identical structure among Arab states only, a "new Arab order" in the aftermath of the second Gulf war. The basis was to have been a "strategic linkage" on the same 6 × 2 premise that underlay the Damascus Declaration of 1991, between the Gulf Cooperation Council (GCC) and the two remaining Arab powerhouses, Egypt and Syria: essentially a "new Middle East" without Israel. The theory of irrevocability that lay behind it is identical to that of Shimon Peres's vision. In the words of Sayed Masri, Egypt's then-ambassador to Saudi Arabia: "Arab unity will be built the same way the Europeans have done it, step by step, *based on concrete economic steps until nobody can break away even if they want to*" (emphasis

added; quoted in David B. Ottoway, "Aid to Egypt, Syria tied to free markets," *Washington Post*, April 6, 1991, pp. A15, 16; for a second rendition during the Netanyahu period see also Issam Hamza, "Eight Arab nations agree on common market," Reuters, June 26, 1997).

74 Interview, Damascus, March 1996.
75 Clawson, "The limited scope for economic cooperation," in Spiegel, *Arab–Israeli Search for Peace*, p. 86.
76 For the economic critique of Middle East economic cooperation, see Clawson's "Mideast economies after the Israeli–PLO handshake," and "The limited scope for economic cooperation."
77 Al-Khalidi, "Israeli integration in Arab world arouses fears."
78 Sara Roy, "Separation or integration: closure and the economic future of the Gaza Strip revisited," *Middle East Journal* 48(1), winter 1994, pp. 11–30.
79 According to one news report, the Peres government had already broached the subject with its Arab counterparts (see Julian Ozanne, "Separation mars Middle East integration," *Financial Times*, February 9, 1995, p. 9).
80 Interview, Tel Aviv, March, 1996. It should be added that this Israeli did not see such fears as ungrounded, given the huge differences in the size and nature of the Arab and Israeli economies.
81 Merhav, *Economic Cooperation and Middle East Peace*, p. 17.
82 Yousef Ibrahim, "Israelis join Arabs in step to broaden cooperation; but money and politics block wide agreement, boycott is maintained," *International Herald Tribune*, November 2, 1994.
83 Rana Sabbagh, "King Hussein marks 60th birthday amid criticism," Reuters, November 14, 1995.
84 Zvi Barel, "The Jordanian model," *Ha'aretz*, July 30, 1995, p. B1.
85 Mounir B. Abboud, *Saudi Gazette* correspondent in Beirut, "Peace bomb is Israeli weapon to invade Arab culture," *Moneyclips*, December 5, 1994.
86 Interview, Beirut II, March, 1996. Indeed, during my own visit to Beirut in 1994 I came across another group of intellectuals with goals identical to those who held the anti-normalization conference later that year. They wanted to help their fellow intellectuals organize a cultural front to save the Arab identity from destruction by the new "Middle Eastern" one being imposed on them from outside.
87 Samih Farsoun, "The Arabs: preparing for the 21st century," *Mideast Monitor* 10(2), spring, 1995, p. 10.
88 Interview, As-Salt.
89 A recent articulation of this complaint occurred, of all places, at the Middle East and North Africa Economic Summit in Amman, held in October 1995, where Peres himself attacked Egypt from the podium for failing to make "economic peace" with Israel (Jack Redden, "Israel says Egypt did not make 'economic peace'," Reuters, October 30, 1995).
90 Amos Perlmutter, "Abandon the dream of a 'new Middle East'," *Jerusalem Post*, August 4, 1995, p. 5.
91 Gerges, "Egyptian–Israeli relations turn sour," *op cit*.
92 Rana Sabbagh, "King Hussein marks 60th birthday amid criticism."
93 The exact charges against Shbeilat were violating the dignity of the king and queen, distributing leaflets that do the same, inflaming religious and ethnic divisions, and undermining the state's moral authority and confidence in the national currency (Suleiman al-Khalidi, "Detained Jordanian wins labor election," Reuters, February 18, 1996).

94 Shbeilat was the joint candidate selected to represent both the Islamist and secular nationalist opposition (the report on the election, *ibid.*).

95 "Domestic debate continues on 'normalization' with Israel," *Jordan: Issues and Perspectives* 22, Jordan Information Bureau, Washington, DC, January/February, 1996, p. 6.

96 David W. Lesch, "Damascus won't accept 'peace at any price'," *Christian Science Monitor*, December 6, 1995, p. 19.

97 Peter Ford, "Unlearning hatred: Syrians ambivalent on peace with Israel," *Christian Science Monitor*, October 20, 1993, p. 3.

98 For the procedural details, see Yoram Meital, "The economic relations between Israel and Egypt: tourism 1979–1984," in Fishelson, *Economic Cooperation in the Middle East*, p. 294.

99 Merhav, *Economic Cooperation and Middle East Peace*, p. 253.

100 Sheikh Hamad bin Jassem Al-Thani, Qatar foreign minister, quoted in "Israel sells $2 billion in goods a year to Gulf states," Reuters, January 18, 1996.

101 Guy Bechor, "The Syrian flute and the peace treaty," *Ha'aretz*, July 30, 1995, p. B2.

102 Naomi Levitsky, "Nasrallah and the seventy suicide bombers," *Yediot Aharanot*, Sabbath supplement, April 19, 1996, pp. 10–12.

103 Interview, Tarrablus.

104 *Ibid.*

105 *Ibid.*

106 Abboud, "Peace bomb is Israeli weapon to invade Arab culture."

107 One *Ha'aretz* correspondent went so far as to refer to an "Israeli–Jordanian axis," which he said has become "a political fact in the Middle East" (Guy Bechor, "The Syrian flute and the peace treaty").

2

COMPETING TRADE AGENDAS IN THE ARAB–ISRAELI PEACE PROCESS

A case studies approach

J. W. Wright, Jr.

> Businessmen tend to harbor a deep distrust of political equality, majority rule, congress, and the institutions of democratic government generally. They seek to use their superior resources – in money, organization, status and access – to protect their possession of opportunities to acquire these superior resources. It is hardly surprising, therefore, that reform efforts directed toward redistributive policies and the effective regulation of money in politics meet with so little success.
>
> Robert A. Dahl[1]

Introduction

The contribution Laura Drake makes above is extremely important, and one of the best I have read on the subject. Even so, it could more fully consider the role mercantilism plays in the Arab–Israeli peace process.[2] This is to say that competing trade agendas form crucial impediments to developing and sustaining peace in the region. The author posits that it is not only the Peres "vision" of the new Middle East which forms the driving force behind the peace process. Rather, it is individuals' and corporations' financial interests in conflict continuation that control the speed at which the negotiations are driven. For example, as Bichler and Nitzan illustrate in Chapter 3, Israel's core conglomerates are clearly unconvinced of the gains to be made from retooling their "war" industries as peacetime production machines and are resisting the peace process. However, they are not outdone by American firms, who depend heavily on the recycled U.S. Agency for International

Development (USAID) funds that flow to them through their Israeli partners and subsidiaries. Certainly the Israeli small and medium-sized enterprises which supply these core conglomerates have an interest in continuing their profit flows. Palestinian Authority (PA) officials also have vested interests in continuing deliberations as opposed to real resolutions, mainly because they have more control over aid funds than corporate profits. The Gulf Arab countries have often been accused of being less interested in the peace process than maybe they should be, but it is important to realize that they are facing serious economic decline issues of their own.

The point is that diplomats (as well as scholars writing on the peace process) have so far too often failed to identify correctly the actors and agencies that are competing most vigorously for controlling positions in the peace process. As such, they have not placed failures in Arab–Israeli negotiations in their appropriate contexts. The goals of this chapter are:

1   to show that the continuing conflict in the Middle East can be linked to commercial interests in the region;
2   to identify players in the peace process who face competing trade agendas and who therefore have vested interests in keeping markets in Arab and Israeli territories less than fair and less than free.

Position 1 is investigated through discussions of political-economic theory. Position 2 is addressed through presentation of a series of case studies. This format is meant to introduce into the debate further discussion of the role merchant interests play in negotiations and to illustrate how economic diplomacy could help dismantle the web of competing trade agendas that form barriers to peace. In sum, I feel that if we do not identify who profits most and least from the peace process we cannot understand who is promoting conflict and why.

Defining the problems

A couple of initial definitions may be useful here. By commercial interests, I mean people who have profit motives within a given funding scenario. This definition obviously applies to corporations operating in the region. As used here, it also applies to government officials who receive either campaign or individual funds from funding entities, ranging from the lobbyist groups to international aid agencies. As an extension of this definition, the phrase 'competing trade agendas' then refers to groups that have competing commercial interests, i.e. governments with conflicting budgetary or economic development structures, corporations with opposing cost or revenue source structures, or service provision groups who must compete for aid or grant funding. Further definition can be made through Louis Cantori's concept of corporate conservatism as it applies to the region, which illustrates that economic structures are often built around family, tribal, or political alliances in the Middle East, as opposed to the more firm-oriented corporate structures seen in the West. He and I both feel that this conservatist system creates variant regional competitive structures.[3]

With the exception of Valerie York's Peace Media project,[4] few publications have presented case studies on trade agendas and their impact on Arab and Israeli diplomacy. Most writers on the peace process have seen barriers on the political landscapes in the Arab countries and Israel as the most crucial impediments to building regional peace. However, the regional kaleidoscope is not this narrowly defined; forcing pundits to ask what makes the Arab and Israeli political horizons so filled with obstacles are not people who oppose peace – meaning that the majority of people throughout the Middle East support a peace process leading to economic and political stability – but people who have ceded their moral integrity to financial incentives which are based on conflict continuation. These incentives lead to the development of competing trade agendas. In the process, trade regimes are built that promote serious economic inequality between the rich and poor on both sides of the Green Line, and on both sides of the North–South divide that exists among the Arab states. A further consequence of these situations has been the development of radical groups from the poorer sectors of both the Arab and Israeli communities who feel they have little to lose by creating conflict. Thus those in power profit from the cycle of violence that is created by those who oppose them.

My position on this subject was reached through association with, and the study of, ideas presented to me via unexpected sources. First, I sat on a series of panels with former American diplomats who were able to give practical insights into how U.S. diplomatic agendas are set. Second, I was teaching a graduate course in economic theory when I came across references to the Middle East situation in a 1971 edition of John Kenneth Galbraith's *Economics, Peace, and Laughter*.[5] I also found work by Gary Becker and William Darity on the economics of crime and welfare that can be applied to the Middle East situation. Third, I attended a lecture by Queen Nour of Jordan, who, rather than speak on cultural exchanges as she often does, pointed out the economic parameters within which the Arab–Israeli peace process was being discussed.[6] I realized that Becker, Darity, Galbraith, and Queen Nour reach three similar conclusions which can be applied to analysis of the peace process:

1 Economic inequality is an impediment to both commercial and political stability.
2 Political solutions written without properly addressing economic realities are not sustainable.
3 The competing industrial interests of individuals with access to negotiators often have a negative impact on the direction of peace negotiations

in troubled areas – indeed they often outweigh collective/national policy agendas.

Ambassador William Stoltzfus ilustrates this third point with an American example, claiming that those interested in U.S. diplomatics must

differentiate between American policies, which might include the promotion of democratic forms of government or programs aiming to facilitate free trade and economic development for poorer nations, and interests, the factors around which U.S. diplomacy really centers; we seem too willing to sacrifice policies if they impinge on our interests in a region. I don't aim to pass judgment on the morality of this fact, but it is naive to believe this is less than the true state of affairs. U.S. policies toward the Middle East reflect our desire to support democratic regimes that promote human rights agendas and that maintain legal and economic equity among all social levels; that promote goals for reducing military aggression and the reduction of chemical and nuclear weaponry in the region; that foster our hopes for addressing medical and environmental issues that threaten to destroy our earth.

Our interests, however, suggest the need for different agendas all together. These interests have historically been driven by our cold war fears about Soviet infiltration of Arab regimes. In addition, they have reflected our perceived need to dominate the geo-political position in the Middle East through our influence on Israeli governments. Since the 1970s we have added to the list of U.S. interests our need for Arab-owned oil, our industries' desires for access to oil-rich commercial markets, and our goal of sustaining American jobs via military exports to our largest clients, the Arabs and the Israelis. On a broader scale, the scope of foreign aid and economic diplomacy has grown enormously through the offering of most favored nation status to "friendly nations." These are examples of situations where American interests have come into conflict with our official policies, and fostered regional disputes.[7]

It is informative to begin with this American commentary because it reveals how political goals and commercial and governmental interests are likely to be in conflict. It also illustrates ways in which economic and financial incentives for conflict can outweigh political interest in peaceful cooperation. Few would argue against the statement that in the Middle East the groups who have profited most from the status quo are not the people or the peacekeepers, but the arms traders, military officers, and black marketeers. Possibly the most distressing part of this scenario is that democratically elected governments like those in the U.S. (and the U.K.)

and Israel are the most obvious supporters of a status quo in the Middle East that promotes conflict rather than cooperation.

This situation leads us to ask what governing people or population of voters would fail to identify and follow policies supporting peace. There are five logical answers:

1   A country whose national interests are in conflict with the ideologies that are supposed to define its political policies.
2   A regime staffed by people whose personal political or individual finan-cial-economic interests outweigh their commitments to stated national agendas.
3   A government facing economic difficulties so great that it cannot (or will not) bear responsibility for inter-regional diplomacy.
4   A voting population which does not (or does not care to) understand the underlying foundations of the economic and political problems it faces.
5   A voting population so prejudiced that it is willing to sacrifice economic well-being for the perceived benefits of discrimination.

Within these possibilities it is clear that we cannot assume that voters understand the economic implications of their actions, but we do know that voters are often willing to allocate their tax dollars in ways that promote policies reflecting their personal biases, even if their professional positions suffer.[8] In the U.S. this has recently been played out in several issues, including a host of referenda on migration legislation and welfare reform. In Israel, Shimson Bichler has studied electoral economics since the 1972 elec-tion and determined that people voted not as an expression of political beliefs but in accordance with the way they thought party policies would affect their occupations and wages. More to the point of this discussion, his work reveals that biased and prejudiced perceptions among Israeli voters often outweighed their pragmatic behaviors. He concludes that

> Israel has in a relatively short period of time undergone a significant restructuring, interlocking its business elite into global capital. However, for the small business sector, where the majority of voters earn their livings, the New Middle East Order was often more a curse than a boon. Lower import barriers and the consequent flood of cheaper imports have undermined profitability. It should be noted, however, that it was not Palestinian imports that have closed these businesses but rather it was Rabin's policies. This segment within the Israeli business sector was the primary victim of repeated closures of the Palestinian territories, because these closures prevented Palestinian workers from selling their services to weaving and finishing contractors.[9]

It is worth mentioning that blocks of voters do learn over time, or, better said, they fine-tune their strategies for opposing government policies that do not suit their economic interests. For example, the labor groups that opposed Rabin in the 1996 election in Israel in response to Netanyahu's promises of substantive economics reforms are the same groups which implemented a massive strike again Likud policies in 1997 and 1998. Their grievance was that Netanyahu had not kept his promises, and indeed that they had learnt that border closures were not in their best interests. Polls show these voting groups will not support Likud again in the 1999 elections.[10]

Even so, according to Bichler (as well as the authors of Chapters 3, 4 and 5), it was voters who felt threatened by the potential influx of Palestinian labor who supported Likud most strongly in the 1996 Israeli election. Thus, while it may be beliefs that lead to the creation of democratic systems and benevolent national ideologies, it is the pursuit of self-preservation that drives voter behavior, and that defines national political and economic agendas. Clearly, however, perceptions of self-interest need not be substantiated by fact or reality, because the popular perceptions held by voters and elected officials can be misguided by media or politics. Herein lies the conflict between promoting national policies and pursuing the interests of the economically and politically powerful in any given nation. While this idea will be illustrated further in cases presented later in this chapter, it is crucial to understand that a nation's benevolent ideals are not always, if ever, reflected in an electorate's voting register or a government's decision-making process.

However, because a majority population can impose both economic and social inequality on a minority group, especially in a system dominated by a theocratically driven electorate, linkage needs to be made between the impact of economic inequality, the political responses made to it, and the development of radical factions. It is illustrative here to review some of John Kenneth Galbraith's remarks, made in the 1960s, on economic diplomacy in the region:

- On the rise of militancy, he urged diplomats "to distrust the man who blames on revolutionaries what should be attributed to deprivation."[11]
- On U.S.–Arab relations, he warned that "circumstances and politics have given us different and relentlessly hostile friends and clients in the Middle East."[12]
- On commerce, he claimed that "the test of economic achievement is not how much we produce but what we do to make life tolerable and pleasant."[13]
- On faith, he recognized that, "among the poor, only religion, with its promise of a later munificence for those who endure deprivation with patience, has been competitive with economic circumstances in shaping the general character of the social, political, and spiritual processes of life."[14]

From Galbraith's perspective, then, conflict is promoted between peoples with widely divergent economic situations. Cooperation is promoted between people who live under equitable and pleasant living conditions. Moreover, trust is the prevailing prerequisite for participatory economics and politics; for instance, once stable economic and social conditions are provided, people are motivated to expand their influence and wealth through trade and commercial cooperation. Without these conditions and the complementary trade structures they engender, militancy and not prosperity are supported, and only the dominant elite factions benefit.[15] He apparently believes, too, that U.S. policy has too often supported the agendas of the elites.

Work connecting poverty and crime is also applicable here. Nobel Laureate Gary Becker produced a series of articles on the economics of crime and punishment.[16] The essence of this series is that people have a threshold after which they become willing to commit a crime. A crime such as petty robbery would not be committed by a millionaire because the potential "costs" are relatively high and the "economic returns" would be too low. However, the millionaire would be more likely to risk a parking fine because the downside risks are relatively small. But the millionaire would be more likely to pursue insider trading, or the wealthy elected official the embezzlement of public funds, for example, because the returns are potentially very high. Conversely, the person earning welfare wages might find the returns of crimes like burglary high as a percentage of available capital. They might also see the relative costs and risks between destitution and detention as low.

Similarly, William Darity identifies failing social services programs with rising crime.[17] While his conclusions and Becker's do not match, his work illustrates how, after being driven into unemployment by unfair public policies, minorities have incentives to pursue illicit activities. The result is that a spiral of negative behaviors can bring about a rapid decline in people's pride and sense of community. This is almost exactly the point that Sara Roy has made about the situation in Gaza: that people who live under conditions of such "economic despair" fall into a pattern where community values begin to fragment and fail to serve positive purposes.[18] The broader set of unfair public policies which drive Palestinians into economic disadvantage is also presented in a series of articles in Eugene Cotran and Chibli Mallat's *The Arab–Israeli Accords: Legal Perspectives*, especially in the section on "Economy and Law."[19] Darity also recognizes that a consequence of high incarceration rates among minority groups is that a family's main wage-earner is usually displaced, forcing children to grow up in an environment defined by both inadequate social support structures, single parent families, and persistent poverty. This position can be related to those Fatimeh Ziai makes (in Chapter 5) about Palestinian detentions in Israel.[20]

Taken collectively, these researchers argue for national development programs that increase people's quality of life, maximize their occupational mobility, and reduce the number of intolerable living situations. In contrast, an opposing set of programs is being implemented in the West Bank and Gaza (and indeed throughout the Middle East, ranging from the Israeli and Syrian occupations of southern Lebanon to the continuing U.S.-led economic blockades being imposed on Iraq and Iran), where the level of poverty has increased significantly since the peace talks began in 1991. The level of social services provision has also declined significantly in these areas, and at a time when refugee populations have dramatically increased. In addition, in the territories the number of male Palestinian detentions has skyrocketed, leaving far too many women (or children) as heads of households. Even more tragically, the murder rate of Palestinian "collaborators" is both tragic and economically significant, as it leaves families bereft of their traditional wage-earner and creates skills losses in Arab occupational markets.[21]

The point is this: The Arab–Israeli conflict is steeped in situations that could have been avoided had negotiators better considered long-standing economic theories which warned against the very policies that have been written and in some cases implemented. Unfortunately, this failure has created situations in which economic sources of conflict are endemic to weaknesses in the commercial, legal and trade structures that are supposed to support the Arab–Israeli peace process. The result of these weak theoretical underpinnings is failed negotiating structures, and, as an extension, rising militarism among the Israeli and Palestinian lower classes, in both of which people see fewer and fewer benefits from supporting the peace process. And why should not either set of groups seek recompense? I am neither agreeing with nor justifying radical activities – and surely neither are Galbraith, Becker, or Darity – but it is naive to believe that people left destitute by the peace process will view radical behavior in the same ways that those of us who are less threatened would see it. And so the downward economic and political spirals that Galbraith warned us would occur in dependent regions typified by economic inequality have clearly developed in both Palestine and Israel. But if these linkages are so clear, why will the key players involved not work toward reversing this downward spiral?

Case studies from the peace process

This section identifies several commercially based disincentives which lead powerful people and groups to be less than supportive of (or in some cases simply less than concerned about) Arab–Israeli diplomatic processes. It also identifies scenarios which lead to an inequitable concentration of wealth among corporate and government elites, as opposed to a distribution of funds to the region's smaller businesses and poorer classes of people. The economic agendas identified in these case studies merge to reveal significant impediments to achieving regional peace.

Because Chapters 3 and 4 provide analysis of structural biases in the Israeli economic and legal structures, I will not do so here. Similarly, discussions of several national commercial agendas are provided in other chapters. We will therefore limit commentary to regional situations:

- economic factors in the Levant;
- declines in the regional labor market;
- difficulties facing the region's aspirations for participating in global markets.

In order to show that the region does not exist in a policy vacuum, the American corporate agenda for the region is discussed in Case 3. In order to illustrate that no part of the peace process is immune to corruption, the PA's inability and/or unwillingness to distribute funds to non-governmental organizations (NGOs) is discussed in Case 4. The primary linkage between cases is the way competing trade agendas support conflict over cooperation as well as provide incentives for avoiding economic reforms and global market integrations.

Case 1: Problems with the regional cooperation presumption

On March 4, 1996, Queen Nour of Jordan was honored at the Kennedy Center for her contribution to world philanthropy. Unlike most of her speeches, which focus on Jordan's cultural wealth, in this address Queen Nour focused on economics. She spoke of the occupational inequities in the former Israeli occupied territories which fueled the intifada (uprising) and other civil strife among Palestinians. She spoke of the high density of refugees in the Levant and the influence their abject poverty has on regional instability. She discussed the Arab regimes' inordinately high budget expenditure on military equipment, and she mentioned both the positive and the negative roles international aid plays in the region. Her husband's people, she said, cared more about occupational advancement than radical politics, and she asserted that investments leading to employment creation are an essential factor in promoting peace. In sum, Queen Nour argued that the critical disincentive against garnering support for the peace process is grounded in the region's persistent poverty, and its failing economic and social service provision structures.

These situations clearly do not provide an environment that will promote economic cooperation between Arabs and Israelis. And yet for sustainable peace to develop the goal of cooperation between both small firms and large corporations is necessary; the modus operandi in the twenty-first century in the Middle East will likely be one of both economic and political dependencies. As Sari Nusseibeh puts it, "Even if a genuinely independent Palestinian state is established, political and economic separation will not be possible...

it is unworkable."[22] The claims of Queen Nour and Nusseibeh are realistic and simple: while the politics of separation is popular, the economics of state-building makes commercial cooperation essential, especially if the resulting trade regimes bring employment to the region's people, allowing them to build wealth worth protecting. Indeed, employment cooperation could lift the Palestinian labor market out of the despair it has faced since the intifada and the Gulf war.[23] The other alternative, lower employment, will lead more Palestinians to lose hope and will surely lead to more violence.

Cooperation is possible. One survey showed that 92 percent of Palestinian firms and 96 percent of Israeli firms felt peace-process protocols on trade would facilitate economic growth.[24] But is cooperation probable? There are several reasons that the answer to this question is most likely negative. The first of these is that the barriers caused by the 28-year Israeli occupation of the West Bank and Gaza are difficult to overcome. Biased legal structures are the most pervasive part of this scenario. According to Kent Ford and Doyle Peterson, the regulatory structure was so biased against Arab economic integration before the peace process that real growth was difficult to achieve (even to imagine).[25] This situation is echoed in Chapter 5, and also in the articles in *The Arab–Israeli Accords: Legal Perspectives*. According to Sharif Elmusa and Mahmoud El-Jaafari, the agreements signed so far during the peace process create a legal and economic web "woven by Israel to serve its own economic and strategic interests, [and which] has kept the Palestinian economy in a state of subordination to the Israeli economy. The Palestinians tried unsuccessfully during the *intifada* to unravel this web,"[26] but in reality this attempt leaves the Palestinian private sector in a more dilapidated condition than ever. At the same time, both the Arab boycott of Israeli products in effect since the 1970s[27] and the Palestinian boycott which began during the intifada served to break long-standing ties with Israeli buyers, suppliers, and employers.

Now the persistence of border closures on the Israeli side, the division of business districts that has been agreed in Hebron, and increasing incidences of human rights violations and detentions on both sides of the Green Line serve to restrict not only people's ability to earn money but businesses' ability to negotiate contracts within the region.[28] This leaves one asking with whom cooperation is possible. For the most part, a positive answer cannot be given on a regional basis. It is true that the Paris protocol sets out initiatives aimed at giving the PA a freer hand in setting trade agendas and creating regulations.[29] But has it used these powers well? Even if it has, the Levant's business environment remains constricted by several things:

- a less than stable money supply in Israel that makes the prospect of recycling any Palestinian deposits unlikely;[30]

- shifting alliances between Jordan and its neighbors, especially Iraq, which continue to alter regional import–export exchanges;[31]
- regulatory systems that impede even middle-class professionals' attempts to mobilize human or financial capital;[32]
- a competitive market for U.S. aid that facilitates economic and political dependencies rather than promotes political or regulatory liberalism.[33]

More specific examples come from the fact that many types of trade are legally limited by the economic protocols signed because they "list the types of goods that Palestinians may import from places other than Israel."[34] Import regulations can be used to illustrate how this regulation could affect economic development. Fertilizers have to be imported from either Egypt or Jordan, leaving Palestinian farmers unable to import fertilizers directly from the region's largest producer, Saudi Arabia. Palestinians can also import construction materials and home appliances only from Egypt or Jordan. For assembled products with mixed input-part origins, the product must have a 30 percent contribution from either Egypt or Jordan. Even products like wheat must come from either Israel or one of a list of preferred Arab or Islamic states. No European nations are on this list, and thus imports from the European Union (EU) have to go through an Egyptian, Israeli, or Jordanian mark-up process before (or if) they are able to reach the West Bank or Gaza. Are such regulations really meant to enhance the Palestinians' ability to develop trade cooperation on either an intra-regional or an inter-regional basis? This seems unlikely. Rather, these regulations severely limit productivity in the Palestinian private sector, and serve to impede the transfer of foreign products or would-be foreign direct investment from Middle East and North African (MENA) countries, from the Palestinian Diaspora, and from the broader global market for investment funds.

The prevailing presumption in these agreements is that Egypt and Jordan were already involved in trade with Palestine and that these protocol edicts would further enhance those relationships. The problem is that this presumption is based on perceptions and not on reality. In practice, sales between the West Bank and Jordan have not exceeded more than 10 percent of Palestinian trade during any time under Israeli occupation.[35] This means there were (and are) fewer marketing contacts and established trading lines between Palestinians and their Jordanian neighbors than one might expect. Moreover, the 50 percent decline in Jordan's gross national product (GNP) growth since the Gulf war will only weaken Palestinians' ability to enhance their commercial positions with either Egyptian or Jordanian buyers or suppliers.[36]

Another trade impediment has been the erosion of the Palestinian production base. Not only are the territory's manufacturing bases and financial structures weaker today than they were a few years ago, but Israel's long occupation "weakened the Palestinian economy and made it increasingly dependent on the Israeli economy."[37] Examination of economic data reveals that the dominant sources in Palestinian economic growth come from income generated via transfers made outside the territories, such as employment in Israel or labor exportation to the Gulf States. While some claim that the intifada has led to an increase in Palestinian self-reliance in numerous markets, the following situations remain:

- the Palestinian labor force is largely dependent on Israeli employment;
- Palestinians have been left with a poor and crumbling infrastructure;
- Israel's attempts to disenfranchise the territories' formal sector succeeded;
- the "strategic investment policy" severely limits available funding from the Diaspora.[38]

Moreover, these strategies were part of the Israeli policy of "communal stagnation," meant to further Israel's expropriation of at least 67 percent of usable land in the West Bank and 40 percent of the usable land in the Gaza Strip. This policy also allowed the Israeli military to exercise complete control over the Palestinian water supply, 68 percent of which was transferred to Israeli settlers. As a result, agriculture's contribution to Palestinian gross domestic product (GDP) fell dramatically in both the 1980s and the 1990s.[39] In addition, legal restrictions on Arab use of water – in areas where climate and topography make only 10.4 percent of the land productive and only then with access to intensive irrigation – make it difficult for Arabs to produce agricultural or other products requiring water.[40] Too often, even productive Arab firms exist only as subcontractors to Israeli firms.[41]

At the same time, one should not look at developments in PA-controlled areas from naive perspectives. Human rights violations, including the deaths of untried people held in detention by the Palestinian police and the seemingly overlooked vigilante murders of Palestinian men suspected of collaborating with the Musa'ad, leave families more susceptible to poverty and/or radicalism. Sustained periods marked by clashes between Israeli forces and Palestinian youths only serve to make this situation worse. Border closures hurt people on both sides of the Green Line. And, from an economic point of view, the degeneration of civil authority and the rights it is supposed to protect is simultaneously inefficient and unproductive.[42] These situations leave peace-process negotiators with few avenues left to travel. They also leave business owners with fewer firms than expected with whom they can expect to develop cooperative commercial relationships or potential partnerships.

Case 2: Competing forces in regional labor supply

Unemployment in the Levant is probably the most critical problem in the region. Indeed, the stakes connected to reestablishing "repatriation, remittance, and reunion" structures between the northern Arab states and the Gulf Cooperation Council (GCC) states are very high.[43] It was hoped that movements toward regional peace, via Arab and Israeli negotiations, would convince the Gulf States to (re)open their economies to more northern Arab labor. This has not happened and is unlikely to happen for several reasons.

Since the 1970s the Gulf States have set a tradition of importing labor. On the one hand, they needed this labor so they could complete ambitious construction and development programs. On the other hand, they paid the price not only in the cost of their own budgetary expenditures, but also through the loss of massive amounts of remittance income. In addition, corruption became an integral part of the system, with national Mafia-type groups extracting vast amounts from Gulf entrepreneurs. As a consequence, the Gulf States paid for most of the region's growth. This is especially true in Jordan and Palestine, where as much as 70 percent of private-sector investment was financed through remittance revenues.[44] In contrast to Jordan, the Gulf States lost enormous amounts of liquidity due to foreign-labor financial transfers. This was apparently a price these then labor-poor countries felt forced to pay in order to meet aggressive plans for industrialization.

The question currently asked by many is whether or not the Gulf States will support the peace process by (re)opening their borders to more Palestinian labor. Indeed, the GCC as a whole has been widely criticized for implementing policies many see as being opposed to this end. However, if the practical situations that exist in the Gulf are examined it becomes difficult to believe that these states could support additional labor transfers from the North. For example, with population growth rates in the Gulf countries averaging over 4 percent, local labor-supply markets have changed in ways which are economically and politically troublesome.

In fact, the Middle East maintains the highest labor-force growth rate of any region in the world. Based on International Labor Organization figures, the annual growth rates of working-age populations were as follows in selected Arab countries between 1975 and 1990: Bahrain 4.61 percent, Egypt 2.58 percent, Iraq 3.57 percent, Jordan 3.33 percent, Oman 4.51 percent, Saudi Arabia 5.17 percent, and Syria 3.52 percent. A particularly noteworthy trend these figures illustrate is that the highest local working-age population growth rates are not in the countries that are traditionally labor suppliers, like Egypt, Jordan, and Syria. Rather, the three fastest-growing workforces between 1975 and 1990 were Saudi Arabia, Bahrain, and Oman, in that order. Projections show that growth rates may be slowing somewhat in the Gulf States, but this is a relative conclusion because these countries are expected to maintain labor-force growth rates of 3 percent between 2000 and 2025.

The obvious implication is that the oil-rich nations are finding it necessary to localize their labor forces. For example, Saudi Arabia included notice of its ten-year schedule for Saudiization as early as 1985 in its Fourth Five-Year Development Plan, but in 1997 it increased the pace for repatriating labor, often held in/working in the kingdom illegally, by enforcement of an "amnesty" program. The United Arab Emirates (UAE) and other Gulf States have also implemented similar amnesty programs. The point is that today all of the GCC is following localization policies because such programs make economic sense in terms of raising citizen employment (at least theoretically), enhancing community-level participation in private-sector production, damming the outward flow of remittance transfers, and lowering the overall costs of import subsidies, social services provision, and immigration and visa application processing.

In contrast to the Gulf States, which need to promote local employment, the Levantine states still need to export labor in order to survive.[45] Their population and workforce growth rates are still high by world standards, and their increasing inability to generate local employment has led to a real decline in regional wages. Egyptian manufacturing wages fell from 181 percent of the 1970 levels in 1985 to 114 percent in 1992; Jordanian wages fell from 157 percent of 1970 levels in 1985 to 111 percent in 1992. Syrian wages had fallen to 92 percent of their 1970 levels by 1992. Much of this decline in wages can be attributed to the presence of too many new job entrants; 78 percent of first-time job seekers in Syria and 76.6 percent in Egypt are persistently unemployed and unable to earn sustainable incomes.

In addition, the sector where the Gulf's projected labor-force entry will most likely take place is in the services. These sectors now comprise significant proportions of the Gulf economies – Bahrain 68.2 percent, Kuwait 74 percent, Qatar 65.4 percent, Saudi Arabia 66.9 percent – which have traditionally relied on university-level labor from Egypt, Jordan, Lebanon, and Palestine. However, statistics for higher education in the Gulf States show that university-level enrollment figures exceed 18 percent in Bahrain, 16 percent in Kuwait, 18 percent in Qatar, and 20 percent in Saudi Arabia. It is also true that these students tend to congregate around studies in business, computer science, English, and engineering, which are also fields traditionally filled by imported labor. This pool of young and well-educated local youth will further facilitate the Gulf States' localization processes, especially in sectors like banking and government services.[46]

The most unfortunate part of this scenario is that neither Jordan nor Palestine wants Palestinians to repatriate because the mass return of Palestinians to Palestine would cause significant economic shocks. As Ishaq Diwan and Michael Walton put it, "For Jordan, the key economic objectives in the short-term remain defensive: to avert a sudden attack on the dinar, to retain Palestinian capital in the host economy, and to avoid the sudden exposure of inefficient industries to competition."[47] On one side of the Jordanian equation, unemployment and declining wages are key problems. Real per-capita income in Jordan had already declined to about 50 percent of its 1980s' level by 1991. The Gulf war hastened this decline because it led to the loss of most of its exports to Iraq, which absorbed 30 percent or more of Jordan's exports in 1989, and it caused massive repatriation of skilled workers who had been living in the Gulf. For these reasons Jordan wants to avoid the absorption of any more people from the regional labor force.

That said, however, on the other side of the Jordanian equation, Palestinian returnees from the Gulf have been the saving grace of the financial sector because they deposited huge amounts of repatriated savings that they had accumulated while working in the GCC markets (with additional savings abroad estimated at over 100 per cent of GDP). These deposits enabled Jordan at least partially to revive financing for the pattern of infrastructure development it developed in the early 1980s. Most of the returnees from the Gulf to Jordan also had more marketable skills than did people trained in the local market. For these reasons the returnees who had been working in the Gulf States, who often had more experience and better skills, became preferable employees in the kingdom to those who had stayed to work in local markets. A paradox has thus developed in Jordan since 1991:

> although there are enticements for allowing this labor to leave — such as a potential reduction of social welfare provision costs — the fact that this movement of Palestinian labor would not be complemented with an inflow of remittances and/or increased external aid, will place a real strain on Jordan's already crowded financial institutions and markets. It would also certainly force a repricing of wage rates, probably leading to inflation. In addition, the resulting decrease in population would reduce consumption demand and in the process will reduce employment in heavily-import-laden markets.[48]

From the Palestinian side of the equation a similar situation is faced. The PA wants to attract deposits to its fledgling but already ailing banking system, as do the Israelis, because their banking system benefits from the expansion of Palestinian deposits. Gaining more professional-level workers would also be of benefit to both the Palestinian and Israeli economies. However, neither the PA nor Israel wants to attract workers who will displace the few people who are still employed in the territories. Moreover, they do not want to see repatriation of the lower end of the Jordanian-Palestinian labor force that would add to the unemployment problem and not bring capital with it. This position, probably more sternly taken in Lebanon, leaves the poor in the region worse off than ever before.

In addition, it is not to either Jordan's or Palestine's immediate advantage to have its Gulf-trained skilled labor return to the Gulf. While such a return would raise remittances in the long run, in the short run it would likely lead to serious capital flight. After all, Gulf banks are more secure than any of the banks which now operate in Palestine,[49] and the rate of financial liberalization is quickest in the former Trucial States, leaving possible returnees from Jordan/Palestine to the Gulf with more investment opportunities in the South. And, since the best candidates for returning to the Gulf are the most highly qualified people in Jordan and Palestine, the potential for a significant skilled-labor "brain drain" also exists.

One can see how incentives for conflict in the region are enhanced in areas where people are most frustrated by unemployment. Gaza is perhaps the most glaring example, as an area where poverty has led to the support of militarism. But it is also easy to see why neither the Levantine nor the Gulf governments are well served by significant labor transfers, at least in terms of meeting their short-term agendas. Thus, within the region's conflicting labor agendas, the Palestinians fall into a category of the Gulf States no longer needing them, Israel no longer wanting them, Jordan not knowing what to do with them, and one in which there is little hope that massive local employment will be developed anytime soon in the homeland.

Case 3: Competition for global investment and finance

That the world had strategic interests in the Middle East and North African region was never in dispute.[50] What has been in dispute is whether the laggard rates of foreign investment into the region could be reversed, and also changed in directions that would funnel funds toward trouble spots. One of the hopes at the beginning of the peace process was that foreign direct corporate investment in the region would increase significantly and that over a decade or so the flow of global funds to the Levant would increase to a level high enough for it to replace international aid. This situation has not developed in any of the states which border Israel. In Chapter 3 Nitzan and Bichler claim that, in order to survive, large Israeli corporations must give up domestic control in return for global alliances, but they go on to illustrate how the core conglomerates have resisted this move. Still, Israeli firms are in a much better position than any others in the region to attract global capital. Will Arab firms be able to develop global access as well? The answer is that several of the conglomerates located in the GCC probably can. But is it as likely that the Arab firms which operate in the more conflict-ridden areas can attract foreign funds?

The answer to the second of these questions is unlikely to be positive for several reasons:

1   the peace process has not brought about in Northern Arabia the peace and stability needed to attract foreign investments;

2   in the GCC there is historically a lack of foreign direct investment, and when there was investment in the Gulf it was usually part of a required joint-venture arrangement related to the oil industry or to a service facilitating import procurement.

The upshot of this situation has been that "The Middle East is receiving little of the massive international flow of investment capital that has developed in the last ten years."[51]

The situation is worst for Palestine and its Arab neighbors. Rodney Wilson asserts that in the Northern Arab states the failure of capital markets to develop

> has increased dependency on foreign aid and decreased the supply of domestic savings. In comparison to the rapidly growing economies of the East and South East Asia, growth rates in the Middle East are poor, the per capita gross national product being negative for most of the region for much of the last decade....[In further comparison,] the newly industrializing countries in the East and South East Asia have high domestic savings ratios, in excess of 30 percent of GDP in the case of Muslim countries such as Malaysia and Indonesia. But in the Middle East savings rates are much lower, especially in Egypt and Jordan, the figures being respectively 5.9 and 3.3 percent.[52]

Michael Fields further asserts:

> Foreign companies find it difficult to invest in the region...[because] local business practices remain unsophisticated, very slow moving and in some ways uncompetitive. [Most local investors want] "pure profit" and few see the benefit of giving themselves "unnecessary costs" by investing in the proper maintenance of their assets or paying good salaries to attract able managers....Governments also fear losing control over their economies [and this causes] bureaucratic resistance...[to liberalization and privatization, and] foreign investment is encouraged only in some sectors but banned in others.[53]

The combination of uncertain and often unfair government regulatory intervention, economic environments producing low savings rates, and widespread management perceptions that do not match Western modes of executive practice place the region in a difficult strategic position in relation to its ability to attract foreign investment. This is not to say, however, that the region does not have its share of large companies, but it suggests that the region's commercial strengths lie in concentrated industries supported by management structures with a short-term focus.[54] For example, Bahrain's Islamic banks have loan portfolios that are, on average, 80 percent concentrated on import financing (those of two banks have figures of over 90 percent). Such concentrated portfolios do not display willingness by Gulf banks – at least the Gulf's Islamic banks – to adopt sophisticated portfolio policies. It is also true that the privatization process in both the Arab countries and Israel has revolved around only a few industries.

As can be seen from Table 2.1,[55] of the top 20 Middle Eastern companies, 11 are based in the Gulf, 4 in Israel, and 3 in Turkey. Only one operates in a location which can be considered a high conflict area: Solidere is a construction company whose primary work is currently the rebuilding of government buildings in Lebanon, even though its wealth was created mainly in the Gulf States. Teva Pharmaceuticals is the only manufacturing firm on the list, but two others in the top twenty-five Middle East companies include Israel's Koor Industries and Turkey's Koc Holdings. Fifty percent of these firms are banks, with the rest working in resources-based operations. The UAE's Etisalat, a telecommunications firm, is the major exception to this rule, but this is heavily backed by government money.

As it relates to this discussion, this list yields interesting details about the ability of the peace process to affect investment flows. First, the regional division of these companies places them in geographical positions with little direct contact with the economies of Gaza, Lebanon, or Palestine, where political instability is a major impediment to finance. Second, this list reveals that comparative corporate advantages have been developed in only a handful of industries, primarily in banking and in petrochemicals, in which governments play primary roles. What is seen, then, are commercial systems in which the core conglomerates are supported by a tightly controlled group of merchants, which are, in turn, supported by a closely related banking sector which can use oil deposits to finance expansion of those same firms. The result is biased markets, on the one hand, and, on the other, the development of dominant firms which are in advantaged positions for recruiting international financing and management partners in the global marketplace.

In addition, for these favored firms the more immediate benefit of the peace process may well have been the lifting of trade embargoes against foreign firms having links with Israel. This change has allowed Gulf Arab firms to trade directly with firms that had been banned, like Coca-Cola and Marks & Spencer. This liberalization is likely to increase foreign direct investment in sectors where cooperative advantages are found, for example financial services in Bahrain and retail merchandising in Dubai.

Unfortunately, in terms of creating comparative advantages, the PA has not set itself up well for supporting the reallocation of local financing to

Table 2.1 Top twenty Middle Eastern companies by capitalization

Rank Company	Country	Capital (US$ billion)
1 SABIC	Saudi Arabia	10.6
2 Etisalat	UAE	4.4
3 Saudi American Bank	Saudi Arabia	3.1
4 Riyadh Bank	Saudi Arabia	3.0
5 Al-Rahji Bank	Saudi Arabia	2.8
6 National Bank of Kuwait	Kuwait	2.6
7 Bezeq	Israel	2.2
8 Solidere	Lebanon	2.2
9 Teva Pharmaceuticals	Israel	2.1
10 Bank Hapoalim	Israel	2.1
11 Bank Leumi	Israel	2.1
12 Sceco-Central	Saudi Arabia	2.0
13 Petkim Petrkimya	Turkey	1.9
14 Sceco-West	Saudi Arabia	1.7
15 Akbank	Turkey	1.6
16 Arab National Bank	Saudi Arabia	1.5
17 Arab Bank	Jordan	1.5
18 Turk Hava Yolian	Turkey	1.5
19 Saudi British Bank	Saudi Arabia	1.4
20 Arab Banking Co.	Bahrain	1.3

Source: Rodney Wilson, 'The effect of the peace process on portfolio investment flows in the Middle East,' *Economic and Political Impediments to Middle East Peace: Critical Questions and Alternative Scenarios*.

the Palestinian private sector, or to the public or NGO sectors for that matter. The base problem lies with the Palestinian Monetary Authority (PMA). When it was established it was supposed to be structured in ways that would encourage financial deepening in the former territories. For example, the agreements actually signed allow the PMA only to "predict its supervision" and work within a "home authority and host authority" approval process. When the PMA collects the reserve requirements it must hold those reserves in New Israeli shekels (NIS); "[t]he liquidity requirements on the various kinds of NIS deposits in banks operating in the area will not be less than 4% to 8%," and "the amount of convertible NIS during a calendar year" will be decided annually by Israel. The PMA must "supply temporary finance for banks operating in the region," including Israeli banks. "The clearing of money orders and transactions between banks operating in Israel will be done between Israel and the Palestinian clearing houses on a same working day basis," but there is no reciprocal agreement forcing Israeli banks to process funds on a daily basis. "The exchange of foreign currency for NIS and vice-versa by the PMA will be carried through the Bank of Israel Dealing Room," but, "[t]he BOI [Bank of Israel] will not be obliged to convert in any single month more than 1/5 of the semi-annual amount."[56]

There are several problems with these monetary-control arrangements. Foremost among these are that without control of real reserve requirements the PMA can neither set money-supply policies nor regulate interest rates. Because it must provide a discount window to Israel as well as to Palestinian banks, it must ultimately target portions of its temporary funds toward lending to Israeli borrowers. This stricture essentially forbids the PMA from reinvesting its entire portfolio in Arab-owned banks or institutions. Because the PMA does not have a foreign-currency dealing room, and because the BOI is only forced to deal with the PMA in limited amounts, the PMA has no emergency conversion facilities. The lack of a currency dealing room also denies the PMA the ability to make trading profits. Because it must deliver Arab interbank funds in one day, without Israeli reciprocity, the PMA may have outstanding funds on which it cannot earn interest.

Without control of interest rates, without the ability to run market operations or to plan its own portfolio investment policies, without the means of creating trading and processing profits, and without the ability even to offer licenses without prior approval from Israel, the new PMA does not seem to have the tools it needs to promote the Palestinians in their bid to compete against U.S., Israeli, and Gulf Arab firms for foreign direct investment. By the same token, few investors in the global marketplace would look on an economic structure with so little control over its own financial system as one that could offer viable investment opportunities. Even if they found such opportunities, the prevailing structure would limit their ability to repatriate earnings to the home office.

In all fairness, some discussion of the American corporate role in these biased structures should be admitted. It is debatable whether or not it would be in U.S. (or U.K.) firms' best interests if either Arabs or Israelis become more dependent on global rather than U.S. funds transfers. It is a misapprehension that Israel is the primary beneficiary of USAID funds. There is no doubt that these funds have allowed Israel to build the most powerful economic structure in the region. They have also allowed nations like Egypt and Jordan to avoid implementing both economic and political liberalization and market reform programs. But the latter – the use of U.S. aid to support the transfer of American tax dollars into production processes that are dependent on supplies from States-side arms manufacturers – is of greater concern. In reality, both aid funds flows and exogenous oil revenues have created a series of unproductive dependencies in the region that promote both authoritarian rule and increased military spending. As Stephen Zunes puts it:

> The prospects for peace will not reduce the close military relationship between Israel and the U.S. because American military support for Israel was never and is not based on any actual concerns for

Israeli security. Indeed, U.S. aid to Israel has increased since the signing of the Oslo Accords and the peace treaty with Jordan, as Israel's strategic needs have lessened. Continuing U.S. arms transfers to both Israel and Arab Gulf States serves important political functions for the recipient Middle Eastern states despite the enormous costs and negative impact on their respective economies. For the Israelis, Arab militarism serves as an excuse for continued control over much of the occupied territories and for maintaining subsidies for its entrenched militarized industrial structure. For the autocratic Arab leaders, Israeli military power provides an excuse for their unwillingness to promote internal democratization programs, and affords them rhetoric allowing them to avoid making badly needed social and economic reforms.[57]

The point being made here is that the U.S. defense and contracting firms which benefit most from the recycling of USAID funds do not want either Israel or the Northern Arab states (or the Gulf States for that matter) to liberalize their financial markets. It places them in a much stronger position if they act as the global representatives of their Israeli (and Gulf Arab) corporate partners, and if these partners are left to control the competitive structure at home as well as in the West Bank, Gaza, and, within their strategies, to allow these firms eventually to expand their control to Jordan, Lebanon, Syria, and Egypt. These core firms and the politicos who support them have an active incentive to stifle Arab access to global markets.

Case 4: Corruption and conflict within the Palestinian structure

This case is the most troubling of the four presented here because it illustrates how misguided attempts to organize a functioning governing system in Palestine by Palestinians have become. The situations illustrated here are just a few of the type that will lead to all of the negative behaviors feared: increasing domestic capital flight, declining multinational aid and foreign investment, and rising militancy. The fact is that the Palestine Liberation Organization (PLO), now the PA, has suddenly become rich and has yet to learn how to handle this wealth effectively. As for Yasser Arafat (and, indeed, Bebe Netanyahu), it might be said that

> until he learns to live with his wealth, he will have a well-observed tendency to put it to the wrong purposes ... [because] as it is with individuals so it is with nations; the experience of nations with well-being is exceedingly brief.[58]

An unexpected consequence of international aid restructuring is that aid distribution has created ineffective divisions between NGOs and the PA. On the one hand, it was necessary for international donors to recognize the PA and treat it as the central distributing authority in the West Bank and Gaza. Had the international community not done so it would have undermined the governing authority it had assigned the PA. On the other hand, by making the PA the focus of aid funding it forced many long-standing charitable and community organizations to seek program funding from Arafat and his authorities instead of dealing directly with their traditional donors. This situation has created numerous political rifts, and in far too many cases the PA either has not distributed the funds or has taken over the service agency and sequestered the funds.[59]

As background information, it is important to realize that during Israel's 28-year occupation of the West Bank and Gaza (even before, since numerous welfare organizations were established in the 1920s and 1930s) the Palestinian NGO "third sector" has traditionally provided the majority of social services offered in the region.[60] The American-Near East Refugee Aid (ANERA) data bank includes 800 Palestinian NGOs – working in education, agricultural extension, housing development, human rights, and charitable welfare, among others – which have participated in its development-oriented workshops. It is estimated that over 1500 Palestinian NGOs were in operation in the West Bank and Gaza at the end of 1995. The Palestinian NGO sector provided approximately 30 percent of educational services, 50 percent of hospital care, 60 percent of primary healthcare services, 100 percent of disability care, and nearly 100 percent of daycare and kindergarten education.[61]

The percentage of services offered by Palestinian NGOs was even higher before the signing of the Declaration of Principles. This decline in Palestinian NGOs is partly due to the fact that several service organizations have been absorbed into the PA structure, others have been dissolved in the transfer of power, and others have failed because the PA has not distributed funds to targeted organizations. By way of an example, the Society for the Care of the Handicapped was forced to reduce its staff by 180 and to cut its Early Intervention Program's services to 2500 children because the group's formerly United Nations-provided U.S.$1.5 million dollars annual budget was redirected toward new PA-established programs. In another case, the Association of Khan Younis lost 60 percent of its funding. These funds had formerly been received directly from the EC but are now received and reallocated by the PA. This forced closure of the Younis Children's Center and its Teen Center.

In addition, in 1995 the PA central administration began to harden its position and drafted legislation that would allow it to consolidate further the control over Palestinian NGO budgets and personnel. The fight for control of Palestinian NGO funds reached fever pitch when the PA issued draft legislation that aimed to restrict an individual from participating in more than one NGO; to prohibit an NGO from holding bank deposits in excess of one month's expenditures; to restrict an NGO from cooperating with any organization outside the jurisdiction of the PA; to grant the Ministry of Social Welfare [MSW] the right to dissolve any NGO, cancel permits, and initiate any type of regulation [it] sees fit to execute. What was particularly frustrating about this restrictive draft law was that it came at a time (August 1995) when Israel ordered the closure of three Palestinian NGOs [PNGOs] based in Jerusalem. PNGOs felt under siege from both Israel and the PA.[62]

The PA apparently felt it could recoup budgetary shrinkages by consolidating Palestinian NGO funds into its accounts. However, after seeing this plan several primary donors had authorized their Palestinian NGO affiliates to operate from foreign bank accounts. While this legislation may have constricted such financial transfers, the obvious potential of this proposed legislation to limit donor flexibility and to blur financial transparency did not go unrecognized by the international community, which eventually forced the PA to withdraw the proposed legislation. In the meantime, the MSW felt it necessary to issue its own draft law. The major differences between the PA and the MSW draft provisions did not concern Palestinian NGO rights, but, rather, location of the funding approval with the MSW. The Ministry of Justice (MOJ) also issued a draft law that would give Palestinian NGOs the right of appeal for final decisions to the MOJ instead of the MSW.

In the end no legislation has been enacted, which leaves this market continually open to corruption. Obviously it was not only the PA and the Palestinian NGOs which were competing with each other, but the ministries as well, which were vying among themselves for control of these surely to be appropriated funds. All this, taken with the PA's inability to redistribute funds to its targeted Palestinian NGOs, has caused considerable hesitance on the part of foreign donors when reviewing new proposals. This has left far too many social service organizations bankrupt. More specifically, with unemployment rates in the West Bank and Gaza persistently high, the lack of basic social services has led to a dangerous situation. Sara Roy places the position of Gaza, where unemployment has reached 75 percent, in the following context:

The most urgent problem facing the Gaza Strip is employment. Between 1987 and April 1996, the number of Gazans working in Israel fell from 80,000 to no more than 7,000. In the past two years, over 2,000 Gazan jobs in Israel were eliminated, costing Gaza's economy at least U.S. $25 million per month in wages and services, a loss that cannot be recreated domestically.... When calculated according to 1987 employment levels, the monthly loss is almost U.S. $44 million in wages alone. Gaza's per capita GNP is now $750, half its 1987 level, and well below the average for developing countries, which stands at $950. Between 14 and 25 percent of the entire Palestinian population live at or below an absolute poverty level of $500–$650 per year.[63]

A vicious circle has developed here because the result of this situation is an increase in the reliance of many Palestinians on Islamic groups for the receipt of social welfare services. Hamas is, of course, the most famous of the Islamic groups operating in Gaza, but it is in fact only one of dozens operating in the West Bank and Gaza. It should be noted that, while Hamas does support many economically focused groups, not all and not even most of the Islamic groups that provide social services support militant movements. But, regardless of these groups' political intentions, as Sara Roy explains further, in the Palestinians' economic climate

> the Islamic role of "alternative provider" becomes that much more significant.... [Palestinians] use Islamic-based services, not because they support Hamas or radical Islam but because they need the services.... The fundamental problem in Gaza, as in many other places, is that the majority of the people are disenfranchised and poor, having no power, access, or future. Radical Islam emerged not because people were opposed to developmental change but because they were unable to obtain it.[64]

At the very least it can be said that "[t]he economic situation has not provided the catalyst for popular public support for the peace process."[65] But here, too, the vicious cycle of hard-line policies against Islamic groups versus the perception of these groups as the primary care providers is enhanced. Given that crackdowns on Islamic groups have recently been as abrupt on the PA side of the territories as they have in Israel, many Palestinians living in Gaza face foreboding circumstances. Because the most readily available form of employment is linked to PA patronage, a primary option is to work for the PA. There are clearly limits to the level of patronage employment the PA can support before donors withdraw their funding.

As an alternative, to support an Islamic group might be the next most feasible means of receiving income or services, but it could also subject the person to a high likelihood of retention or imprisonment. It would most certainly mean that one's travel and work permits would be revoked, thereby insuring a dependence on the nearest social services provider. To be associated with neither the PA nor an Islamic group would raise suspicion of collaboration, which could leave one in the hands of vigilantes wanting to end all cooperation with Israel. This type of economic environment will foster increasingly violent barriers to the peace process.

Conclusion

These cases – four out of ten being developed for inclusion in a case book I am developing – illustrate that each of the region's political dynamics are surrounded by competing economic agendas. They present, first, a call for further inquiry into the roles commercial and corporate agendas play in conflict continuation and resolution in divided societies like those in Israel and Palestine. However, they additionally show that those who seem to be the key players in a political sense – heads of state and the like – may not be as significant when viewed in an economic sphere; the power base is not with the peacemakers, but lies within both national and global corporate-economic structures that will not benefit from peace. Whether one believes that those structures are controlled by regime elites who want to sequester aid fund for private uses, by corporations which profit enormously from the arms trade, or simply by oil-rich sheikhs who are unable to manage the problems facing their own weak economies, the fact remains that economic and financial incentives rule the process and its negotiators. It is therefore unreasonable to believe that national leaders will do much more than promote the status quo. The cynic might even claim that some of the politicos who are now in power may be wanting to promote further decline in the peace process. To do otherwise would mean certain loss of power and self-promotion opportunities in the market for international aid, on the practical side, and in the market for prejudice-bound votes on the political side.

The problems to date in the peace process are twofold. First, negotiators have too often blamed on radicalism what should have been blamed on depravity. The primary example of this is the Israeli policy of border closures, which is misplaced in terms of both means and ends. If the end goal is to create a more secure environment for Israelis, then enforcing policies that further displace Palestinians from jobs will not satisfy that end; rather, it will serve to strengthen the position of radical groups because they are increasingly becoming the only source of economic (and emotional) solace available. Similarly, if the means of providing a peaceful environment is to provide peace dividends that will raise Israeli incomes, then further restricting the supply of inexpensive Arab labor and products circumvents that productive process.

Second, the peace process's designers have not been willing to contest corporate forces that have had a negative influence on negotiators. In taking this approach policy-makers have assigned importance to people and groups who need not be seen as important, and they have ignored people who could potentially be given incentives to change their positions and change their strategies so that they could support a peacetime transfer of funds to the region. Hamas, Hezbollah, and their leaders would not be as influential as they are if they were not identified as the enemy on a daily basis. More specifically, this influence would be greatly reduced if the PA was forced to use the money it collects from donors to provide essential social services; if Israel was forced to share the water supply with Palestinian farmers on a remotely equitable basis; if Lebanon was made to spend more of the reconstruction aid dollars it receives on building adequate housing for refugees living in the South. If these policies were followed, agents able to provide employment could replace the influence of the radicals.

Still, it is more difficult to find economic than political common ground at the government level. All rational people want to live in peaceful and stable living environments, but we are less likely to pay the price, or to trust our competitors in the transition. And so you see, the remaining obstacles to peace revolve around conflicting budgetary, labor, and social services agendas, which are the real impediments to peace. While the activities of the revolutionary groups may be impeding long-term economic growth and significant foreign investment, such groups appeal to people living in abject poverty because they provide necessary support and social services. In this context, purely political approaches are neither working nor appropriate. We must create new and dynamic styles of Middle East diplomacy, styles that do more than throw unmanaged money at the problem.

It is easy enough to recognize the ruses issued by the Netanyahu cabinet. It is much more difficult to determine where the real power lies, what the real sources of capital are, and what agencies are willing to bend to their influence. But identify these powers and influences is what we must do if we really want to create affluent societies between Israel and its Arab neighbors in the "liberal hours" that have been hailed as the coming result of the Middle East peace process.[66]

Notes

1 Robert A. Dahl, *A Preface to Economic Democracy*, University of California Press, Los Angeles, 1991, pp. 109–10.
2 Laura Drake and the author have debated this issue on several occasions, but most recently in the commentaries entitled "American strategy and an Israeli vision" and "American malaise and an American corporate vision," at the end of *Structural Flaws in the Middle East Peace Process*, which the author edited for Macmillan (1999). Laura Drake co-edited volume I of that series, *Economic and Political Impediments to Middle East Peace: Critical Questions and Alternative Scenarios* (1999).
3 Louis Cantori, addresses at the Center for Contemporary Arab Studies, Georgetown University, 1995. Further references for papers he has delivered on this subject can be received by contacting Dr. Cantori at the Department of Political Science, University of Maryland–Baltimore County, 5401 Wilkins Avenue, Administration building #632, Baltimore, Maryland 21228, U.S.A.

4 See *Peace Media*, a publication series supported by the European Union's Peace Media Programme, which is edited by Valerie York, London School of Economics and Political Science.

5 John Kenneth Galbraith, *A Contemporary Guide to Economics, Peace, and Laughter*, Houghton Mifflin, Boston, 1971. This book presents a collection of essays and lectures, edited by Andrea D. Williams, written by Professor Galbraith between 1963 and 1969. They are reprinted in this volume, sometimes with additional or revised commentary on the contemporary states of affairs.

6 The author would like to thank Kevin Connelly for providing tickets.

7 This quote was taken from a panel discussion the author shared with Ambassador Stoltzfus at Rutgers University. The ambassador has assimilated his panel comments into the "Epilogue" of *Economic and Political Impediments of Middle East Peace: Critical Questions and Alternative Scenarios* J. W. Wright and Laura Drake (eds), Macmillan, London, 1999.

8 This point has been proven numerous times and from numerous perspectives. However, it does not imply that voters understand that their positions will be negatively affected. For example, in Becker's *The Economics of Discrimination* he shows quite clearly that the exclusion of minority groups from the mainstream occupational structure constrains both the occupational expansion and production growth processes. Barry Chiswick shows how this exclusion drives minorities into entrepreneurial activities, which eventually lead them into higher earnings classes over the long run (for a more complete discussion of this phenomenon see the author's dissertation, cited in the bibliography). Still, the general population of workers in the U.S. sees minority economic integration as threatening in the short run and votes for politicians who oppose equal-access legislation. Shimson Bichler has identified an almost identical process of voter discrimination in his article "Political shifts in Israel, 1997 and 1992: unsuccessful electoral economics or long range realignment?" (*Science and Society* 58, winter 1994–1995, pp. 415–39), which was revised for publication as "Between capitalism and Jewish voters: electoral economics in Israel, 1977 to 1997," vol. II.

9 Shimson Bichler, "Political shifts in Israel, 1977 and 1992," pp. 438–9.

10 BBC news coverage of the December 1997 labor strike in Israel, December 12, 1997.

11 Galbraith, "Poverty and the way people behave," *Economics, Peace, and Laughter*, p. 223.

12 Galbraith, "Foreign policy: plain lessons of a bad decade," *Economics, Peace, and Laughter*, pp. 169–70.

13 Galbraith, "Economics and the quality of life," *Economics, Peace, and Laughter*, pp. 4–5.

14 Galbraith, "Poverty and the way people behave," *Economics, Peace, and Laughter*, pp. 212–13, 226.

15 Galbraith, "Economics and the quality of life," *Economics, Peace, and Laughter*, pp. 4–6.

16 For a general discussion of this work and a list of supporting research publications, see Gary S. Becker, "An economic approach to behavior: the Nobel lecture," *Journal of Political Economy* 101(3), June 1993, pp. 385–409. Other works that should be reviewed in relation to the points that could be applied to the situation in Israel include: Gary S. Becker, *The Economics of Discrimination*, University of Chicago Press, Chicago, 1971; Gary S. Becker and Kevin M. Murphy, "Human capital, fertility, and economic growth," *Journal of Political Economy* 98(5), 1990, pp. 12–33; Gary S. Becker and Kevin M. Murphy, "The

division of labor, coordination costs, and knowledge," *Quarterly Journal of Economics* cvii(4), November 1992, pp. 1137–60.

17 See the following publications as examples of Darity's work: William A. Darity, Jr., "The undesirables, America's underclass in the managerial age: beyond the Myrdal theory of racial inequality," *Daedalus* 124(1), winter 1995, pp. 145–66; William A. Darity, Jr., "How do we reach the civil rights goals in the 1980s?," *Rutgers Law Review* 37(4), 1995, pp. 977–83; William A. Darity, Jr., and Samuel L. Myers, Jr., with Emmett D. Carson and William Sabol, *The Black Underclass: Critical Essays on Race and Unwantedness*, Garland Publishing, New York, 1994, p. 1; William A. Darity, Jr., and Samuel L. Myers, Jr., "Impacts of violent crime on black family structure," *Contemporary Policy Issues* 8, October, 1990, pp. 15–29; William A. Darity, Jr., and Samuel L. Myers, Jr., "Public policy and the condition of black family life," *Review of Black Political Economy* 13(1–2), summer/fall 1984, pp. 165–87; William A. Darity, Jr., and Arthur H. Goldsmith, "Unemployment, social psychology, and unemployment hysteria," *Journal of Post Keynesian Economics* 16(1), fall 1993, pp. 55–71; Barbara R. Bergman and William A. Darity, Jr., "Social relations, productivity and employer discrimination," *Monthly Labor Review*, April 1981, pp. 47–9.

18 Sara Roy, "The political economy of despair: changing political and economic realities in the Gaza Strip," *Journal of Palestine Studies* 20(3), spring 1991, pp. 58–69.

19 See Eugene Cotran and Chibli Mallat (eds.), *The Arab–Israeli Accords: Legal Perspectives*, Kluwer International Law, London, 1996, with special reference to C. W. Fassberg, "Legal aspects of Israeli–Palestinian economic relations," pp. 157–72, and Sharif Elmusa and M. El-Jaafari, "Power and trade: the Israeli–Palestinian economic protocol," pp. 173–98, both of which outline inherent biases in both the current Israeli legal system and the economic agreements assented to by the Palestinians.

20 See also Sara Roy, "Beyond Hamas: Islamic activism in the Gaza Strip," *Harvard Middle Eastern and Islamic Review* 2, 1995, pp. 1–39.

21 See Sara Roy, "Between Hamas, Israel, and the Palestinian Authority: the role of the Islamic movement in Palestinian development in the Gaza Strip," *Structural Flaws in the Middle East Peace Process*, J. W. Wright, Jr. (ed.), Macmillan, London, 1999.

22 Daoud Kuttab, "The peace process and the Palestinian interest: an interview with Sari Nusseibeh," *Palestine–Israeli Journal of Politics, Economics, and Culture* 1(4), autumn 1994, pp. 69–73.

23 Gil Feisler, "Palestinian employment prospects," *Middle East Journal* 47(4), autumn 1993, pp. 633–51.

24 Samir Hazboun and Simcha Bahiri, "Palestinian industrial development and Israeli–Palestinian attitudes to cooperation," *Palestine–Israeli Journal of Politics, Economics, and Culture* 1(4), autumn 1994, pp. 74–81.

25 Kent Ford and Doyle Peterson, "Conducting business in the West Bank and Gaza," *Developing Alternatives* 5(2), fall 1995/winter 1996, pp. 1–6.

26 Elmusa and El-Jaafari, "Power and trade: the Israeli–Palestinian economic protocol," p. 172.

27 Some provisions of the Arab boycott were aimed at making sure Israel did not re-export products to the GCC through Palestinian distributors. Palestinian suppliers were therefore required to show that products were either produced by or significantly enhanced by Palestinian manufacturers. They could also not have a majority of parts that were bought through Israel for assembly in the territories. While this kept Israeli products from reaching Arab countries as

easily as they might have otherwise, it also, inadvertently, severely limited the Palestinian firm's ability to sell goods and services to the region, and thus limited their commercial contact with other Arab business people and firms.

28 Fatimeh Ziai, Chapter 5.
29 "Developing the Palestinian economy: an interview with George T. Abed," *Journal of Palestine Studies* 23(4), summer 1994, pp. 41–51.
30 Avrahman Ben-Basset and Arie Marom, "Is the demand for money in Israeli stable? (1965–1983)," *Bank of Israeli Economic Review* 60, January 1988, pp. 52–71; Rafi Melnick, "Two aspects of the demand for money in Israel, 1970–1981," *Bank of Israel Economic Review* 60, January 1988, pp. 36–51; Rafi Melnik, "Financial services, co-integration, and the demand for money in Israel," *Journal of Money, Credit, and Banking* 27(1), February 1995, pp. 140–53.
31 Laurie A. Brand, "The economics of shifting alliances: Jordan's relations with Syria and Iraq, 1975–1981," *International Journal of Middle East Studies* 26(2), May 1993, pp. 301–26; Michael R. Fischbach, "The implications of Jordanian land policy for the West Bank," *Middle East Journal* 47(4), summer 1994, pp. 492–651.
32 Glenn E. Robinson, "The role of the professional middle class in the mobilization of Palestinian society: the medical and agricultural communities," *International Journal of Middle East Studies* 25(2), May 1993, pp. 301–26.
33 Both Bradley Glasser and Stephen Zunes have written a series of articles on this topic, the first with financial and the second with political focus. They are contributors to *Structural Flaws in the Middle East Peace Process*.
34 Elmusa and El-Jaafari, "Power and trade: the Israeli–Palestinian economic protocol," pp. 178–81.
35 Three chapters in *Economic and Political Impediments to Middle East Peace: Critical Questions and Alternative Scenarios* survey the potential for regional and global trade participation, and in the process dispute the claim that Jordan and Palestine will have significantly increased trade. See Emma Murphy, "The Arab–Israeli peace process: can the region benefit from the economics of globalization?," Stanley Fischer and Mohamed El-Erian, "Is MENA a region? The scope of regional integration," and Elias Tuma, "Will the Arab peace process bring a trade dividend?"
36 Sarah Roy, "The political economy of despair."
37 Fadle M. Naqib, "The economics of the Israeli occupation of the West Bank and Gaza Strip," address to the 1995 Middle East Studies Association, Washington, DC. The author notes that this paper draws on his contribution to a UN Conference on Trade and Development (UNCTAD) report on "A quantitative framework for the future prospects of the Palestinian economy."
38 See Emma Murphy, "Structural inhibitions to economic liberalization in Israel, proceedings of the 1992 British Society for Middle East Studies (St Andrews: St Andrews University, 1992), 217–34."
39 Fadle Naqib quoting the "Report of the Secretary General on assistance to the Palestinian People in the light of the Cartagena Decision", UNCTAD TD/B/39(1)/4 20, August 1992.
40 On negotiations over water inequities, see Alwyn Rouyer, "Between desert countries: the political-economy of water under the Israeli occupation of the Palestinian territories and beyond," *Structural Flaws in the Middle East Peace Process*. For statistics on typography, see Fawzi Asadi, "How viable will the agricultural economy be in the new state of Palestine?," *GeoJournal*, a special issue of *Geographical Aspects of the Israeli–Palestinian Conflict* 21(4), 1990, pp. 375–83. See also Naqib, UNCTAD report, p. 41; Jacob Meltzer, "The Arab economies in

mandatory Palestine and in the administered territories," *Economic Development and Cultural Change*, 1992, pp. 844–65.

41 George T. Abed, *The Palestinian Economy: Studies in Development Under Prolonged Occupation*, Routledge, London, 1988, p. 165.

42 Fatimeh Ziai, Chapter 5.

43 This was considered a "core issue" from the beginning of the peace process by Jordan and Palestine, in particular, when they entered negotiations. See J. S. Birks and C. A. Sinclare, "Repatriation, remittances, and reunions: what is really at stake for Arab countries supplying labour to the Gulf Co-operation Council States?," in Charles E. Davies (ed.), *Global Interests in the Arab Gulf*, University of Exeter Press, Exeter, 1992, pp. 86–116. However, this article takes a more "global" labor-supply scope, and does not dwell on the policies and growth rates of GCC-national labor.

44 J. W. Wright, Jr., "Islamic banking in practice: problems in Jordan and Saudi Arabia," *University of Durham Centre for Middle Eastern and Islamic Studies Occasional Papers Series*, no. 48, May 1995. An earlier discussion of the importance of remittance in the northern Arab countries is presented by J. S. Birks and C. A. Sinclare, in "Repatriation, remittances, and reunions."

45 The statistics in this report come from the Regional Perspectives on World Development Report 1995, "Will Arab workers be left out in the twenty-first century?," Washington, DC, 1995.

46 Dahi Hassan, "More nationals set to get jobs in banks," *Gulf News*, November 13, 1997, p. 29.

47 Ishaq Diwan and Michael Walton, "Palestine between Israel and Jordan: the economics of an uneasy triangle," *Structural Flaws in the Middle East Peace Process*.

48 Nora Coulton, "Between supply-shocked markets: Palestinian returnees in Jordan", in *Structural Flaws in the Middle East Peace Process*.

49 April Wright, "Are Middle Eastern banks safe?," *International Journal of Commerce and Management* 5(3), 1995, pp. 90–105.

50 For a historical perspective on these interests, see Peter A. Davies and Paul J. Stevens, "Oil in the Gulf – internal and external interactions: past, present, and future," in Charles E. Davis (ed.), *Global Interests in the Arab Gulf*, pp. 67–85. The role of global interests in the demarcation of regional borders is discussed in the articles in Richard Schofield (ed.), *Territorial Foundation in the Gulf States*, UCL Press for the University of London School of Oriental and African Studies, London, 1994. For articles specific to Saudi Arabia, see J. W. Wright, Jr. (ed.) *Business and Economic Development in Saudi Arabia*, Macmillan, London, 1996.

51 Michael Field, "Modernizing the Arab economies," an occasional paper published by Stabsabteilung Friedrich-Ebert-Stiftung, January 1996.

52 Rodney Wilson, "The effect of the peace process on portfolio investment flows in the Middle East," *Economic and Political Impediments to Middle East Peace: Critical Questions and Alternative Scenarios*. The author discusses Jordan's dependence on the Gulf States for financial flows, which is a case that applies to Palestine as well. See Wright, "Islamic banking in practice."

53 Field, "Modernizing the Arab economies," pp. 2–3.

54 Their loan portfolios are also very short term. For example, the most popular product line is "*murabaha*," import finance contracts, which last no longer than the shipping period: 79.9 percent of Albaraka's outstanding investments are in "commodity *murabaha* financing"; 55.9 percent of Faysal Islamic Bank's non-cash and equivalents are held in *murabaha* contracts; and 95.3 percent of the Bahrain Islamic Bank's and 89.9 percent of the Islamic Investment Company of the Gulf's are short-term *murabaha* contracts. This data was gathered from

annual reports and presented first in lectures entitled "Islamic banking at the crossroads," which the author gave at Al-Isra and Al-Il-Bait Universities in Jordan in May 1997.

55 Rodney Wilson, "Will the peace process affect portfolio investment flows in the Middle East?" *Economic and Political Impediments to Middle East Peace: Critical Questions and Alternative Scenarios.*
56 The quotes in this section come from "Special supplement to Annex V: protocol on economic relations, Israeli–Palestinian Interim Agreement," *Palestine Report*, December 1995, pp. 15–25. This is a revised discussion found first in the author's article "American trade and Islamic banking in the Israeli occupied territories," *International Journal of Commerce and Management* 5(4), 1995, pp. 71–94.
57 Stephen Zunes, "Between the arms race and political lobbyists: how pax Americana threatens Middle East peace," *Structural Flaws in the Middle East Peace Process.*
58 The quote comes from John Kenneth Galbraith, *The Affluent Society*, Houghton Mifflin, Boston, 1958, p. 13. Although it did not refer to the Middle East, it seems to fit amazingly well here.
59 Denis Sullivan, "International aid and the peace process: the Palestinian Authority vs. civil society," *Structural Flaws in the Middle East Peace Process.*
60 Peter Gubser, President of ANERA, notes that the history of Palestinian NGOs extends to the Ottoman empire and consisted of "waqs, sufi orders, churches and synagogues, guilds in urban areas, and occasional water associations in rural regions." See "The role of civil society in Middle East socio-economic development during the transition to peace," *Economic and Political Impediments to Middle East Peace: Critical Questions and Alternative Scenarios.*
61 Sullivan, "International aid and the peace process."
62 *Ibid.*
63 Roy, "Between Hamas, Israel, and the PA."
64 Roy, "Between Hamas, Israel, and the PA," and "Beyond Hamas."
65 Barbara Balaj, Ischac Diwan and Bernard Philippe, "External assistance to the Palestinians: What went wrong," *Economic and Political Impediments to Middle East Peace: Critical Questions and Alternative Scenarios.*
66 The phrase "liberal hours" was used as an economic term by John Kenneth Galbraith in *The Liberal Hour*, Houghton Mifflin, Boston, 1960.

Part II

NATIONAL AGENDAS

3

THE IMPERMANENT WAR ECONOMY?

Peace dividends and capital accumulation in Israel

Jonathan Nitzan and Shimshon Bichler

Introduction

Since the end of the 1980s Israel appears to have begun a fundamental trans-formation. From a militarized economy characterized by large government deficits, heavy dependency on the United States and intense stagflation there is also now a decisive move toward peace and regional integration, coupled with continued economic growth and declining military spending. These developments come amidst a deep ideological and cultural change which sanctions the centrist/liberal world-view of the Labour and Meretz parties. Increasingly, there are calls not only for a more open foreign policy but for an entirely different regime based on political democratization and economic liberalization. The emphasis is on small government, sound finance, and market reform; the acceptance of laissez-faire brings lower income taxes, smaller fiscal deficits, scaled-down social services, and a heightened process of privatization. The Zionist-collectivist ethos seems finally to have given way to the universal culture of business enterprise.

The purpose of this article is to offer an alternative analytical framework for understanding this long-term transformation. First, we argue against the conventional separation between the "political system" and the "economic system." This separationist approach has been popular among Israeli scholars but its analytical value is open to doubt. Second, instead of the common aggregate/statist approach, we take the disaggregate route of political economy, accentuating the historical role played by key power groups. And, finally, rather than focus merely on domestic considerations, we claim that both the earlier military economy and the current trajectory into "peace markets" are part of broader global developments, particularly the internationalization of business institutions and the changing nature of the capitalist nation-state. In our opinion, the sharp "U-turn" in Israeli history is intimately linked to the changing nature of "capital accumulation" and "corporate concentration," both in Israel and in the United States. For the large core firms at the center of the economy, which we view as principal actors in this process, accumulation and concentration are two sides of the same process. With the evolution of modern capitalism, the leading firms are increasingly driven not to maximize their profits but rather to "beat the average." Specifically, they seek to achieve a "differential rate of accumulation" – that is, to *exceed* the average rate of return in the economy. However, since a differential growth in profits implies control over a growing share of the aggregate capitalized assets, for these firms the goal of accumulation means a quest for rising corporate concentration.[1]

Differential accumulation can be achieved in two ways. One is to raise the "depth of accumulation" by maintaining profit margins above the economy's average. The other is to focus on the "breadth of accumulation" by expanding market share. Although the two methods are not mutually exclusive, economic conditions which are conducive to one often undermine the other. During the 1970s and much of the 1980s Israel and the United States were both characterized by a political-economic structure in which a combination of corporate concentration and stunted growth gave rise to "military Keynesianism." Under these circumstances, corporate concentration is typically maintained and enhanced by expanding the "depth of accumulation"; the large corporations try to raise their profit margins above those of smaller periphery firms and the ensuing "profit competition" often culminates in a stagflationary spiral.[2]

However, since the mid-1980s, and particularly with the disintegration of the Soviet Union and the opening to business of China, India, and Southeast Asia, the large firms both in Israel and in the United States have changed gear, moving toward an alternative model of peaceful expansion.[3] Under this latter regime the core corporations advance their differential position by expanding the "breadth of accumulation"; instead of competing over profit margins, the differential increase in profits now depends on a rapid intrusion into new markets, where the large firms succeed in expanding their market shares faster than their smaller counterparts. This mode of differential accumulation is accompanied by falling military spending, disinflation, and revived growth.

The focus on the process of accumulation sheds new light on the history of Israel. The first section examines some of the fundamental assumptions underlying the Israeli political and economic literature since the late 1960s. According to this literature, Israel represents a "special case" – but that is so only because most writers chose to ignore the process of accumulation. If the latter is put at the center of analysis the forces underlying the Israeli war economy, as well as its current transition to peace markets, no longer seem unique. The second section examines briefly the "military bias" of mature capitalist economies, with specific emphasis on the United States. In the third section we argue that until the late 1980s the Israeli military bias was similarly affected by pressures emanating from growing corporate concentration, as well as by the country's role in the superpower confrontation. These considerations could then help explain the current peace process. In the fourth section we claim that fundamental changes in the global pattern of accumulation have left the Israeli elite (and many of the Arab ones) with little choice but to accept the imperative of open borders and global ownership. In a certain sense, the current enthusiasm for peace is similar to the earlier obsession with national security – they both serve the quest for differential accumulation.

Theoretical background

The Israeli literature dealing with the economics and politics of war and peace suffers from several related shortcomings:

- an emphasis on the "statist" frame of reference;
- a view that the historical development of Israel was predetermined by "unique" circumstances;
- a belief that as a consequence of these circumstances Israel has developed into a "special case" of classless society – a society in which the process of capital accumulation and the role of elites could be safely ignored.

We deal with these issues in turn.

The "statist" or "state-centered" approach grew increasingly fashionable in the 1970s.[4] The basic unit of analysis here is the nation-state, whose actions are dominated by an amorphous group of "central decision-makers," "state officials," or "rule-makers." This group is supposedly driven by the national interest and seeks to achieve broad macroeconomic goals such as growth and a favorable balance of payments, or macropolitical aims like military prowess and social stability.[5] These broad ends are perceived as independent of the particular interests of various societal groups and, indeed, are often emphasized for their universal nature.

The aims of the state are formulated in "aggregate" terms – a habit of thinking which emerged and consolidated with the Keynesian paradigm.[6] In this aggregate framework it is customary to subdivide society into two systems of "economics" and "politics." In the Israeli context, it is assumed that the economic system would guarantee universal welfare – that is, if it were allowed to function "efficiently." The political system may undermine that efficiency when it seeks to achieve additional goals such as "national security" but fails to find the optimal rate of substitution between security and economic growth along the nation's production-possibilities frontier.

With its foundations deeply embedded in this neoclassical paradigm, the focus on "aggregate welfare" enables the writer to remain within the boundaries of the national consensus,[7] and has driven many Israeli academics to accept the supremacy of the political echelon.[8]

The total subjugation of the economy to the state is manifest throughout the writings of the economists and other scholars who have "studied" and opined on the issue.[9] Indeed, the Hobbesian view has been so thoroughly accepted in the Israeli political literature that some researchers have decided to skip the analysis altogether and turn directly to policy implications. Klieman, for example, still has little doubt about the militaristic course of Israeli society. For him, the main issue is the benefit to the "state," and the principal questions are how Israel could best respond to mounting challenges in the global weapon market and how it should preserve its position and competitive advantage. The answer is succinctly summarized in Klieman's own words: "In order for the Israeli arms industry not to perish, it should continue with its tradition of domestic dexterity and external cunning." In his opinion, the key is a proper reading of the world arms market, leading to a most revealing conclusion that "those who foresee the future and respond adequately will get the juiciest market share."[10]

The substitution of advice for serious research is typical of an academic community captured by rigid consensus. Perhaps the clearest expression of this consensus is the repeated use – often unconscious – of terms such as "we," "us," and "ours," usually coupled with a need for "sacrifice."[11] And once defense cuts are put out of the question (due to the supremacy of "national security" concerns) an economist can self-assuredly step in to announce that "if we want to enjoy this kind of growth in the future, we must begin immediately by rapidly reducing the standard of living."[12]

The adoption of this state-centered approach by Israeli academics was greatly facilitated by the view of Israel as *sui generis*. The first basis for this characterization is the challenge to Israel's right to exist, which has always presented a constant threat to Israel. Among others articulating this very notion are Peri, on the one hand, and Horowitz and Lissak, on the other, who respectively write: "Since its establishment, and in fact even prior to 1948 Israel has been in a state of war" and "the all-encompassing nature of war in Israel and the centrality of security to national existence have created a situation whereby numerous spheres, which in parliamentary democracies are considered 'civil,' fall within the security gambit and are enveloped in secrecy."[13] And so, "[b]eyond the ideological and political disagreements prevailing in the Israeli public, there was always a broad consensus regarding the threat for survival embedded in the Israeli–Arab dispute."[14] The consequence was that Israel became a unique case.[15]

The second and perhaps more important reason for the uniqueness of Israel stems from its own "primordial sin": the East European founding fathers instituted an authoritarian "socialist" culture which, according to the overwhelming majority of Israeli social scientists, lies at the heart of the "Israeli malaise."

Beginning in the 1920s, the political system seized control of the economy, first through the Labour party and the Histadrut (federation of labor unions), which then transferred their power to the government of the newly formed state. The result was the institutionalization of an authoritarian/statist culture, which resulted in Israel failing to maintain the requisite separation between economics and politics, and allowing the public political domain to impinge upon the private economic sphere.[16] The model is fairly simple. Most broadly, it argues that a socialist tradition inevitably gives rise to a statist bureaucracy, which in turn depresses the spirit of private enterprise and ends in a lack of vitality and chronic stagnation. From the new-right perspective of Sharkansky:

> the predominance of the government in Israel's economy makes it the most socialist country outside the Eastern Bloc. Along with a government budget that exceeds gross national product (GNP), there are numerous detailed controls on the activities of government officials, private-sector companies, and individual citizens.... It is Israel's fate to suffer the worst from the centrally controlled east and the democratic west.[17]

In short, Israel is like no other capitalist society. Its history is the result of "the trilateral relationship between the settlement movement, the pioneering elite which exercised its control through the political parties and the bureaucratic stratum which recognized its hegemony."[18] It is "a party state in which almost everything is determined by political parties."[19] According to Arian, power, and hence the historical course of Israeli society, lies within the formal political sphere, in the hands of the political elite.[20]

This conventional "wisdom" of the primacy of politics and "decision-makers" serves not only to separate the study of politics and economics, but also to divert attention from the class structure of Israeli society. Indeed, since control is in the hands of politicians and former army officers, and since these people do not generally come from a capitalist background, it goes without saying that class conflict is irrelevant to the Israeli case. Israel, so it seems, is a classless society in which the process of capital accumulation, the growth and consolidation of a ruling class, the ownership of resources, the distribution of income, the control of economic power, the methods of persuasion, legitimization, and the means of violence could all be safely ignored. Paradoxically, if there is any recognition of "class struggle" in Israel, it has been largely limited to the pre-independence era – a period in which the society was hardly industrialized, in which there was barely any accumulation of capital or a meaningful working class, in which the most organized groups were the agricultural cooperatives, and in which the army and the police were those of a colonial power.[21] Since the 1970s, however, when these characteristics where long gone – replaced by a highly concentrated business structure, international economic integration, a developed industrial system of mass production, and an urban amalgamation of wage-earners – there has been no single study about the Israeli ruling class or the process of accumulation, let alone the connection between them.

The "military bias"[22]

An alternative assessment of Israeli history could begin from a theoretical framework linking the process of capitalist development and the budgetary crisis arising from military spending, expansionary foreign policy, and armed conflict. Early Marxist writers such as Hilferding and Luxembourg, and institutionalists like Veblen offer some insight into the analysis arising from such an approach. They saw the tendency toward economic and military expansionism as an outgrowth of the concentration of capital in the leading industrialized countries of their time.[23] Later authors, such as Kalecki, Tsuru, Sweezy, and Steindl, further claimed that a rising "degree of monopoly" created a tendency for the societal surplus to rise while at the same time limiting the extent to which this surplus could be offset by profitable investment outlets.[24] The historical solution appeared in the form of "military Keynesianism," where a "Keynesian coalition" between big business and organized labor administered rising military spending and a more aggressive foreign policy as a means of maintaining aggregate prosperity and high employment.[25] Other writers even went a step further, suggesting that the militarization of the economy was driven not by the aggregate needs of employment and output, but rather by the profit requirements of the largest "core" firms of the "monopoly sector"[26] or "monopoly capital."[27]

Conceptually, much of this research was concerned with the effect of economic structure on military spending. However, after the 1950s and 1960s, with the American involvement in Korea and Vietnam, it became increasingly clear that causality ran both ways, and that military expenditures were in turn a factor of restructuring. One of the first to recognize this double-sided link was Michal Kalecki. In his articles on "The fascism of our time" and "Vietnam and U.S. big business" he predicted that the growing American involvement in South-east Asia would shift the balance of power from the "old" civilian industries on the east coast to the "new" military-oriented groups in the west. Rising military budgets, he argued, would redistribute income in favor of the latter and fortify the "angry elements" within the U.S. ruling class, leading to what Melman later called a "permanent war economy."[28]

It now appears that Kalecki was right, and that the war economy, which in the United States lasted until the late 1980s, has indeed shifted the center of gravity of U.S. business in favor of arms contractors. With the post-war decline of the American economy *vis-à-vis* Europe and Japan, the large U.S.-based companies were faced with a growing predicament of excess capacity – which was then counteracted, first, by rising aggregate concentration via mergers and acquisitions, and, second, by a growing reliance on government budgets, particularly in the area of military, space, and medical technology. An analysis of differential accumulation by the "Arms Core," comprising the sixteen largest military contractors based in the U.S., reveals that these developments have resulted in a heightened process of classic differential accumulation; when measured as a share of the Fortune 500 total, the net profits of these firms soared to over 10 percent in the mid 1980s, up from around 5 percent during the Vietnam war.[29]

These considerations prove significant for the Israeli case in two ways. One is a striking structural similarity. The military bias of the U.S. economy suggests that there is a direct link between military spending and market structure. The Marxist thesis of "military Keynesianism" – that is, the counter-cyclical use of military spending to achieve macroeconomic goals – may have been adequate for the 1950s and 1960s when rising defense spending came together with overall economic expansion;[30] this thesis seems less robust, however, from the 1970s onward. Military procurement has become concentrated in a relatively small number of large firms (with the 100 leading contractors typically accounting for about 70 percent of the total prime contract awards), and as the dependency of these firms on military budgets tended to increase, the flexibility of the U.S. administration in manipulating these budgets tended to decline.[31]

If we can generalize, it seems that under certain historical conditions, particularly in an early state of development or after a severe structural crisis, military spending can play a macroeconomic role. But as the economy "matures," and the concentration of capital and centralization of ownership passes a certain threshold, military spending becomes less able to serve "overall" economic goals, and is catering more to the interest of "dominant" political and business groups. In this latter stage the macroeconomic impact of such expenditures often becomes stagflationary,[32] but that is tolerated given their positive effect on the most powerful firms at the core.[33] The Israeli economy, we shall argue, followed a similar historical pattern, with military spending initially associated with overall growth, and subsequently accompanied by rising corporate concentration and heightened stagflation.

Second, beyond the structural similarities there is also a direct connection between the military bias in the two economies. Since the late 1960s Israel has become increasingly integrated into the U.S. orbit – a process which was partly a result of global expansion by U.S. arms producers. During the period between the late 1960s and late 1970s, when U.S. domestic military spending experienced a cyclical downturn, arms exports became increasingly crucial to the well-being of the defense contractors – first, as a stop-gap measure for falling orders at home and, second, because they usually provide far higher profit margins.[34] Moreover, the most significant factor affecting the rise of arms exports has been the global redistribution of income following the 1973 oil crisis. The explosive growth of oil revenues made the countries belonging to the Organization of the Oil Producing Countries ideal clients for weaponry and in 1974, after the U.S. exit from Vietnam, the Middle East became the world's largest importer of armaments.

The result of these situations was that the military bias of the Israeli economy coincided with this U.S. foray into the armament market of the Middle East. Israel accepted its role as a U.S. satellite in this hostile region in return for massive military aid and U.S. consent for economic protectionism. For the large U.S. arms contractors military sales to Israel quickly became part of a heightened arms race, which drew even larger clients such as Iran and Saudi Arabia into the cycle. For the large Israeli firms the combination of a war economy and trade barriers proved equally beneficial, generating rising profit margins and a rapid surge in differential accumulation.

The structure of the Israeli economy

In assessing the parallels and interactions between the U.S. and Israeli economies it is instructive to begin with a bird's-eye view of Israel's economic structure during the height of its militaristic phase. Our analysis follows the dual-economy approach which emphasizes the firm rather than the industry; furthermore, given our focus on differential accumulation, we look specifically at the distribution of profits rather than standard proxies such as sales or value added.[35] During the mid-1980s the Israeli dual economy was characterized by a "big economy" of about fifty firms, surrounded by a "small economy" comprising the rest of the business sector and nonprofit organizations. The perimeter of the "big economy" is composed of large firms which enjoy a leading position or even a monopoly in a given industry, while the center consists of a core of five conglomerates: Leumi, Hapoalim, Israel Discount Bankholding (IDBH), Koor, and Clal (the latter being controlled by the first three).

The history of the core conglomerates mirrors that of Israel. Bank Leumi was established in 1902 to finance colonial settlements by the Zionist movement. Bank Hapoalim was formed in 1921 in order to finance cooperative activity in agriculture, construction, and industry. IDBH began as a private bank in 1936, when capital flight from recession-hit Europe and British preparations for the Second World War fueled an economic boom in Palestine. Koor was established in 1944 as the industrial subsidiary of Solel Bonhe, after war spending had turned the latter into the largest contractor in the Middle East. Clal was set up in 1962 as a joint venture designed to lure foreign investment through tax incentives and subsidies, and eventually became a "gravity center" for the domestic core groups, the government, and foreign investors. During the 1950s there were also other relatively large groups, but these declined or merged with the five core conglomerates; since the 1970s the latter have come to define the center of the Israeli economy.[36]

By the 1980s the core groups were dominant in almost every significant business activity – from raw materials, through finance, consumer- and investment-goods industries, services, and merchandising, communication, and advertising – usually with the backing and cooperation of the government.[37] According to Dun & Bradstreet, in 1984 the core groups and the government controlled about half of the 100 leading industrial firms – 23 were controlled by Koor, 8 by IDBH, 8 by Clal, and 9 by the government. Based on this listing, the core and the government controlled 28 of the top 50 and 14 of the top 20 firms.[38] A similar picture emerges in the banking sector, where Leumi, Hapoalim, and IDBH controlled 80 percent of all assets, employment, and branches, and 70 percent of all net profits (excluding foreign subsidiaries). The core groups also control many of the non-industrial sectors, such as fuel and gas, merchandising, construction, insurance, shipping, and real estate. The perimeter of the "big economy", with its smaller investment groups and medium-sized firms (some of which are foreign subsidiaries, mostly of U.S. conglomerates), is associated with the core through numerous ownership, trade, investment, and credit ties. These associations were strengthened during the "gilded age" of the Israeli stock market, and are now boosted further with the wholesale privatization of government-owned enterprises.

Since the 1970s the cohesion of the core groups has been reflected in the high correlation that exists between their separate performance indices, such as sales, value added, subsidies, taxes, executive compensations, and, most importantly, net profits.[39] Moreover, this cohesion extends beyond the dry statistical picture. Underlying the numbers lies the power/class structure of Israeli society. Since the 1950s this structure has been consolidated through a growing web of reciprocal business ties, as well as through personal, kinship, and cultural bonds among the Israeli business, political, and military elites – ties which eventually led to the emergence of an Israeli ruling class.[40] The amalgamation of this class is embedded in cross-ownership, procurement rights, credit arrangements, and endless unwritten conventions and rules which define the "natural state of things" in Israeli society.

A thick cloak of silence normally covers the nature of this institutional structure; its existence comes to light, however, on the rare occasion of intra-elite conflict. Thus, after a heightened redistributional struggle among the leading business groups precipitated by the 1983 stock market crisis, the Bejsky Commission – nominated to carry out an inquiry into the collapse – "suddenly" discovered that the large banks had for years cooperated, and rather tightly, in many of their diversified activities. Among other things, the banks' managers collaborated in manipulating share prices, in predetermining real rates of return on such stocks, in offsetting excess supply, and in maintaining a common front against an unpredictable finance minister. The banks had also concealed information, window-dressed their financial reports, and engaged in illegal foreign-exchange activity – none of which could have been done without collusion.[41]

In contrast to the "big economy," which in many respects acts like a single "bloc," the "small economy" is much more amenable to standard industrial analysis. Firms are small, usually operating in a single industry, and often consist of a single plant; performance is subject to wide fluctuations with little or no inter-company correlation. While in the big economy, the separation between "economics" and "politics" has little meaning, in the small economy the distinction is much more evident, with the link established only indirectly through loose professional associations and pressure groups. For example, until the early 1970s net profits (after taxes) for the five core conglomerates and the rest of the business sector moved in the same general direction. During the subsequent period, the mid-1970s to the mid-1980s, however, the patterns were no longer similar; profits for the core firms were rising rapidly, while those for the rest of the business sector were actually falling.[42] The consequence was a rapid process of differential accumulation by the core firms.

The period after the 1967 war saw a parallel duality developing in the labor market. The first analysis of this process was provided by Farjoun, who emphasized the unequal exchange between the developed Israeli economy and the underdeveloped Palestinian one.[43] Attempts to create a dual labor market began even before independence in 1948, with the Israeli elite striving for a separate agricultural economy based solely on Jewish labor. However, with the 1967 occupation of the West Bank and Gaza Strip, and the concurrent militarization of the big economy, the emphasis shifted. From then on, writes Farjoun, there was a growing need "for a cheap, mobile labour force, with no social rights; a free labour force in the classical meaning of the term." This was achieved by the proletarianization of the Palestinian population, which was rapidly becoming the main labor pool for a growing number of small-economy sectors, such as agriculture, construction, services, and low-technology civilian manufacturing.[44] During the time of the study, wages in the small economy were only half those paid in the big economy and, according to Farjoun, the survival of this sector was more or less contingent on the availability of Palestinian workers.[45] The other side of this process was that the big economy, particularly its financial and military branches, came to rely solely on Jewish, unionized workers, with much higher earnings and relatively extensive social security.[46]

Yet, through the use of "aggregates," standard analysis of Israeli society has managed more or less to ignore this marked duality. The ruling ideology has masked the true economic regime. Viewed through macroeconomic and

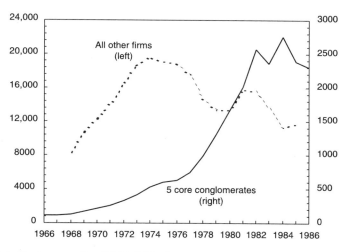

Figure 3.1 Real net profits (1980 NIS; three-year moving average)

Source: *Statistical Abstract of Israel* and company financial reports.

macropolitical spectacles, the nation-state is seen as inhabited by an amorphous body of "private" and "government" agents, who are subject to the
equilibrating influence of economics ("civilian" in the Israeli case) and to
distortions emanating from politics (mainly in the "security" and "welfare"
domains). The central questions are concerned with "societal" welfare – how
to maximize overall growth and minimize inflation while assuring national
security. Since the 1970s, however, this framework has become gradually less
useful. Both the economy and security seem to have deteriorated. Growth
plummeted, inflation soared, the external accounts plunged into crisis, and
Israel's military superiority was put in question. But the apparent curtail-
ment of aggregate welfare was misleading, for while the small economy was
feeling the brunt, the large conglomerates at the core of the economy were
actually thriving.

The aggregate approach offers a useful abstraction only when the underlying phenomena are commonly shared *across society*. However, when there
are systematic divergences in the experience of different groups the assumption of structural stationarity no longer applies. Under these latter
circumstances – for instance when military expenditures cause stagnation in
most sectors but prosperity for the arms contractors, or when government
credit policy stifles the small economy while subsidizing the core conglomerates – the aggregate view serves to conceal the underlying process of
differential capital accumulation and its consequent ramifications for social
restructuring.

The interaction between macroeconomic development and differential accumulation in Israel could be perceived as belonging to three distinct "regimes":

- the period between 1955 and 1972, characterized by emphasis on the differential breadth of accumulation, with rapid macroeconomic growth and a "latent" structural consolidation;
- the 1973–84 era, in which the emphasis shifted to the differential breadth of accumulation, accompanied by severe stagnation and rapid inflation;
- the post-1985 era, distinguished by retrenchment for the big economy, followed by a shift toward an open "peace economy" and a return to the differential breadth of accumulation.

During the 1955–72 period the economy expanded at an average annual rate of 10 percent. Differential accumulation by the core conglomerates, on the other hand, was relatively contained, and between 1966 and 1972 their profit share of gross domestic product (GDP) remained below 0.5 percent. The post-1973 period was fundamentally different; there was a marked drop in overall growth rates, to an average of 3 percent between 1973 and 1985, and as stagnation lingered the profit share of the core firms started to rise rapidly, climbing to nearly 2.3 percent of GDP in the early 1980s. From the mid-1980s onward, differential accumulation for the core firms turned negative, and over the 1986–1990 period their profit share of GDP collapsed to less than 0.75 percent. The political-economic shift since the late 1980s has contributed to revived overall growth, now accompanied by a parallel recovery for the core companies. In this section we deal with the first two regimes. The third phase is discussed in the last section of this chapter.

Until 1972 economic growth in Israel was disproportionately affected by two "external" stimuli: the unilateral capital inflow of German compensation between 1955 and 1965 and the "Palestinian boom" in the immediate years after the 1967 war. During the 1955–65 period unilateral transfers from Germany accounted for most of the capital import, and until the early 1960s their levels were almost identical to the annual change in gross national product (GNP). Indeed, the end of these transfers in 1965 was followed by the severe recession of 1966–7. The situation changed again in 1968, when the Israeli market suddenly expanded to include 1 million new consumers from the occupied territories of the West Bank and Gaza Strip. Furthermore, the post-war years, roughly until 1973, saw very rapid increases in the number of Palestinian employees working in Israel – from zero to over 60,000 in just five years – and a consequent increase in purchasing power. This combination of an overnight expansion of markets and a rapid process of proletarianization had a decisive multiplier effect on the Israeli economy. Indeed, by 1974, when the growth in the number of

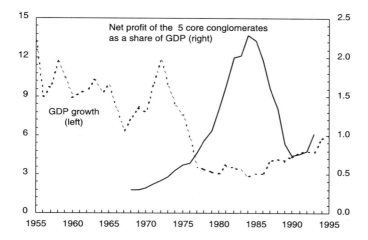

Figure 3.2 Macroeconomic growth and differential accumulation (%; five-year moving average)

Source: *Statistical Abstract of Israel* and company financial reports.

Palestinians working in Israel stabilized at a lower rate (eventually peaking at 140,000), the economy reverted back to stagnation.[47] These external impetuses acted to mitigate the latent process of aggregate concentration, primarily through their positive impact on the expansion of the small economy. However, after 1974, with the growing differential accumulation by the big economy, the picture began to change. The concentration process came into the open, accompanied by a fundamental political shift and the gradual decline of the government as a central economic force. The right-wing Likud bloc, which assumed power in 1977, adopted an aggressive foreign policy and high military spending, while its "liberal" economic agenda of laissez-faire hastened the ascent of the core conglomerates.

The core conglomerates of today were consolidated during the mixed-economy period after independence. During the 1950s and early 1960s investment was almost entirely financed by unilateral capital transfers and managed more or less exclusively by the government. The allocation of capital was determined partly by the government's import-substitution poli-cies, but also (and often more so) by political and family ties. The government developed "special relationships" with several rising business clusters, which were originally considered to be "national agents" and even-tually grew into the core groups of today.[48] The pattern of these relationships started to take shape immediately after independence, with the distribution of land and other properties belonging to the Palestinians who left during the war; it developed further during the austerity period of the

85

early 1950s, which saw the allocation of exclusive certificates, monopolies, procurement, and other forms of "goodwill" to well-connected domestic groups and foreign investors;[49] and it was consolidated with the inflow of German compensation payments, which financed a decade of growth between 1956 and 1965.

The 1950s was a period of sharp contrasts. On the one hand, massive Jewish immigration from Europe, Asia, and Africa more than doubled the population in just a few years. These were mainly impoverished refugees, with few marketable skills, often without knowledge of the language. Their harsh conditions in 1951 were vividly captured in the memoirs of David Horowitz, then general director of the Finance Ministry:

> As the immigration waves rose, the economic problems imposed themselves on us with enormous might, forceful enough to break the backs of those in charge with immigration absorption. Tens of thousands of people were crowded in the *ma'abarot* [transit camps] and the camps for the ailing. They were grieved by war, tormented with the horrors of the Holocaust and often burdened with large families. Within a short while, 60,000 people, or 10 percent of the [Jewish] population, were congested into the camps. A similar number stayed in decaying buildings of abandoned Arab towns and villages. The tent and hut camps were damp and cold during the winter and burning hot through the summer. The congestion, filth, and stench exhausted their strength and shook their souls.[50]

However, the population grew at over 9 percent a year, which meant that even with no per-capita growth overall economic activity was nonetheless rising very rapidly. And so, while most of the population suffered acute shortages and hardship, the business potential for well-placed companies was huge. It is hence hardly surprising that where David Horowitz saw misery and despair Harry Recanati, then owner and director of the Discount Bank (later IDBH), perceived business success:

> By 1951, I had good reasons for being satisfied with the completed task. The bank left to us by our father had prospered and constituted the base for a first-rate Israeli financial group.... I had striven thinking about new initiatives in Israel, but in vain. We already had in our group all the subsidiaries appropriate to our basic operations.[51]

The Discount Bank, established only fifteen years earlier by tobacco merchants and realtors, grew rapidly to become the second largest bank and fifth largest industrial concern, with a wide variety of investments in areas like rubber, paper, fuel, shipping, aluminum, insurance, construction, mortgage banking, citrus orchards, and electrical equipment. Such an expansion, experienced also by a select number of other groups, would have been inconceivable without solid and consistent government backing.

The first years of statehood were crucial, for it was during this period that the central institutions of accumulation, particularly the relationship between the government and corporate sector, were set. Harry Recanati, who was later unseated from his position as the IBDH group's chairman following a family feud, was not entirely comfortable with these cozy relationships:

> I said to myself that our bank had completely changed. It was no longer the family bank founded by my father. My brothers turned it into an industry, against my will. There were other things that caused me anguish: the flattering advertisement, much of which was created under our own aspiration, the charity organizations and institutions established under our auspices with tax deductible donations, the indiscriminate support of all political parties, left and right, to acquire the friendship of each and every one, and the stock market maneuvers where share prices were jointly determined in collusion among several banks. Even less cherished was our managers' friendship with government officials in Jerusalem. I resented their constant striving for government benefits of every kind, all under the pretext of the national interest. Our group was a private business, not a public institution. It was unjust and undignified to bank on government grants for the benefit of shareholders who were mostly affluent capitalists. I was well aware that my views were uncommon in Israel. This was a country where too many financiers and businessmen enjoyed the allocation of public wealth and were continuously nourished by German payments, U.S. grants and donations from the Jewish Diaspora.[52]

The rapid expansion of public services and the acceleration of the Israeli–Arab conflict after the 1956 Suez war accentuated the centrality of the government and boosted the significance of the military elites. However, under the surface these developments ushered in a more fundamental process of corporate concentration. Foreign unilateral transfers and loans, which induced aggregate growth, were not equally allocated across the economy, but, rather, were channeled disproportionately to a selected number of firms. Indeed, during the 1950s and 1960s growth was propelled not by the "animal spirits" of local or foreign capitalists, but through "administrated" capital formation. Capacity was rising not because of an eager entrepreneurial quest to tap a growing market, but rather through directed government grants or subsidized loans. For the leading capitalists at the receiving end, accumulation often took place before production even started.

87

This allocation system, known as the "Sapir method," after the finance minister of the time, encouraged the formation of binding institutional arrangements and enhanced centralization – though for a while its negative effect on economic growth was more than offset by the continuous flow of immigrants and foreign assistance. Only after 1970 or so, when these external stimuli were no longer available, did the economy enter its monopolistic stage of "militarized stagflation."

Since the early 1970s economic activity has rapidly converged around two related poles – defense and finance. Earlier forays into military-related manufacturing were often explained by Israel's political isolation, though economic considerations were at least equally important. Initially, domestic production of weapons fitted nicely with the Labour government's import-substitution effort, while, later, military exports were seen as a possible solution to the country's chronic current-account deficit. Financial activity became increasingly significant, much as in other capitalist countries, as a consequence of a merger wave during the 1960s and early 1970s. At the center of this process stood the would-be core conglomerates, which started to form during the 1950s with the amalgamation of small family banks and saving and loans cooperatives.[53] Their expansion began in earnest, however, only during the 1965–6 recession, when the government's austerity policy triggered a massive wave of business consolidation[54] and stripped labor cooperatives of their remaining autonomy.[55] In the early 1970s the government also started liquidating its direct industrial holdings, moving toward indirect intervention through subsidies and military contracts.

After the early 1970s the growth of the large conglomerates came to depend increasingly on the differential "depth" rather than "breadth" of accumulation. This was achieved in three principal ways. First, mergers and acquisitions brought a larger share of the profit under the control of these firms, enabling them to better control competition and prevent an unruly rise in capacity. Second, with civilian production entering a period of protracted stagnation, resources started shifting into financial activity and inflation began to rise. This inflated the conglomerate's financial assets relative to the economy's total and eroded the share of labor. Finally, and perhaps most importantly, the intensification of the Israeli–Arab conflict contributed to rising military spending and growing arms exports (mainly to dictatorships and peripheral countries such as South Africa, Panama, Taiwan, Ecuador, Zaire, Thailand, Nigeria, and Iran). This burdened the aggregate economy but, much as in the United States, the ensuing "military bias" was highly beneficial, both relatively and absolutely, to the leading arms contractors of the big economy. Moreover, high tariff barriers, capital subsidies, grants, and tax exemptions to support the militarized economy contributed further to the ascent of its large conglomerates.

This pattern of "military/financial accumulation" was typical to all of the core firms. The Discount group (IDBH), for example, entered the military sector during the late 1960s, when rising superpower tensions in the region created lucrative business opportunities in the arms industry. After the 1967 Israel–Arab war it recruited Dan Tolkowsky, a former commander of the Israeli air force, to head its newly reorganized industrial subsidiary, Discount Investment Corporation. A descendant of the pre-independence bourgeoisie with close ties to the Labour party leadership, Tolkowsky was well situated for the task, and as his company expanded he moved to recruit other high-ranking officers from the army, Shin Beit (security service), and Mossad (spy agency) as heads of many of its subsidiaries.[56] In a short time Discount Investment Corporation acquired numerous holdings in the military sector – usually in association with tax-exempt foreign partners[57] – and within a few years it began to account for a rising share of IDBH's overall profits. The main outlet for these profits was the flourishing stock market, where IDBH-run mutual and pension funds were increasingly active in stock manipulation – another major source of profit for the group.

Much like IDBH, Koor too was enjoying the post-war prosperity. Riding the military multiplier and boosted by cheap credit from Bank Hapoalim, the group's labor force more than doubled to 22,000 in 1974, up from only 10,000 in 1967, while its net earnings rose to $16 million from a loss of $4 million. Koor's numerous operations, which until then did not have any coherent structure, were grouped into thirteen "brigades" according to military-bureaucratic principles. Top managerial positions were staffed by retired army officers and financial decisions were centralized. Although still nominally owned by its own workers (as well as by all other members of the Histadrut), the company was now behaving much like any other capitalist enterprise, with the ratio of executive compensation to factory-floor wages rising. Strategically, Koor concentrated on acquiring companies rendered vulnerable by the 1965–6 recession. Dozens of firms in areas such as chemicals, steel, edible oil, pharmaceuticals, and the automotive industry were taken over. The biggest incursion, however, was into defense – particularly through Koor Trading, which dealt with arms exports, and Tadiran, which acted as a principal weapon producer.[58] The Clal group also began to grow during the 1960s, and its expansion was not much different from that of IDBH or Koor. After a few difficult years (in which losses were covered by the government) the group was taken over by Bank Hapoalim (42 percent), IDBH (33 percent), and others. From 1969 onward Clal expanded via mergers and acquisitions, financed largely by subsidized government loans.[59] As in the cases of IDBH and Koor, the expansion brought Clal into every corner of the economy, with holdings in diverse areas such as textile, cement, frozen food, paper, and rubber. Most significantly, Clal developed into the "gravity center" of the big economy – both by virtue of its ownership structure and through a dense network of joint ventures with the other core conglomerates. For instance, Clal is a joint owner, together with Discount Investment, of the paper monopoly Hadera Paper; together with

Koor, it controls the cement monopoly Nesher; and with Elron, from the Discount group, it controls the electronic-imaging giant Sitex. Finally, much as the other groups, Clal, too, became dependent on both the military and finance sectors. For instance, its Urdan subsidiary manufactures land platforms for the army, including Israel's main battle tank (Merkava), its automotive subsidiary supplies armored vehicles and trucks, while its ICI subsidiary provides military communication gear. In the financial branch, Clal entered the insurance sector, where, after taking over many of its mid-size competitors, it became the leading company.

The interaction between the military and financial sectors in Israel was not coincidental. The country's large military-related deficits were financed partly by grants and loans from the U.S., but mostly by a bulging domestic debt. The arrangement was doubly beneficial for the core conglomerates, which enjoyed not only the benefit of massive military spending, but also the consequent investment outlet opened through the issuance of inflation-indexed government bonds. Capitalists often object to large government deficits on the grounds that these serve to "crowd out" private investment, though in the closed war economy of the 1970s and early 1980s the large Israeli capitalists had little to lose from this type of arrangement. True, massive government borrowing contributed to three-digit real rates of interest, but these hardly hurt the core conglomerates. First, their virtual monopoly over credit helped them maintain the real spread between lending and borrowing rates at 20–50 percent and, second, the effect on their profit of a high-interest-rate regime was more than offset by political ties which assured cost-plus government contracts, subsidized credit, and low taxes.

Moreover, to the extent that monetized deficits contributed to inflation, for the core conglomerates inflation's positive effect on profits and the value of financial assets far outweighed its impact on rising wages. Despite these benefits, after the 1970s there was growing pressure for greater "liberalization" of the capital market. The goal, though, had little to do with improving "allocative efficiency." Indeed, when the government began to withdraw from the market, reducing the role of its directed loans, gross investment started to drop – falling to about 15 percent of GDP in 1985, down from 30 percent ten years earlier. The real reason behind the liberalization push was that the core conglomerates discovered a new gold mine – the stock market. Tight collusion, particularly among the large banks, enabled them to manipulate the price of their own shares – as well as those of many others – to the point of guaranteeing investors *a predetermined real rate of return*! In the words of the Bejsky Commission, the banks were able to create a "new type of security" combining the properties of shares and indexed bonds in the same paper. But in order to maximize the benefit of this invention the government had to be pushed out, and that required "liberalization."[60]

The gradual withdrawal of the government gave rise to a "parallel monetary policy" managed by the big banks; on the one hand, their systematic stock manipulation was tantamount to printing money, while, on the other, the consequent market buoyancy enabled them to "absorb" much of this newly created money by issuing new stocks. The consequence was a rapid inflationary redistribution of income. In broad terms, the principal winners were shareholders, whose financial assets appreciated much faster than the rate of inflation (stock-market capitalization increased from 8 percent of GDP in 1973 to 99 percent by 1982).[61] But even that fails to convey the full extent of the ensuing redistribution. Although Israel has no official data on the distribution of wealth, it is clear that the main beneficiaries of the inflationary process were the three largest banks. These banks became the biggest owners of their own stocks, which by 1982 rose to account for a full 44 percent of the economy's aggregate liquid assets, up from only 7 percent in 1973.[62]

The concentration process, which remained latent during the 1950s and 1960s, had now emerged with all of its consequences. After the 1970s the external stimuli of immigration, capital inflows, and market expansion were all gone, and as a result the focus of accumulation shifted from breadth to depth. By now the economy had already accumulated a dense network of "distributional coalitions" whose interests lay in *stagflation* rather than growth and price stability. The process of corporate concentration and income redistribution undermined the political power of organized labor and restricted purchasing power. The economy began to suffer from "excess capacity" – that is, an excess over what could be sold at *profitable* prices. For firms in the big economy, business success was thus increasingly dependent on limiting the growth of capacity while using inflation to raise their distributive share in the stagnating pie. Indeed, after the early 1970s there was a drastic drop in net investment – to a mere 5 billion NIS (New Israeli Shekels) in 1986, down from 21 billion NIS in 1973 (figures in constant 1980 prices) – coupled with a rise in inflation to over 400 percent in the mid-1980s, up from less than 20 percent in the early 1970s.[63] Yet despite the stagflation – or rather because of it – the large Israeli conglomerates were now experiencing their fastest expansion ever.

In summary, after the 1970s the Israeli economy was increasingly characterized by a dual economy dominated by several large core conglomerates whose differential accumulation was sustained mainly by raising the depth of accumulation. The principal vehicles were armaments and finance – the first supported by the accelerated Israeli–Arab conflict and the growing superpower involvement in the region, the latter by intensifying stagflation. The Israeli government was getting deeper into debt – with domestic debt servicing accruing principally to the big economy, and with foreign payments helping to support the export drive of U.S.-based military contractors. In the process the structure of power in Israel underwent a fundamental transformation, whereby the core conglomerates grew increasingly intertwined through a web of cross-ownership, business, political, and kinship ties, while the government was gradually reduced to the role of a mere intermediary.

Significant as it was, this transformation has made little impact on the conventional wisdom of power, which still sees the subjugation of the "private" to the "public" as the key ill of Israeli society. The main problem, we are still told, is the superiority of politicians over businessmen, of parties over companies, and of the state over the economy. According to Shapiro, Arian, Aharoni, and numerous others, it is the socialist tradition perpetuated by a dominant party system which undermined the economy and threatened democracy.[64] Unfortunately, by mistakenly equating the *effective* structure of power with its *formal* appearance, this approach became increasingly anachronistic; while the effective locus of power has shifted, interpretations based on its formal appearance remained mired in a bygone past.

During the 1950s and 1960s, with the government controlling most capital inflows and investment, and being involved in diverse fields such as agriculture, industry, construction, and mass public services, the notion of Israel as a "dominant-party system" offered a useful analytical framework. However, with the growing "military bias" after the 1970s, the government gradually lost its central role in the economy, moving from direct economic involvement to indirect support and subsidization of the big economy, and eventually to passive mediation between the large domestic conglomerates, the leading American-based armament companies, and the U.S. Administration. During the late 1980s, as a consequence of its mounting institutional obligations toward the big economy in both of these countries, the Israeli government lost control over its own fiscal and monetary policy, and eventually gave up the initiative even in matters of foreign policy. Much as in the United States of the 1960s, the "military bias" of Israel's big economy served to enhance militaristic tendencies among the country's elites. Unlike the old "political" militarism of pre-independence, the new brand was driven by "economic" considerations rooted in the very process of accumulation. Moreover, Israel was becoming important, both directly and indirectly, to the profitability of U.S. military contractors, and they too were having an impact, albeit an indirect one, on the course of foreign policy. As a consequence of these changes, it seems fair to say that from the mid-1970s onward the dominant-party system had given way to a new system of "dominant capital."

In many ways, the Israeli regime of "militarized stagflation" was self-propagating. Rising military expenditures and debt servicing, on the one hand, and weaker labor unions and wage erosion, on the other, contributed to a differential accumulation by the big economy, and hence to its growing political leverage. For almost two decades, from the late 1960s to the mid-1980s, the rising power of the core conglomerates more or less guaranteed the continuation of this regime.

But then the militarized order collapsed. The early signs of this collapse appeared in 1986. First came the cancellation of the "Lavi project" – a domestically produced fighter aircraft which fell prey to vehement objections from the U.S. arms lobby. Then Israeli arms producers started losing money. After years of hailing the aggregate benefits of military production and exports, the tone suddenly changed. Journalists, politicians, and academics, who had previously labored to demonstrate the technological, economic, and cultural contributions of arms sales, were now turning to attack the armament industry. After having been subsidized for decades, these industries suddenly became a "burden." The most vulnerable were government-owned companies, whose chronic losses of up to $1 billion annually made them an easy target for massive layoffs and outright closure.

The questions revolve around what and why. What made the military business elite reverse its course? Why was the old order of war profits falling apart and what brought the new regime of "peace dividends"?

From war profits to peace dividends: the new order

Israel's transition into a new era of peace has been affected by several domestic and regional developments, but these must be understood within the broader transformation of global capitalism. Until recently, globalization occurred mainly in the realm of *production*, with companies spreading their factories around the world and shifting their sources of output in line with changing expectations about cost and profit. The current phase extends globalization into the realm of *ownership*. Increasingly, the spread of multinational companies into emerging markets involves not only the creation of new productive capacity, but also the establishment of ownership ties. The pace of this process has been greatly enhanced, first by the rapid growth of equity and money markets in the emerging economies, and, second, by their ongoing process of privatization. As a consequence, the expansion of multinational companies is increasingly becoming a matter of "business as usual," with far less nationalistic overtones on the receiving end.

The globalization of ownership is intimately linked with a worldwide shift from the differential depth of accumulation to the differential breadth of accumulation. For the local elites in the emerging markets, the first stage of this transition often appears in the form of severe economic crisis and a threat to the institutions underlying the differential depth of accumulation. Thus in Brazil the debt crisis of the 1980s undermined the arrangement of an *entreguista* (collaborator) state, in which public spending and government-owned corporations in the resource sector were underwriting the expansion of multinational companies and private capital; in India the foreign-exchange crisis of the early 1990s brought an end to the protectionism of the "license raj"; in South Africa the nose-dive of gold prices after 1980 put a seal on the "labor shortage" rationale of apartheid; and in Israel the collapse of the war economy and the bursting of the stock-market bubble eliminated the main mechanisms of internal redistribution.[65] Following the crisis, the second stage is almost invariably associated with a fundamental rethinking of the link between capital and the state. With the ideological collapse of socialism and Keynesianism, there is a growing recognition that the "natural right of investment" – that is, the customary right to control a portion of the societal surplus – can no longer be secured solely by "domestic legitimization" and must increasingly rely on "global market power." Thus the depth of accumulation declines in significance and the breadth of accumulation comes to the fore. The external manifestation of this process is the falling of trade barriers and the opening of previously closed economies to foreign investment. The heightened significance of balance-of-payments and currency considerations means that foreign invest-ment can no longer be considered unwelcome. Most developing countries run a current-account deficit, and, given that intergovernmental loans and transfers are on the decline, financing this deficit must increasingly rely on *private* investment flows.

For the local business groups, the initial effect often comes in the form of disintegrating institutional arrangements and a resulting collapse of the "normal rate of return." This stage is usually short-lived, however, and is quickly compensated for by the ability to "go global"; for large compa-nies with relatively limited foreign investment, the advantage of outward expansion is that differential accumulation is no longer constrained by the inherent barriers of domestic redistribution. Examples abound. In South Africa, for instance, the large conglomerates such as Anglo-American are under pressure to disinvest in some of their diverse local holdings and consequently lose their stranglehold over the local market. Such disinvest-ment, however, is likely to help rather than hinder profitability. In contrast to their U.S. counterparts, whose foreign subsidiaries account for over 25 percent of their overall net profits, South African corporations receive only 5 percent of their earnings from abroad, and are eager to raise this percentage significantly. Indeed, the process of disinvestment is intimately linked with the removal of capital controls, allowing local firms to take their first unconstrained steps into the world economy.[66] The situation of the Israeli core firms is not much different, for they too are under growing pressure to disinvest in order to accommodate pent-up demand from foreign investors. The solution is outward investment, particularly in the emerging markets of Asia, Latin America, and the former Eastern Europe.

Renewed emphasis on the differential breadth of accumulation – a fore-gone conclusion among the leading multinational corporations for quite some time – is rapidly becoming an article of faith in the periphery coun-tries as well. The main consequence of this new consensus is the globalization of ownership – initially through cross-border corporate alliances and subsequently also through the diffusion of transnational owner-ship. In this sense, the current phase of globalization implies a higher level of absentee ownership. Although the process is still dominated by Western-based firms, the nationality of owners becomes not only increasingly difficult to ascertain but also increasingly irrelevant to the process of capital-ization. First, there is the growth of pension- and mutual-fund investments, the owners of which are not one but several stages removed from the produc-tion process. Second, with the rapid capital accumulation occurring in emerging markets and with the growth of their own middle classes, outward financial investment by Taiwanese, South African or Brazilian conglomer-ates, mutual funds, and eventually also by pension funds will augment the absentee nature of global investment.

On the face of it, globalization seems to imply greater competition. Although global alliances are on the rise and the large corporations continue to grow in size, these factors seem to be more than counteracted by the rapid decline in trade and investment barriers. Moreover, the opening of the world economy is accompanied by significant technological changes and macroeco-nomic growth. Large populations undergo a rapid process of proletarianization, which in turn facilitates the mushrooming of a vibrant small economy. The growth of the small economy is also assisted by the labor-intensiveness of the information revolution, so that software companies in Bangalore, India, for instance, need only minimal capital outlays in order to achieve annual growth rates in excess of 50 percent. The process is not limited to the computer industry, and is common wherever production is affected by the falling cost of communication and control.

One has to be careful, however, not to equate growth in the number of small firms or in their share of sales with rising competition. The real test of the latter is the direction of differential accumulation — that is, the extent to which the rate of return of the world's largest firms exceeds or falls short of the average. So far, there is little evidence that this has been undermined by globalization. In fact, freer trade and investment may very well contribute toward faster differential accumulation. First, the growth of the small economy is at least partly a consequence of a more effective system of outsourcing by large corporations. In contrast to the "putting-out" system in eighteenth-century England, today's multinational companies are able to enforce universal standards and low profit margins on their suppliers, and can shift from one supplier to another (indeed from one country to another) in a matter of days. Seen from this perspective, the relative growth of the small economy is to some extent a barometer of the progressive absenteeism of ownership; instead of extracting the surplus from its own subsidiaries, today's giant corporation operates more as a profit center, appropriating the surplus via a long chain of small suppliers. The fact that the latter system is preferred to the former suggests that it may well be more profitable.

Second, free trade makes it difficult to object to horizontal mergers and acquisitions. Since the end of the nineteenth century there have been roughly four merger waves in the U.S. The 1990s may mark the beginning of a fifth, global wave. The consequence could be the emergence of "global dominant capital" – this time with little countervailing powers and no regulatory body. If that happens, by the end of the twentieth century differential accumulation may accelerate and the degree of global aggregate concentration may well exceed current levels.

The shift of emphasis from depth to breadth in the process of differential accumulation, together with the consequent globalization of ownership, carries significant political implications. Although these cannot be analyzed here, it seems clear that the main consequence is a heightening of the conflict between "McWorld" and jihad[67] – that is, between the advent of democratic institutions and conciliatory foreign policy, on the one hand, and a backlash of religious fundamentalism and xenophobic nationalism, on the other. The move from a war economy to peaceful accumulation in Israel is part of this conflict.

Conclusion: the needed transitions

The 1980s marked a severe economic crisis in Israel, with the differential depth of accumulation running into external and internal barriers. The principal cause was the demise of the Soviet Union and the changing political-economic arithmetic of the Middle East. Relative to the heyday of the 1970s and 1980s, the oil slump of the 1990s has pushed GDP per capita in the region's oil-exporting countries down by as much as 30–80 percent. At the same time, the populations of these countries have more than doubled.[68] The result has been an ongoing socioeconomic crisis and growing political vulnerability and a shift in perspective on who is the enemy. Western governments now see their main threat as Islamic fundamentalism, and, with the old communist menace gone, their principal solution is a geopolitical realignment. The basis of this realignment is a pro-Western axis extending from Turkey, through Syria, Lebanon, Jordan, Israel, and Egypt (and possibly even Morocco, Tunisia and eventually a post-Hussein Iraq). This axis is expected to serve a number of purposes. Militarily, it will constitute an effective wedge in this hostile area and help ensure stability in the Persian Gulf. Economically, this axis fits well into the emerging-markets agenda of multinational corporations and, assuming the peace drive prevails, U.S.-based companies are eager to secure their regional position *vis-à-vis* competitors from other countries. Politically, the hope is that lower trade and investment barriers will boost macroeconomic growth, and that rising standards of living will then provide an alternative to the anti-Western rhetoric of fundamentalist Islam.

This changing international framework has fatally undermined the Israeli war economy. Up until the mid-1980s U.S. military contractors (and oil companies) gained from Middle East militarization.[69] A proportion of their weapon exports went to Israel, which was also instrumental in maintaining regional tension, in assisting U.S. arms exports, and in subversive activity around the world.[70] In return, the "deal" was for the U.S. to let Israel maintain its own military industries (provided these did not undermine U.S. arms shipments) and to allow it to keep a tightly oligopolistic market with high tariff, import, and investment barriers. However, since the mid-1980s world recession and a massive drop in global demand for arms forced U.S.-based producers to fight vigorously for contracts, so Israeli contractors had to give. The consequences were a decline in domestic military procurement, as opposed to arms imports (which have remained relatively stable), as well as a very rapid collapse of Israeli arms exports.[71] In order to win export orders Israeli weapon-makers now find it necessary to team up as subcontractors with American groups. In parallel, since the 1990–1 Gulf war Israel is no longer seen as a U.S. watchdog in the region, so U.S.-based companies can now demand the opening of the Israeli economy to more imports and foreign investment. From this perspective, one could argue that the same U.S. interests which earlier supported an oligopolistic war economy for Israel are now promoting its transition toward an open peace economy.

For the Israeli core conglomerates, these external developments came on top of growing internal constraints. Until the mid-1980s differential accumulation by these companies was supported by militarized stagflation, which kept their profit margins way above the economy's average. However, like any system of redistribution, this was limited by its own barriers. First, inflation threatened to throw the fiscal management out of balance, and the stock-market collapse of 1983 was a clear sign that business management too was getting out of hand. Second, in order to continue fueling differential profits in the big economy, military spending had to rise in *relative* terms, but that could not be done without eventually suffocating the economy. Moreover, military exports, which were for a long time considered an economic panacea, were now running into increasing difficulties. Part of the problem was growing international competition from the U.S., as well as from smaller "emerging" suppliers such as Brazil and South Africa, but that only masked the larger internal limitation. In absolute terms, Israel's domestic demand for major weapon systems is far below the necessary threshold for cost-efficient development. Under these circumstances, arms exports required either massive subsidies, which Israel could decreasingly afford, or captured markets, which the new world order no longer supports.

Finally, since 1987 the Palestinian intifada (uprising) has tested the dual-market relationship between Israel and the occupied territories. Until the mid-1980s the West Bank and Gaza Strip were seen as political and business gold mines of which the benefits, in the form of cheap labor and captured markets, far exceeded the maintenance cost. However, with the collapse of oil prices these costs began to mount. Lower income remittances from Palestinian workers in the Persian Gulf put growing pressures on a population already besieged by a rate of unemployment in excess of 50 percent, mass seizure of land, administrative barriers, and constant humiliation. The eventual backlash turned the territories into a net burden. Under these conditions, continued occupation threatened the very social fabric of Israeli society and the legitimacy of its so-called "national consensus."

The convergence of these forces coincided with an economic slump the severity of which paralleled the recessions of 1965–6 and the early 1970s. In contrast to the previous downturns, however, the prospects for the core conglomerates now looked particularly dim. The earlier periods of stagnation were accompanied by a heightened military bias and accelerating inflation, which contributed to differential depth of accumulation by the core groups and *augmented* the aggregate concentration of profit; this time neither military spending nor inflation were viable options. A change of regime seemed imminent. And, indeed, much as in the aftermath of the South African, Indian, or Brazilian crises, the Israeli business elite, too, realized that the old order had finally reached its limits and had to go. The new path was fairly clear. The Israeli conglomerates now had to focus on expanding their differential breadth of accumulation, which implied an end to the war economy, liberalization, "flexible" labor markets, lower trade barriers, and capital decontrols. None of this could be sustained without peace, and so from 1990 onward the core conglomerates grew increasingly vocal in their support of regional reconciliation.[72]

The implications are twofold. First, it is necessary to remove the Arab boycott and create a perception of a stable regional environment in order to enable Israeli companies to expand business connections *outside* the region. The Middle East itself offers future potential for Israeli firms, but the immediate gains are limited; GDP per capita in most neighboring countries is very low, there is little overlap between the Arab demand profile and Israeli production lines, and suspicion and hostility still linger.[73] The main promise lies outside the region, particularly in the emerging markets, and the effects are already evident in the data. The growth rate of Israeli exports has gradually declined, falling from 20 percent in the 1950s (from a very low base) to 8 percent in the 1980s. The geographical distribution between industrial and developing countries was fairly stationary until the late 1980s; however, since 1990 growth patterns have diverged. Growth in exports to industrial countries has remained stationary at less than 8 percent per year, but with the unfolding of the peace process and the weakening of the Arab boycott export growth to the emerging markets has surged to nearly 14 percent per year.

Second, the process of outward expansion is intimately related to the changing ownership structure of the core conglomerates. Since the early

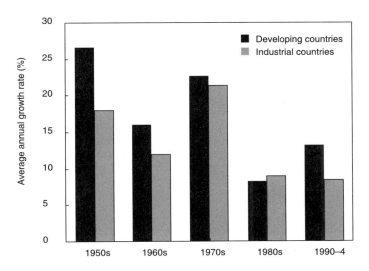

Figure 3.3 Israeli exports (US$)

Source: *Statistical Abstract of Israel.*

1990s direct foreign investment in Israel (as well as of Israeli companies abroad) has increased. The nature and extent of this investment marks a sharp departure from past experience. Whereas earlier most foreign investors had to be attracted by large grants and generous tax exemptions in order to compensate for Israel's high country risk, the current trend is driven by a desire to establish regional footholds in preparation for Middle East development. Companies which have never before operated in Israel – such as Volkswagen, Nestlé, Citicorp, Cable & Wireless, Shamrock, Enron, Bechtel, Toyota, and many others – are now teaming up with the Israeli conglomerates, either through direct investment or via the secondary market.

This process coincides with growing pressure on the core conglomerates to disinvest their holdings. In preparation for such disinvestment there is increasing criticism of the "excessive" power of the large firms. In 1995 a government-commissioned study *suddenly* discovered that the Israeli economy was "too concentrated" and recommended that the key holding groups be dismembered by separating financial holdings from industrial operations. The main target is Bank Hapoalim, which according to the study has ownership stakes in over 770 non-financial companies across the economy – including 34 percent of Clal and 25 percent of Koor.[74] In addition, the bank holding groups themselves are up for sale. The three largest banks – Hapoalim, Leumi, and Discount – have been under government

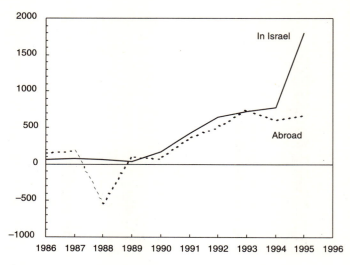

Figure 3.4 Foreign direct investment (US$ million)

Source: Statistical Abstract of Israel.

control since the stock market crash of 1983 and are now being set for re-privatization.

Officially, disinvestment and privatization are sanctioned in the name of "competition" and "efficiency," but this merely serves to conceal the changing nature of absentee ownership. Much as in South Africa, the attack on big business is at least partly driven by pressure from the United States and Europe to open the Israeli market to foreign investment. However, as in South Africa, the Israeli business elite, too, is set to benefit from the ensuing restructuring. The rigid cross-ownership structure of the core conglomerates was adequate for the earlier regime of a closed militarized economy. The emphasis was on the differential depth of accumulation by maintaining above-average profit margins. This necessitated an intricate system of mutual "understandings" and institutional arrangements such as coordinated stock manipulation, synchronized price increases, a common front against labor demands, and a closed system of military procurement – all of which were facilitated by cross-ownership and multiple holdings. The end of this regime, however, eliminated some of the need for close coordination and reduced the need for conglomerate structures. Direct investment is no longer seen as the only means of controlling the flow of profit; this can now often be done more effectively and with far greater flexibility through portfolio stock ownership.

These conjectures suggest that we should be careful not to misinterpret the apparent decline of the core conglomerates. On the face of it, the pending dismembering of these groups, the entry of foreign investors, and the rise of smaller (mainly high-technology) groups seem to imply that the Israeli economy is entering a period of falling concentration and greater competition. Such conclusions may prove too hasty for two principal reasons. First, with Israeli outward investment on the rise, differential accumulation will increasingly depend on the company's global position and the strength of its international ownership ties. On these counts, the core groups are already far ahead of their smaller counterparts, and their differential pace of outward expansion suggests that the gap will only widen.[75] Second, with corporate realignment becoming more commonplace and frequent – via takeovers, mergers, and acquisitions – our existing definition of Israel's dominant capital may prove too rigid. As the pattern of ownership grows more fluid and unstable it may be necessary to go beyond corporate entities and identify the holdings of key individuals. Such data may be hard to collate, but the evidence it would provide would be well worth the effort.

Notes

1 The concept of differential accumulation was first introduced in J. Nitzan, "Inflation as restructuring: a theoretical and empirical account of the US experience" (unpublished doctoral dissertation, Department of Economics, McGill University, Montreal, 1992), where it was used as a basis for understanding inflation as a process of corporate restructuring. The significance of differential accumulation for international political economy, with special emphasis on energy conflicts in the Middle East, is analyzed in J. Nitzan and S. Bichler, "Bringing capital accumulation back in: the weapondollar-petrodollar coalition – military contractors, oil companies and Middle East 'energy conflicts'," *Review of International Political Economy* 2(3), 1995, pp. 446–515, and S. Bichler and J. Nitzan, "Putting the state in its place: US foreign policy and differential capital accumulation in Middle East 'energy conflicts'," *Review of International Political Economy*, forthcoming. An analytical model and econometric analysis of differential accumulation in Israel is given in S. Bichler and J. Nitzan, "Military spending and differential accumulation: a new approach to the political economy of armament – the case of Israel," *Review of Radical Political Economics* 28(1), 1996, pp. 52–97.
2 Nitzan, "Inflation as restructuring."
3 This pattern of accumulation has been labelled "ultra imperialism" by some Israeli writers.
4 See C. Tilly (ed.), *The Formation of National States in Western Europe*, Princeton University Press, Princeton, New Jersey, 1975; S. D. Krasner, *Defending the National Interest*, Princeton University Press, Princeton, New Jersey, 1978; and T. Skocpol, "Bringing the state back in: strategies of analysis in current research," in P. B. Evans, D. Rueschemayer and T. Skocpol (eds.), *Bringing the State Back In*, Cambridge University Press, Cambridge, 1985, pp. 3–37.
5 See, for instance, A. Arian, *Politics in Israel: The Second Generation*, 2nd edition, Chatham House, Chatham, New Jersey, 1989.

6 S. Tsuru, "Keynes versus Marx: The methodology of aggregates," in D. Horowitz (ed.), *Marx and Modern Economics*, Modern Reader Paperbacks, New York and London, 1968, pp. 176–202.

7 J. Robinson, *Economic Philosophy*, Penguin, Harmondsworth, Middlesex, England, 1962, pp. 117–18.

8 Thus E. Berglas, in "Defense, standard of living and foreign debt" (in Hebrew, *Economic Quarterly* 17(67), September 1970, pp. 191–202), asserts that "the central problem of the economic policy in Israel is choosing the right point on the curve [production-possibilities frontier]," yet he immediately adds that this choice must be determined by "security considerations" which are "beyond the domain of this article." That particular article was written at a sensitive period, right at the end of the Israel–Egyptian war of attrition – though time has done little to change the author's basic presumption. Thirteen years later, after the 1982 Israeli entanglement in Lebanon, Berglas still claimed that "the purpose of military expenditures [in Israel] is both to deter potential enemies from starting a war and to achieve superiority once a war has started," and that "it is thus difficult even in retrospect to assess the success or failure of a military expenditure program" (E. Berglas, "Defense and the economy: the Israeli experience," discussion paper 83.01, the Maurice Falk Institute of Economic Research, Jerusalem, 1983). Likewise, Hasid and Lesser, while working as senior economists at the Ministry of Security, asserted that although "Israeli society is democratic, free, peace seeking and striving for a standard and quality of living much like the progressive western states, Israel is coerced into a permanent state of war." In this context, they explained, "the allocation of resources for security involves national risks which are very difficult to assess in any objective way" (N. Hasid and O. Lesser, "Economic resources for Israel's security," in Hebrew, *Economic Quarterly* 28(109), 1981, p. 243). These assertions may all be true, of course, but then there arises the simple question: If the size of the military budget, decisions about the occupied territories, the fate of the settlements, and the dependency on the United States are all determined by "autonomous" state officials, uncompromising Arab regimes, and ideological inclinations, why the scientific pretensions of rational "economism"?

9 According to E. Sadan, an economics professor and general manager of the Finance Ministry at the time, "In Israel economic goals arise naturally from the general goal of the survival of the state." Indeed, "planning for survival includes economic growth, and even when this is not an objective in and of itself, it is a means for making possible the establishment of the defense system required for future wars" (E. Sadan, "National security and national economy," in Hebrew, in Z. Lanir (ed.), *Israeli Security Planning in the 1980s: Its Politics and Economics*, Tel Aviv University, the Jaffee Centre for Strategic Studies, Tel Aviv: Ministry of Defense, 1985, p. 119). (Sadan has since converted to advocating peaceful regional integration.)

10 A. Klieman, *Double-edged Sword: Israel Defense Exports as an Instrument of Foreign Policy*, in Hebrew, Am Oved, Tel Aviv, 1992, p. 326.

11 On the concept of "we," see R. J. Barnet, *Roots of War: The Men and Institutions Behind US Foreign Policy*, Atheneum, New York, 1972, p. 7. Additionally, Aharoni, for example, describes how "we are required, and justly so, to demonstrate resilience and hold out against political and economic pressures," while "our young are called for a long reserve service and bloodletting" (Y. Aharoni, "Institutional rigidity and resource utilization," in Hebrew, *Economic Quarterly* 16(62), July 1969, p. 157). Although Aharoni hinted that the Labour government of Golda Meir should reevaluate its priorities, he was also quick to add

that this was "not to doubt the need to devote whatever is necessary in order to assure our very survival" (Aharoni, p. 160).

12 Berglas, "Defense, standard of living and foreign debt," p. 195.

13 Y. Peri, *Between Battles and Ballots: Israeli Military in Politics*, Cambridge University Press, Cambridge, 1983, p. 1; D. Horowitz and M. Lissak, "Democracy and national security in a continuous conflict," in Hebrew, *Yahadoot Zemanenu* 4, 1988, p. 28.

14 Horowitz and Lissak, *Trouble in Utopia: The Overburdened Polity of Israel*, State University of New York Press, Albany, New York, 1989, ch. 6.

15 See D. Horowitz, "The Israeli defense forces: a civilianized military in a partially militarized society," in R. Kolkowitz and A. Korbonski (eds.), *Soldiers, Peasants and Bureaucrats*, George Allen & Unwin, London, 1982, p. 96. See also A. Mintz, "The military-industrial complex: the Israeli case," in M. Lissak (ed.), *Israeli Society and its Defense Establishment*, Frank Cass, London, 1984, p. 104; and G. Ben Dor, "Politics and the military in Israel in the seventies," in Hebrew, in M. Lissak and E. Gutmann (eds.), *The Israeli Political System*, Am Oved, Tel Aviv, 1977, p. 431.

16 Y. Shapiro, for example, believes that, contrary to the basic individualistic liberal principles of Western society, Israel has failed to adopt the requisite economic perspective to encourage private enterprise (Y. Shapiro, *The Organization of Power*, in Hebrew, Am Oved, Tel Aviv, 1975, pp. 207–8; see also, Y. Shapiro, *The Democracy in Israel*, in Hebrew, Massada, Ramat Gan, 1977; A. Arian and Y. Aharoni, *The Political Economy of Israel*, in Hebrew, Am Oved and the Levi Eshkol Institute, Tel Aviv, 1991). The consequences for Israeli society were detrimental. The petrifying effect of political dominance since the British Mandate era has created grave "distortions," mostly associated with the evils of a "socialistic tradition" and excessive "government intervention" (N. Halevi and R. Klinov-Malul, *The Economic Development of Israel*, Praeger, New York and Jerusalem, 1968, p. 4). "The socialist ideology," writes Ben Porath, "included a distrust of the market, a view of profits as mere rewards to parasitism, and (paradoxically) a view of services as unproductive" (Y. Ben-Porath (ed.), *The Israeli Economy: Maturing Through Crises*, Harvard University Press, Cambridge, Massachusetts, and London, 1986, p. 14).

17 I. Sharkansky, *The Political Economy of Israel*, Transaction Books, New Brunswick, New Jersey, 1987, p. 5.

18 Y. Shapiro, *An Elite Without Successors: Generations of Political Leaders in Israel*, in Hebrew, Sifriat Poalim, Tel Aviv, 1984, p. 45.

19 G. Goldberg, *Political Parties in Israel: From Mass Parties to Electoral Parties*, Ramot, Tel Aviv University, Tel Aviv, 1992, p. 16.

20 A. Arian, *Politics and Government in Israel*, in Hebrew, Zmora-Bitan, Tel Aviv, 1985.

21 D. Giladi, *The Yeshuv During the Fourth Migration 1924–1929: An Economic and Political Examination*, in Hebrew, Am Oved, Tel Aviv, 1973; and G. Yatziv, *The Class Basis for Party Association: The Example of Israel*, in Hebrew, Research in Sociology, Department of Sociology, Hebrew University, Jerusalem, 1979.

22 For a detailed analysis of the "military bias" in the U.S., see Nitzan and Bichler, "Bringing capital accumulation back in," and Bichler and Nitzan, "Putting the state in its place."

23 R. Hilferding, *Finance Capital: A Study of the Latest Phase of Capitalist Development*, edited with an introduction by T. Bottomore, from a translation by M. Watnick and S. Gordon, Routledge & Kegan Paul, London, 1910, 1981; and R. Luxemburg, *The Accumulation of Capital*, translation from German by A.

Schwarzschild, with an introduction by J. Robinson, Monthly Review Press, New York, 1913, 1951.

24 M. Kalecki, *The Last Phase in the Transformation of Capitalism*, Monthly Review Press, New York, 1972; S. Tsuru, "Has capitalism changed?," in S. Tsuru (ed.), *Has Capitalism Changed? An International Symposium on the Nature of Contemporary Capitalism*, Iwanami Shoten, Tokyo, 1961; P. M. Sweezy, *Modern Capitalism and Other Essays*, Monthly Review Press, New York, 1972; and J. Steindl, *Maturity and Stagnation in American Capitalism*, Monthly Review Press, New York and London, 1976.

25 D.A. Gold, "The rise and decline of the Keynesian coalition," *Working Papers on the Kapitalistate*, vol. 6, 1977, pp. 129–61.

26 J. O'Connor, *The Fiscal Crisis of the State*, St. Martin's Press, New York, 1973.

27 P. Baran and P. M. Sweezy, *Monopoly Capital. An Essay on the American Economic and Social Order*, Modern Reader Paperback, New York and London, 1966.

28 Michal Kalecki, "The fascism of our time," 1964, and "Vietnam and US big business,"1967, both reprinted in M. Kalecki, *The Last Phase in the Transformation of Capitalism*, Monthly Review Press, New York, 1972; and S. Melman, *The Permanent War Economy: American Capitalism in Decline*, revised and updated, Simon & Schuster, New York, 1985.

29 Nitzan and Bichler, "Bringing capital accumulation back in."

30 See Melman.

31 The Reagan years saw a sequence of publicized corruption scandals in the defense sector, but even modest attempts to regulate procurements were quickly aborted. Indeed, the drop in military spending since the late 1980s would have been far more difficult to implement had it not been for the collapse of the Soviet Union and the rise of global investment outlets through the North American Free-Trade Agreement (NAFTA), the General Agreement on Tariffs and Trade (GATT), and the "emergence" of Latin America and Asia.

32 As described in R. P. Smith, "Military expenditure and capitalism," *Cambridge Journal of Economics* 1(1), March 1977, pp. 61–7.

33 J. L. Griffin, J. A. Devine and M. Wallace, "Monopoly capital, organized labor, and military expenditures in the United States, 1949–1976," in M. Burawoy and T. Skocpol (eds.), "Marxist inquiries: studies of labor, class and states," *American Journal of Sociology* 88, 1982, supplement.

34 For the military contractors, arms exports became paramount again in the 1990s, when the long-term ascent of global military expenditures gave way to a downward trend in the wake of a new world order of "peace dividends."

35 The dual-economy literature dates back to the 1940s (see, for example, J. Steindl, *Small and Big Business*, Basil Blackwell, Oxford, 1945). Notable dual-economy analyses of the U.S. economy are offered by R. Edwards, *Contested Terrain: The Transformation of the Workplace in the Twentieth Century*, Basic Books, New York, 1979; and J. Bowring, *Competition in a Dual Economy*, Princeton University Press, Princeton, 1986. Most studies on the structure of the Israeli economy tend to deal with the plant and focus on "real" activity, using standard industrial classifications. The firm and its finances are usually seen as belonging to the sphere of business administration and rarely bear on such analysis. However, the growth of the large Israeli conglomerates since the 1970s, with thousands of diversified holdings and complicated inter-conglomerate links, have rendered this framework largely inadequate for the study of accumulation and business power. Of course, this methodological problem is hardly unique to Israel and complicates the analysis whenever an economy enters its conglomerate stage. According to Scherer and Ross, for example, the standard industrial clas-

sification for U.S. firms became decreasingly useful after the 1960s (F. M. Scherer and D. Ross, *Industrial Market Structure and Economic Performance*, 3rd edition, Houghton Mifflin, Boston, 1990, p. 418).

36 For details on the British Mandate period, see T. Gozansky, *Formation of Capitalism in Palestine*, Miphalim Universitaim, Haifa, 1986, ch. 3.

37 A detailed statistical analysis of the performance of the core groups is given in R. Rowley, S. Bichler and J. Nitzan, "Some aspects of aggregate concentration in the Israeli economy, 1964–1986," working paper 7/88, Department of Economics, McGill University, Montreal, 1988. The emergence of the Israeli business elite and its interaction with the political and military elites since the turn of the century are examined in S. Frenkel and S. Bichler, *The Rich Families*, in Hebrew, Kadim, Tel Aviv, 1984. On the relations between the Israeli big economy and the government, see Y. Aharoni, *Structure and Performance in the Israeli Economy*, in Hebrew, Cherikover, Tel Aviv, 1976, ch. 6.

38 Dun & Bradstreet, 1984.

39 For details, see Rowley, Bichler and Nitzan, "Some aspects of aggregate concentration in the Israeli economy, 1964–1986."

40 Frenkel and Bichler, *The Rich Families*.

41 M. Bejsky, V. Ziller, Z. Hirsh, Z. Sarnat and D. Friedman, *Report of the Commission of Inquiry into the Manipulation of Banking Shares*, in Hebrew, Government Printer, Jerusalem, 1986, pp. 32, 35, 38, 40, 73–4, 82, 102, 159.

42 The series for "all other firms" reflects the profits of large firms other than the five core conglomerates, in addition to profits in the small economy. However, given the close correlation between the profits of the core corporations and those of the large satellite firms (see, for example, H. Levi, "Capital structure, inflation and the price of capital in Israeli industry, 1964–1978," in Hebrew, discussion paper no. 795, the Maurice Falk Institute of Economic Research, Jerusalem, 1979, and "Capital structure, inflation and the price of capital in Israeli industry from 1964 to 1978," in Hebrew, research paper no. 122, the Maurice Falk Institute of Economic Research, Jerusalem, 1981), the exclusion of the latter from the category of "all other firms" will have had the effect of making the divergence even greater.

43 See, E. Farjoun's works: "The Palestinian workers: an economic reserve army," in Hebrew, *Red Papers*, no. 5, Jerusalem, 1978; "Palestinian workers in Israel: a reserve army of labour," *Khamsin*, London, no. 7, 1980, pp. 107–43; and "Class division in Israeli society," *Khamsin*, London, no. 10, 1983, pp. 29–39.

44 Farjoun, "The Palestinian workers," p. 4.

45 The paramount role of Palestinian workers became patently clear after 1987, with the intifada (uprising) in the occupied territories. Repeated closures of the territories after Palestinian attacks in Israel have proven detrimental to the small economy. With construction and agricultural wages too low for Jewish laborers, the government had to replace the Palestinians with over 80,000 "guest workers" from Eastern Europe and Asia.

46 Farjoun, "The Palestinian workers," p. 17.

47 Note that this view, which attributes the post-1967 economic growth to the rapid expansion of markets and proletarianization, is generally rejected by mainstream Israeli economists. Indeed, many tend to see the occupied territories as a net cost to the Israeli economy – first, because the availability of cheap Palestinian labor reduced the incentive to invest in new technologies and, second, due to the need to spend heavily on security. Tuma (p. 594), for instance, estimated in a recent symposium on "The Economies of Israel and the Occupied Territories" that the occupation reduced Israeli annual economic

growth by 1.07 percent between 1967 and 1982. In the same symposium, Berglas and Klieman argued that the forced integration between the two economies contributed a mere 2 percent to Israel's GDP. According to their computations, the real winners – in terms of standard of living – were the Palestinians (E. H. Tuma in "The economies of Israel and the occupied territories: war and peace – a panel discussion," in Hebrew, *Economic Quarterly*, no. 139, pp. 593–606). Underlying this calculus lies the same logic as that which sees slavery as an economic loss to the United States and colonies as a net burden on empires; taken *ad absurdum*, such logic implies that over the past five millennia of power civilization humanity was merely busy accumulating losses. The problem, again, is in the aggregates. It is only in the fictitious world of Pareto that an *entire* society can lose or gain. In the real world of occupation and domination the negative aggregates always conceal some definite winners – in the Israeli case, these were the small economy and the expanding middle class. But even that description fails to reveal the whole story. If we were to compute economic surplus on the basis of *unequal* exchange, the Palestinian contribution to Israeli GDP would turn out to be much higher. Indeed, without the occupation the very development of the Israeli economy, as well as its income distribution, would have been far different. As for the Palestinians, a quarter-century of Israeli occupation prevented their industrialization, forestalled the creation of monetary and fiscal systems, confiscated land and water resources, hindered technological education, and encouraged the emigration of skilled workers. Although we will never know for sure, it is not unreasonable to conclude that they would have done better without this occupation.

48 On the paramount role of government during the 1950s, see D. Patinkin, "The Israeli economy in the first decade," 1965. The pattern of sectoral capital allocation is discussed in H. Barkai, "The public sector, Histradrut sector and private sector in the Israeli economy," sixth report 1961–1963, the Maurice Falk Institute of Economic Research, Jerusalem, 1964.

49 Many of today's established companies (now often controlled by the core conglomerates) were born during the austerity era, while many members of parliament and politically connected individuals became millionaires in a matter of only a few years.

50 Horowitz, *In the Heart of Events*, in Hebrew, Massada, Ramat Gan, Israel, 1975, pp. 23–4.

51 H. Recanati, *Recanati, Father and Son*, in Hebrew, Kenne, Jerusalem, 1984, p. 71.

52 *Ibid.*, pp. 92–3.

53 During the 1920s Palestine had seventy commercial banks and 100 savings and loan cooperatives; by the 1970s only five banking groups remained.

54 Some of the largest corporate casualties included the Central Company for Trade and Investment, Gass-Rasko and Israel Holdings (all absorbed by Clal), PEC (by IDBH) and Africa–Israel (by Bank Leumi). Many banks, including the fourth largest (Britain–Israel), went bankrupt or merged with the largest banking groups.

55 During the recession, the Histadrut (confederation of labor unions) took over the workers' pension funds. The immediate purpose, backed by the finance minister, Sapir, was to boost the ailing finances of companies such as Koor, Solel Bonhe and Teus. Jacob Levinson, then chief executive officer of the Histadrut-affiliated Bank Hapoalim, took over seven such pension funds, merging them all into a single giant fund named Gmool. By making Gmool a department within his bank, Levinson was able to bypass the Histadrut's regulatory procedures, so

he could use the fund as a leverage for takeovers. The consequence was a massive redistribution whereby hundreds of millions of dollars of workers' savings were converted into incomes for a limited strata of ex-army officers, financiers, and politicians. (Levinson committed suicide in 1984 after his plan to siphon assets from Bank Hapoalim to U.S. investment companies controlled by his associates was discovered.)

56 The officers were everywhere. Koor, for example, entered the arms business in the late 1960s and in 1968 nominated Meir Amit, a former head of both military intelligence and Mossad, as its chief executive officer. Amit was later replaced by another former army general, Ysha'ayahu Gavish. The "crown jewel" of Koor – the high-technology manufacturer Tadiran – was headed by Elkana Caspy, a deputy commander of the communication corps. Tadiran's board of directors included another former head of military intelligence, Yehoshua Sagee, as well as his deputy Eli Halakhmy. Similarly, when the Clal group entered the military business it got itself a former chief of staff, Zvi Zur. Politically, many of these figures were associated initially with the Raffi party (established in the 1960s by General Moshe Dayan and Shimon Peres) and later with Dash (a political party formed in 1975 by major military contractors and financiers, and headed by Ygael Yadin, another former chief of staff).

57 These partnerships included Elron (jointly owned by TRW), Elbit (with Control Data) and Iscar and Iscar Blades. Investment in the latter two companies was shared with Stephen Wertheimer, a former member of Knesset and a leading advocate of Ian Rand's laissez-faire philosophy, who skillfully combined the benefits of massive government contracts with the glory of free enterprise.

58 Tadiran was originally owned jointly by Koor, GTE, and the government. In 1969 the government transferred its share to GTE, which finally left the partnership in 1987. The company's business success turned it into a semi-autonomous unit within Koor, and, as with the other contractors, its management was rapidly staffed with ex-army officers. A newspaper article from the mid-1980s provides insight into the pattern of political and military business linkages within Tadiran:

> After the chief executive officer, the strong man in Tadiran is the head of international trading, Itzhak Raviv. Raviv recently moved into arms exports, a change which caused some uproar in the company. The main reason is the pending retirement of Yehoshua Sagee [an ex-head of military intelligence who was given a dishonorable discharge after the 1982 Lebanon war]. Sagee was brought to Tadiran for his connections and put at the helm of a special marketing unit of 16 people. Raviv now wants to replace him with Eli Halakhmi, who served in the army under Sagee and was [also] given a dishonorable discharge under humiliating circumstances. After leaving the army, Halakhmi was nominated head of police intelligence, but was dismissed after revelations about his involvement with companies convicted of criminal offenses. Halakhmi was also entangled in the sale of forged Bank of Israel certificates; his partner in the central bank was sentenced to six years in prison, though Halakhmi was not charged. Halakhmi's girlfriend during that time was Leah Levi, deputy senior prosecutor at the Tel Aviv district attorney's office, where the charges were laid. She was forced to resign after being convicted for falsifying receipts.... After leaving the district attorney's office, Halakhmi brought her to work in Tadiran.
>
> (*Hadashot*, March 22, 1985)

59 Aharoni, *Structure and Performance in the Israeli Economy*, Am Oved and the Levi Eshkol Institute, Tel Aviv, 1976, p. 299.

60 Bejsky *et al.*, *Report of the Commission of Inquiry into the Manipulation of Banking Shares*, p. 59.

61 Bank of Israel, *Annual Report* and Central Bureau of Statistics, *Statistical Abstract of Israel*, various years.

62 Bejsky *et al.*, *Report of the Commission of Inquiry into the Manipulation of Banking Shares*, p. 61.

63 Data are from the Central Bureau of Statistics, *Statistical Abstract of Israel*, various years.

64 Shapiro, *The Democracy in Israel*; Arian, *Politics and Government in Israel*; and Aharoni, *The Political Economy of Israel*.

65 Bichler and Nitzan, "Putting the state in its place"; J. Nitzan, "Israel and South Africa: prospects for their transitions," *Emerging Markets Analyst* 4(10), 1996, pp. 12–18.

66 Nitzan, "Israel and South Africa."

67 B. R. Barber, "Jihad vs. McWorld," *The Atlantic*, March 1992, pp. 53–5, 58–63.

68 Nitzan, "Israel and South Africa," pp. 13–15.

69 Nitzan and Bichler, "Some aspects of aggregate concentration in the Israeli economy, 1964–1986".

70 A. Sampson, *The Arms Bazaar. From Lebanon to Lockheed*, Viking Press, New York, 1977; and A. Cockburn and L. Cockburn, *Dangerous Liaison: The Inside Story of the US–Israeli Covert Relationship*, Stoddart Publishing, Toronto, 1991.

71 J. Nitzan, "The Israeli defense industry: a peace dividend for stock pickers?," *Emerging Markets Analyst* 3(1), 1994, pp. 8–9.

72 An analysis of public statements by the various elites since the late 1980s suggests that the first to endorse the new order of peace and globalization was the military echelon, followed by the business elites. The politicians were last in joining the peace wagon (R. Hakeynee, "The political process and elites: statements by the elites regarding the peace process from the mid-1980s until the Declaration of Principles (September 1993)," in Hebrew, mimeograph, Hebrew University, Jerusalem, 1994). The new position of the core conglomerates was succinctly summarized by Benjamin Gaon, chief executive officer of Koor (formerly controlled by the Histadrut): "It is the responsibility of the Israeli business community to assist political leaders by cementing peace on the solid ground of business" ("Koor's Mr. Turnaround builds bridges in the Middle East," *Financial Times*, February 13, 1995, p. 12).

73 E. Sagi and Y. Sheinin, "Opportunities for trade with Arab countries," in Hebrew, *Economic Quarterly* 41(1), April, 1994, pp. 15–27.

74 *Ha'aretz* 4, December 13, 1995.

75 A recent newspaper article showed that since the beginning of the peace process fewer than twenty companies enjoyed systematic long-term profit growth. Most of these were associated with the core conglomerates (*Ha'aretz*, January 10, 1995).

4

THE ISRAELI DILEMMA OVER ECONOMIC DISCRIMINATION AND LABOR-MARKET COMPETITION

Noah Lewin-Epstein and Moshe Semoyanov, with J. W. Wright, Jr.[1]

> The very fact that there is economic discrimination constitutes an added motive for every individual majority group to maintain such discriminatory practices. Discrimination breeds discrimination. The effect creates a circular process which causes job limitations and that keeps the minority group's economic status low.
>
> Gunnar Myrdal

Introduction

This quote comes from Myrdal's famous commentary on "The mechanics of economic discrimination" in his book *An American Dilemma: The Negro Problem and Modern Democracy*.[2] This 1944 book initiated the still unresolved U.S. debate over the roles, agencies, markets, and social institutions play in maintaining ethnic economic inequality. This chapter further contributes to this debate, but with special reference to the Israeli dilemma over the Arab position in Israel.

While Nitzan and Bichler illustrate in Chapter 3 how the core conglomerates in Israel have created structures which allow them "to protect their possessions of opportunities to acquire...superior resources,"[3] we will investigate the structural dynamics that cause ethnic inequalities on the socioeconomic level. For example, workers from the superordinate group who are employed in lower-status jobs tend to support policies meant to confine minority workers and entrepreneurs. While the elite business group is most concerned with controlling international financing mechanisms, the average Jewish Israeli voter wants legal regimes that support biased market structures at occupational, social, and residential levels.

As a combined structure, ethnic economic inequality has become an integral part of local market mechanisms – machines that will not so easily yield to the forces of change that peace might bring. This chapter is premised on the notion that focusing only on Israel's major corporations as a source of resistance to the peace process is too limiting. What is required is an understanding of the uncertainties that Arab and Israeli economic integration present to majority workers in a variety of labor markets. More specifically, we intend to identify the structural foundations of different occupational sectors, and to analyze how these employee communities may react to the promises and problems offered by an era defined by peaceful cooperation.

On the Israeli side of the equation, the possibility of peace creates a primary dilemma: should more economic freedoms be granted to Arabs – Israeli citizens with Arab ancestry, and especially those Arabs residing in the West Bank and Gaza – Jewish labor may have to cede its pay scales in the face of more abundant and less expensive Arab labor; but Israeli businesses will be able to cut costs by hiring Arab labor and they should then be able to pass those savings on to consumers. On the Arab side of the equation, the anticipated level of investment that may flow into the former territories – from the international aid community, from an array of foreign-owned companies, including Jewish investors, and from Israeli businesses – is apt to create unfair competition for Arab entrepreneurs; but greater access to Israeli markets could open new windows of opportunities for Arab entrepreneurs, managers, and workers.

These paradoxes are not easily resolved, especially in the case of Arab citizens in Israel. Israeli Arabs are not as readily excluded from economic activity as is often the case with West Bank Palestinians via border closures (which is not to say that the authors find this policy position either justifiable or progressive). Indeed, it is within the Israeli-dominated structure that mutual links between the political and economic systems could create severe difficulties for entrepreneurs in the Arab sector. This is especially true since, at the current time, they are restricted in their access to means of production and resources, and their ability to pursue modernization is highly dependent on government decisions – ranging from unevenly applied military service requirements to the maintenance of unnecessary bureaucratic procedures. Still, in order for the peace process to reach a successful conclusion, the constraints of economic discrimination should be removed. This is a necessary condition for Arab entrepreneurs becoming productive players in Israeli markets. That said, however, it is important to realize from the outset that Israel is a highly segregated society divided along ethnic and religious lines, and is likely to remain so.

The theoretical structure of Arab economic inequality in Israel

The patterns of economic discrimination against the Arab minority are quite evident, and are supported by a web of corporate and legal constraints which force most Arabs to work in peripheral industry sectors, where – even there – they are disadvantaged in attaining socioeconomic rewards in all segments of the labor market.[4] In some cases the reasons are found in practical bases, i.e. Arabs lag behind Jews in educational achievement, and they support a traditional social structure which impedes the economic development process through the constraint of subgroups, namely limiting women and subgroup minorities like the Druze. But in most cases it is discriminatory policies that constrain Arab entrepreneurial and occupational development. Therefore, on the one hand, on the path to Arab and Israeli economic integration Israeli entrepreneurs, as well as employees, must yield the perceived benefits they receive from the economically restrictive laws which protect them and constrain Arab business owners, and, on the other hand, Arab entrepreneurs must yield their conservative values in response to modern economic and labor-market demands.

Unfortunately, at the present juncture the forces which support the patterns of ethnic economic inequality appear unyielding. It is our aim in this chapter to reveal reasons why Arab ethnic economic inequality should be addressed as a barrier to peace. First, we present a theoretical framework for understanding the nature of labor and occupational market discrimination in Israel. Second, we present a discussion of data we have published in other studies on the socioeconomic positions of Arab citizens in Israel. Along with this presentation we reveal who benefits from maintaining biased market structures. Third, we link these factors to the peace process by drawing attention to the fact that no facet of the Israel economy (nor Arab sectors within it) can escape the peace process's influences. The structural perspective on ethnic economic inequality, we argue, is an important aid in meeting the challenges peace may bring. We hope the information presented here will serve as a catalyst to make planners and pragmatists more aware of competitive barriers within Israel and the threat that they pose to peaceful relations between Jews and Arabs.

There is a growing body of literature which reveals how members of subordinate ethnic groups are kept economically disadvantaged. This writing shows that ethnic-group disadvantages usually extend beyond what can be explained by variations in human capital resources. Recent research underscores the roles agency, commercial enterprises, and institutional structures play in biasing labor and resource acquisitions markets to the disadvantage of minorities. By agencies we mean government-affiliated policies or procedures which draw influence from legal authority. Commercial enterprises are firms or groups that seek to enhance their ability to gain profit and influence through industrial expansion. Institutions are defined by a broader set of structures and networks that serve to maintain prevailing cultural and social orders within a community's stratification system.[5]

According to this line of inquiry, the social and economic rewards an individual receives from selling skills in the workplace are determined not only by human capital achievements but also by the non-pecuniary attributes which the labor market wishes to employ, i.e. tastes for race, religious, or gender discrimination.[6] Hence structural features of a nation's labor market must be viewed as significant factors when investigating socioeconomic inequalities and the conflicts that may arise in response to a community's exclusion from mainstream markets. One of the first modern economists to make this link was John Kenneth Galbraith, who said:

> The most serious friction that can arise between two persons occurs when one denies the right of the other to exist. It is in such a denial of the right to exist that the classic capitalist dispute [over finance and labor] has its origins. However, when the principle of co-existence is conceded by both groups, the nature of the dispute is fundamentally altered.... [Thus when] appraising the state of conflict and agreement in economic life the nature of accommodation in the labor market is, perhaps, the most important datum of all.[7]

First published in 1955, this observation could easily have been written in 1995 about employment accommodation and labor coexistence between Israeli Arabs and Jews – indeed, about their relationship to each other in general. Galbraith's comment on economic inequality, while not aimed at Israel, is germane to the Arab–Israeli situation and provides an interesting dialectic within which the framework for Arab–Jewish economic conflict can be analyzed. This is to say that we see two structured areas in which the dominant impact of ethnic economic discrimination in Israel lies: the ethnic labor markets and the industrial employment sectors. We further assert that structural biases in Israel's labor markets negatively affect patterns of Arab minority socioeconomic growth. The response to this has, too often tragically, been expressions of frustration by Arabs.

Several scholarly attempts have been made to untangle the web of complex relationships which lead Arab and Jewish Israelis to hold widely different socioeconomic positions, but no convincing means of reversing the growing divisions between the two groups has been put forward. Rather, the cumulative result of this research has been to underscore the complexity of the problem, within at least three different paradigms: the cultural perspective, the pluralism perspective, and the class-based economic perspective. Following a brief review of research in Israel carried out within the framework of these paradigms, we will propose the economic-competition model for analyzing Jewish–Arab relations in the Israeli labor market.

In the 1960s S. N. Eisenstadt, in *Israel Society*,[8] focused on the process of economic development as a structure for conflict reduction. He felt that growing commercial contact between non-Jewish minority groups and the Jewish business community would facilitate both cultural change and economic modernization. According to this view, economic progress would serve as an integrative force, which would diminish levels of ethnic conflict. The problem with this framework is that it fully considers neither the historical-political circumstances within which Jewish–Arab relations are mired nor the ways increasingly discriminatory legislation would impede the emergence of such a construct.

In contrast, Smooha conceptualized ethnic conflicts in Israel as stemming from competition over (often government-controlled) scarce resources. He then identified exacerbating factors such as the level of inequality and the presence of mechanisms of exclusion or inclusion. This approach emphasized the predominant polity agenda as the arena in which opposing ethnic groups struggle for control.[9] Ian Lustick took the control framework a step further by linking it to "sophisticated systems" and "regimes" meant to "manipulate the Arab minority, to prevent it from organizing on an independent basis, and to extract from it resources required for the development of the Jewish sector."[10] He then identified three main components of Israeli control over the Arab population: segmentation, dependence, and cooption. Segmentation is defined here as the exclusion of Arabs from the economic, political, and social cores of Israeli society. Dependence is defined as the enforced economic reliance of Arabs on the Jewish majority, especially when it comes to the collection and distribution of important resources. Cooption refers to "the use of side payments to the Arab elites or potential elites for purposes of surveillance and resources extraction."[11] Lustick's control framework makes it possible to study economic activities among Arabs in Israel as a dimension of Jewish–Arab relations, albeit an essentially political model.

A further extension of this line of inquiry focuses on Jewish–Arab commercial relations within the context of a state-controlled economy. Rosenfeld asserted in 1978 that Israeli agencies aimed to insure that Arabs "live in one place and work in many others, live among Arabs, work among Jews and are employed by Jews," so that a schema of restrictions and appropriations could be imposed on the Arab minority. The "appropriations" were of special importance because they intervened in wage-demand market operations, which, as a result, relegated Arabs to lower-class opportunity access via job restrictions.[12] This thesis underscores the role that dependency plays in policies enacted by state agencies to maintain economic and social supremacy over Arab communities. It is interesting how similar this strategy for internal control over the Arabs is to Shimon Peres's regional strategy, which Drake analyzes in Chapter 1. One can imagine that the success of this strategy for control in the domestic economy has made it a planning tool for gaining effective control over the regional economy.

Perspectives on the corporate role in the control process was added by Zureik in 1979, when he evoked the phrase "internal colonialism" to characterize Jewish–Palestinian relations in the Israeli state.[13] Following Hechter, Zureik employed the colonialism concept to develop a model in which the exercise of political control has more to do with government policies concerning resource allocation than it has to do with goals of enhancing economic expansion or national maturation.[14] Hence obstacles for both majority- and minority-group development lie in attempts by the elite, via influence on elected officials and policy-makers, to maintain a tightly controlled and ethnically pure core.

In 1988 Khalidi offered another economic framework for studying Arab and Israeli relations. Published during the intifada (Palestinian uprising), Khalidi's study identified four class-defining sets of regulations that separated Arabs and Israelis, commercially and cordially:

- state policies and popular attitudes which underline the differential treatment of Arabs in Israel;
- spatial separation of the Arab population from the Jews whereby Arabs are concentrated in specific geographical regions, mostly distant from the center;
- unique social and cultural features which clearly distinguish the Arab from the Jewish population;
- economic, political, and social differentiation along ethnic lines, i.e. "a functional economy" polarized by social distance, and controlled by a "systemization context of Arab–state relations in Israel and the existence of specific state policies toward Arabs."[15]

In combination, what Zureik and Khalidi provide is a structure allowing for the development of a dual economy whereby the Arab region is expecting to (or threatening to) "integrate" as an external force in Israel's national (and decidedly state-controlled) economy. More importantly, the review of the literature upon which their positions are based reveals that the occupational and earnings inequalities between Arabs and Jews are to a very large degree imposed by the state, and that differences in education and work experience cannot by themselves account for the gaps in wages and professional mobility. This argument takes on increased significance in the case of Arabs in Israel because of the nation's political-economic history and the fact that the position of Arabs in the system's social stratification has been embedded in the Israeli structure from the beginning. Therefore the economic disadvantages of the Arabs in Israel cannot be separated from that minority group's legal and political subordination to superior majority rights.

A further point needs to be made at this time about the rise of conflict within a system that is characterized by conditions of unequal access to opportunities and resources. Such a competitive structure can be maintained indefinitely as long as there are acceptable living standards at the lower end of the market and an acceptable level of control at the higher end of the market. This state of affairs will begin to falter whenever the terms of inequality change. For example, when one views the rates of corporate earnings decline, as presented by Nitzan and Bichler in Chapter 3, it is clear that those dates coincide with three other market shocks in the region: the rapid decline in oil revenues in the Gulf States; the implementation of labor repatriation programs in the Gulf States, as mentioned by Wright in Chapter 2; and an increase in Jewish immigration to Israel. These events – which forced Israeli firms to lay off Palestinian labor at a time when fewer Palestinians could make remittance payments received from relatives who were working in the Gulf, and which also meant that Israeli government revenues were falling at a time when social services costs were rising dramatically – fundamentally altered the balance of competition and control both in Israel and in the West Bank and Gaza. As the responding contractions of the economy and the declining opportunities for jobs intensified, competition between ethnic groups turned into antagonism and eventually to resistance in the form of the intifada.

The structure of ethnic economic inequality in Israel

In 1990, around the end of the intifada, the Arab population in Israel comprised about 18 percent of the Israeli population, and the Arabs were subordinate to the Jewish majority in almost every aspect of life; they trailed behind in education, income, life expectancy, occupational status, and political power. They also lived in segregated communities and in different neighborhoods within mixed cities. The peculiar nature of this socio-economic imbalance finds it roots in the 1948 war. This situation was put into perspective by Y. Peres:

> Until 1948, there was a clear majority of Arabs in Palestine, although they had no sovereign power ... a village people which had been accustomed to following the leadership of towns such as Jaffa, Nablus, and Beirut. The 1948 war emptied some of these towns and severed the connections with the rest. The resulting lack of trained and accepted leadership increased the vulnerability of the Arabs to Jewish economic and cultural influences.[16]

The Palestinians have never recovered from this defeat, and in times when they tried the result was devastating setbacks. In the periods in between, the

Israeli government pursued economic, legal, and social agendas aimed at restricting the influence of Arab communities. By promoting the interests of the Arab Christian and Druze sub-minorities, the Israelis facilitated fragmentation along religious lines. The means by which housing permits and permits for the development of enterprises were issued ensured residential segregation in ways that kept Arab labor dependent on Israeli employment and also met a number of security criteria. Also, through cooption, the career of Arab political leaders often became closely tied to the influence of Zionist political parties. (As recently as 1988, 40 percent of Israeli Arabs voted for Zionist parties.)[17]

Moreover, the legal status of Arabs is clearly limited. In his exhaustive review of the legal status of Arabs in Israel, Kretzmer identifies three areas in which discriminatory regulations are written into Israeli law.[18] First, overt discrimination, which refers to explicitly prejudicial statutory instruments, is found in laws such as the Law of Return and Nationality. This law provides that any Jews from any nation or origin may "return" to Israel and receive "nationality," but Arabs may acquire nationality only by birth, residence, or naturalization. In addition, many Jewish "national institutions" are entrusted with tasks which are typically managed by government agencies, except that in their case the mandate is to provide services in Jewish communities. This situation leaves a social services void in many Arab areas.

Kretzmer describes covert discrimination as instances when biased laws are disguised through administrative policies. For example, the Defense Service Law of Israel "requires every resident who reaches the age of 18 to serve in the Israeli Defense Force." However, in practice the state refrains from admitting Arab-ethnic Israelis into the armed forces. The implication is that most Arabs (only Druze, and to a lesser extent Christian, Arabs are recruited into the military) do not receive the benefits which accrue to those who have served in the military: child allowances, preference in public-sector jobs, funding for higher education, training program support, easier access to business capital, and subsidized loans for housing. In other cases state-funded economic and tax incentive programs are/were restricted to geographical areas where Arabs were not allowed to live. These areas are often designated as "development zones," where Arabs do not live.[19]

The third form of discrimination Kretzmer describes is institutionalized in bureaucratic decision-making, such as the distribution of budgets and resource allocation by location as opposed to need or population. Other noteworthy areas of discrimination resource allocation are found in educational allotments, the construction of public housing, the location of healthcare facilities, residential finance, infrastructure placement, and government planning, and in the prioritization of application approval processes for items like business licenses and building permits. Biases are even found in the way the government collects census data on Arabs.

Therefore, over a period of fifty years an intricate structure has been developed which determines the direction of both employment and trade in Israeli markets. More specifically, these administrative and legal structures provide, at any given point in time, for an overrepresentation of Jews in higher-status occupations (professional, scientific, and managerial), and they maintain an overrepresentation of Arabs in manual-labor positions. In addition, a deliberate attempt has been made within this structure to make Arab labor dependent on Jewish-owned employment. For example, between 1960 and 1990 Arab employment in agriculture fell from 50 percent to less than seven percent. This transfer placed the majority of Arab workers in blue-collar positions in Jewish-dominated sectors. This makes Arab Israelis continually (and strategically) dependent on Jews for employment.

The results are many. For one, the economic disadvantage caused to Arabs is nowhere more evident than in figures on poverty. In 1986/7 (the last year for which comprehensive data is available) 57.2 percent of all Arab families reported incomes below the national poverty line.[20] After government welfare transfers are taken into account, over one-third (37.5 percent) of Arab families still had a total family income which was below the poverty line. To put these figures into perspective, it is noteworthy that during the same year 23.3 percent of all Jewish families were below the poverty line, but only 7.3 percent remained there after receiving welfare payments. This means not only that a higher proportion of Arab families were poor, but also that government policies were far less likely to remedy the situation for Arab families. The fact that Arab families are generally larger than the Israeli norm makes their situation all the more difficult.

Two other areas where the impacts of discrimination are obvious are "community segregation" and "socioeconomic inequalities." In order to illustrate this point, the authors rely heavily on research published by Lewin-Epstein and Semoyanov in Chapters 4 and 6 of *The Arab Minority in Israel*, presented here as a means of illustrating the influence of Arab-ethnic inequality on the peace process. These chapters describe the empirical and statistical processes taken to insure the validity of the numerical analysis the authors had developed. Here, the authors present only the findings of this research and conclusions; the authors discuss the socioeconomic attainment of employed Arabs and the extent to which their positions are determined by individual versus labor-market characteristics.

Arab workers face restricted occupational opportunities. One reason is that the market within which they are hired lacks diversity with respect to the number and variety of jobs available to them. Another reason is that the Arab marketplace is composed mainly of low-status populations (although this is not entirely their fault, as was illustrated above), which typically lack the resources and political power needed to develop lucrative opportunities. These situations have primary impacts on the economic rewards Arabs can expect to receive in the marketplace.[21] Moreover, when this situation is

NOAH LEWIN-EPSTEIN AND MOSHE SEMOYANOV

coupled with the severe residential segregation they face, the practical consequence is that limited opportunities and skewed industrial structures
necessitate high levels of commuting among Arab Israelis. Some 62 percent
of the Arab workforce and 67 percent of the Arab male workforce are
employed outside their community of residence. This is compared to 50 and
57 percent for Jewish workers, respectively. Arabs also have to commute
longer distances than Jews and, as a result, must spend higher percentages of
their wages on transportation costs. Still, commuting raises the incomes of
both Arabs and Jews because it expands the realm of job opportunities for
both groups. However, the rewards are much higher for Jews. While
commuting adds 9.5 percent to Jewish wages, it adds only 6.5 percent to
the earnings of Arabs working in similar positions.

The sectoral structure of a market also tends to have a different impact on
Arab and Jewish earnings. In determining the factors that should be applied
here the authors used ordinary least squares regressions in order to identify
labor-market characteristics that affect the level of earnings. The categorizations used included weekly hours of work, occupational status, commuting,
community size, people-to-jobs ratios and labor-intensiveness. The
following points are worth special consideration:

- Community size has a positive effect on Jewish earnings, but a negative
  and highly significant impact on Arabs' earnings.
- The people-to-jobs ratio has a negative effect on both Arabs and Jews,
  although the effect is much weaker for Arabs, which suggests that Arabs
  are employed in less desirable jobs; hence their earnings are less affected
  by the overall supply of labor in the market.
- Job diversity tends to increase the incomes of Arabs and decrease the
  incomes of Jews.
- The presence of capital-intensive industries tends to increase the earnings of Jews, but has no effect on the earnings of Arabs.
- When construction constitutes a significant part of an industry's performance the wages of Jews tend to be reduced.
- The proportion of finance and business industries in an area has a strong
  positive impact on the earnings of Arabs and a weak negative impact on
  those of Jews.
- The size of the personal services industry in the labor market has a
  strong negative impact on the earnings of Arabs and a weak but positive
  impact on the incomes of Jews.
- The size of commerce and utilities in the labor market affects income
  positively, and this effect is somewhat stronger among Arabs.

In addition, a striking part of our analysis of Arab participation in Jewish-
dominated labor markets revealed that differences in income and
occupational diversity could not be explained only by variant human-

resource attributes. For example, an additional year of schooling beyond the average increases the income of Jews by 2.87 percent and that of Arabs by 2.29 percent. More revealing is the fact that Jews enjoy an additional 1.36 percent of income for each additional hour of work, whereas the return for Arabs is only 0.49 percent. Jews also enjoy higher income returns based on the occupational status of the jobs they hold, and the income returns for married people are lower for Arab workers than for Jewish workers.

Further evidence of systemic income inequality is revealed by taking the income gap between the two groups and evaluating the mechanisms through which this gap is generated. Regression analysis was used to determine factors in earnings disparities. A decomposition technique allowed the authors to identify the portions of the income gap that were due to mean differences in individual-level labor-market characteristics, as well as differential returns on individual-level and labor-market characteristics. Again, readers can refer to *The Arab Minority in Israel* for more details, but for this discussion it is adequate to note that the income gap between Jews and Arabs is made up of several mutually exclusive components – such as education, hours of work, industrial composition, job diversity, and size of the market. Some of the market inequalities found are provided in Table 4.1.

Obvious discrepancies exist between Arab and Jewish workers. For one thing, the incomes of commuters are relatively high compared to those of residents. This seems odd given that the years of schooling are higher for those who work near their place of residence. This likely means that commuting is an exchange of occupational status for higher income. It could also mean, however, that the net costs of working near one's residence are

Table 4.1 Characteristics: means and category (commuter/resident) percentages of Jews and Arab population groups of the Israeli labor force population, age 25–64

Variables	Jews total	Arabs total	Live and work in Arab communities	Commuters	Residents
Monthly income	33,760	21,117	22,604	21,065	19,362
Occupational status	46.16	38.45	42.94	32.92	37.72
Years of schooling	12.00	9.90	10.30	8.70	10.00
Hours of work	42.00	42.40	40.00	45.20	43.30
Percentage in major occupational categories					
Professional managers	32.00	22.10	32.00	9.00	20.00
Clerical and sales	27.00	16.20	17.00	10.00	20.00
Manual and service	41.00	61.70	51.00	81.00	60.00

Note: A primary category for discussion has been left out here, which is those Arabs living and working in segregated markets, i.e. those who work in the ethnic enclave.

119

high enough to justify foregoing the added income. It may also be that Arab workers, especially those with higher education, have taken the higher-status jobs in Arab communities and have therefore pushed others into the Jewish marketplace. Others may simply be willing to take lower wages as a means of avoiding discrimination and the frustration of working for majority employers.

In addition, commuters are seen to be grossly underrepresented in both managerial and clerical/sales occupational groups. However, they are over-represented compared to both Jews and residents in manual-labor/service jobs. This may be attributed partly to their lower levels of education compared to Jews and residents of Arab communities. It may also be caused by intense competition with Jewish labor.

Having raised this possible explanation, it is instructive to review data generated by decomposing the mean differentials in occupational status between Jews and Arabs. Here, variations due to market discrimination, composition of resources, and interaction were incorporated into the analysis. The data lend firm support to the argument that Arabs living and working in Jewish localities suffer detrimental consequences of occupational discrimination. About 70 percent of the occupational gap between Jews and either Arab commuters or Arab residents can be attributed to the composition of resources in the different groups and, more specifically, to the lower level of education. About 20 percent of the gap resulted from different returns on resources in each of the groups, or what is more accurately labeled labor-market discrimination. First, the magnitude of the composition effect is more than twice the size of the overall status gap (257 percent) in favor of Jews. Second, only a portion of the income disparity between Jews and Arabs is attributable to human resources. In the case of commuters this factor accounts for only 13 percent of the differential. In contrast, the discrimination component identified through this analysis accounts for 82 percent and 61 percent of the income gaps between Jews and Arab residents and Arab commuters, respectively. Furthermore, our estimates show that nearly 40 percent of the income gap between groups can be attributed to differential returns on human resources and group membership, i.e. market discrimination. The real implication is that, had the earnings of Arabs been determined in a similar way to those of Jews with similar resources, the earnings of Arabs would have been considerably higher. At the same time, Arabs and Jews clearly face different opportunity structures in Israel.

These findings are further supported by a report for the Institute of Economic and Social Research written by Hendeles and Gripple;[22] they found that even when Jews and Arabs were employed in blue-collar jobs in the same firms in the food, textile, and hotel industries, Arab men earnt 80 percent of what Jewish men earnt, and Arab women earnt 77 percent of the mean earnings of Jewish women (which was only 69 percent of the earnings of Jewish men). In addition, Wolkinson provides supporting material and attempts to study job discrimination systemically in 48 factories in four cities located in proximity to Arab population centers at Haifa, Petah Tikva, Netanya, and Hadera:[23] 45 of the 48 plants surveyed in the study employed over 100 people, but only 26 employed Israeli Arabs; in only one instance was an Arab found in a managerial position; Arabs were found in professional or technical jobs in only 6 plants; the personnel managers in many of the 26 firms that did hire Arabs claimed they would only do so after they found they could not recruit Jewish workers – this was sometimes a response to union or "workers council" demands that only Jews be hired in a particular facility. This preference for supporting "Jewish work" was revealed by data collected in a 1989 study of Jewish attitudes toward labor-market integration, in which two-thirds of the respondents supported the view that employers should give preference to Jewish workers over Arab workers. Over half of these respondents/potential voters expressed the view that Arab workers occupy jobs that would otherwise be made available to Jews.[24]

In sum, this analysis reveals substantial inequality in occupational status and earnings between Jews and Arabs, especially in the case of Arabs who have to work in Jewish-dominated sectors of the economy. Regarding wage discrimination, the analysis reveals earnings disparities even when controlling for the socioeconomic status of jobs. It also appears that some of the Jewish Arab differences in earnings can be explained by job segregation. Since these inequalities cannot be entirely explained away as the result of differences in personal attributes relative to the labor market, many of these disparities are considered to be reflections of labor-market discrimination against the Arab minority. More importantly, they indicate that two distinct ethnic groups are competing for social and economic rewards, albeit with unequal resources, that this competition is conducive to labor market discrimination, and that control is won by the exclusion of Arabs.

Who benefits from discrimination?

The intention which is common to the state, business enterprises, and Jewish workers is to deny or "close" Arabs' access to lucrative markets and prestigious jobs so that Jews can maximize opportunities and rewards. The question remains: Who benefits from the exertion of labor-market discrimination? The answer depends on the forces of competition and the rigor of labor-market processes. In Israel, for example, there is clearly a two-tiered market geared toward the majority worker's benefit. However, this type of market can be maintained only if the higher-cost (dominant-group) workers can succeed either in raising the earnings of the lower-cost (dominated-group) workers or in developing mechanisms for minimizing competition between the two groups. If the second strategy is chosen the low-cost group must be excluded from the labor market or segregated into jobs the high-cost group does not want to occupy. It is unlikely that Jewish-dominated unions will make serious attempts to raise the pay scales offered to Arab workers. Rather, the two sub-strategies of labor-market exclusion and job segregation are employed simultaneously.

Two alternative views have been proposed of the causal mechanisms underlying the negative relationship between the proportion of members of subordinate groups in occupational markets and the earnings enjoyed by members of superordinate groups in the same market. The two viewpoints have been formalized as the competition model and the segregation model. Hodge and Hodge contend that the entrance of subordinate groups into an occupational labor market tends to depress wages and thereby threaten the income base of the superordinate group.[25] This is referred to as the competition effect. In contrast, Taeuber *et al.* argue that workers who held lucrative positions would attempt to maintain control of these occupations by means of the systemic exclusion of subordinate groups from the supply market. This is labeled the segregation effect.[26] In addition, since the characteristics of both models are apparent in the Israeli market, the situation is consistent with the "split labor market" model which Bonacich posits controls divisions in markets which are primarily divided along racial lines. (In Israel's case, of course, the division is primarily religious.) According to this position, antagonism toward minority markets grows out of their willingness to work for lower wages, which threatens the income of majority workers.[27]

In the current authors' analysis, the question was raised as to whether or not Jewish workers (the superordinate group) actually benefit from discrimination against Arab workers (the subordinate group). And, if so, which sector benefits most. The economic well-being of the Jewish workers is estimated by two indicators, income level and income gain. The first is the mean income of Jewish workers. The second focuses on the residual income of Jewish workers, net of their human resources, or the portion of income which remains after adjusting for human-resource variations. Duncan's indirect standardization method was used to estimate the income gain (or loss).

Our first observation was that there was, indeed, a correlation between income gain and discrimination, with Jewish workers enjoying higher income gains in areas where market biases against Arabs were the most pronounced. More specifically, in the four statistical tests the authors performed, the effect of the market-discrimination variable was both positive and substantial. The results therefore demonstrated that Jewish employees benefit economically from discrimination against Arabs, and that this benefit is reflected in higher earnings in both absolute and relative terms. Second, it is important to examine whether or not the income gain for Jewish workers was actually the result of occupational segregation. To this end the authors re-estimated market discrimination taking into account differences in occupational status. These new estimates were obtained by applying the decomposition analysis to the data collected. This procedure was repeated using information collected from thirty-three local labor markets.

The results indicated that adjusted market discrimination was positively correlated with income gains and average income for Jewish workers. That is, even after controlling for variations in job status between Jews and Arabs, the income of Jewish workers tends to be higher in labor markets characterized by high levels of market discrimination. Indeed, in all of the equations used to test the effect of discrimination on income levels, correlations were found in favor of Jewish employees and against Arab employees in markets where both worked.

These findings raised an interesting question as to whether or not Jewish workers participated equally in the gains made by market discrimination. It was of both practical and theoretical importance to know whether Jewish workers at the top of the economic distribution gain more from economic discrimination against Arabs than those at the bottom of the distribution. In order to examine this relationship the author computed two measures of economic inequality between Jewish groups, one for the top 5 percent of Jewish workers and one for the bottom 20 percent of Jewish workers in a particular locality. The regression analysis revealed that the impact of market discrimination on the top 5 percent was positive, significant, and stronger than it was for any other group. For the four equations that were estimated, the effect of market discrimination on income inequality is over two and a half times the size of the standard error. These findings consistently support the view that the highly paid workers, compared to the lower paid workers, gain disproportionately from market discrimination against minority members.

The implication of these findings is that, while most Jewish workers in Israel appeared to gain economically in labor markets where discrimination against Arabs was most pronounced, discrimination against Arab workers also amplifies income inequality among Jewish workers. Discrimination and segregation of Arabs increases the income share of Jewish workers at the upper end of the income scale; they tend to decrease the income share of Jewish workers at the low end of the income scale.

Ironically, then, those who benefit most from economic discrimination against Arab workers in Israel are those workers who are least likely to compete with them. Indeed, in a more elaborate chain of analysis, the author further subdivided the samples into the top 5 percent, the top 15 percent, and by quintiles thereafter. This revealed, again, that while most Jews working in Israel benefit from market discrimination against the Arabs, the gains decline as one descends levels of income distribution.[28] In fact, analysis of the change in earnings across occupations reveals a decline in the earnings of Jews employed in occupations with high proportions of Arabs. This directly supports the arguments presented by Nitzan and Bichler in Chapter 3.

In combination, then, it can be seen that, while lower-income voters see the most intense threat from Arab workers, it is the elite – the same top of the core conglomerates – that gains the most from the status quo; our findings revealed that the competition and segregation processes were exhibited in both the periphery and the core of Israel's economy.

The Israeli dilemma

From Israel's inception, Jewish–Palestinian relations have been defined by economic competition and political conflict, and both factors remain inherent parts of the current dialectic. By now it should be clear to the reader that the position of Arabs in Israel's stratification system cannot be reduced to personal attributes or individual attainment. Rather, Arabs are actively held back by the system. Key factors here, the authors argue, are employers' hiring decisions and the legal frameworks that set the rules within which biased labor markets are maintained. In many cases the resulting frustration has led to conflict and violence, and to neither peaceful coexistence nor progressive integration of the Arab and Israeli economies or societies. Maybe the reason is that until the recent peace initiative the incentives for designing and/or implementing changes where insufficient. Indeed, as the authors have demonstrated, it has been to the majority's advantage to discriminate actively against Arab workers.

However, in the wake of the intifada and the Gulf war, and in the face of massive waves of international aid as a result of the peace process, the parameters have changed and the stakes have risen to unforeseen levels. Even so, the fact remains that the elites benefit most from both the aid contributions that are flowing into Israel and the revenues gained via the country's toleration of and/or its promotion of ethnic economic discrimination.

Herein lies a key dilemma for Israelis. The dependency of a subordinate group on resources controlled by a superordinate majority supports an economic structure defined by ethnic economic inequality. On the one hand, employing both groups in the same market creates a semblance of economic and social integration. On the other hand, the presence of a subordinate ethnic minority in the labor market gives members of the superordinate group the ability to exercise, if not institutionalize, discrimination. Such a divisive system accentuates the realities of discrimination and deprivation, and fuels discontent between Arabs and Israelis.

Which is more costly, the loss of revenues generated by discrimination, or the gains made by enhanced trade in freer and fairer markets (and possibly gains made as well from reduced security costs)? The central dilemma derives from the fact that resource allocations, market controls, and political power are so closely interrelated in the Israeli system. In Jewish Israel's consciousness the Arab minority is viewed as a foe and an ever-present threat. According to this view, Israeli Arabs with an opportunity to accumulate resources would encourage further competition, and hence they would be able to challenge the superordinate group's control of the market.

Is this view a realistic one? As we have demonstrated, Arabs and Israeli compete for educational access, labor-market entry, legal equity, professional mobility, political representation, and residential positions. In each case there are community and economic structures which bias related markets against Arab citizens in Israel. Moreover, in electoral markets the Arabs are outnumbered and Arab voters are usually confined to districts with few resources to use for leverage. And, as Bichler describes, it is unlikely that majority voters will see the value of ceding their microeconomic benefits for the sake of macroeconomic gains: "for the small business sector, where the majority of voters earn their livings, the New Middle East Order was often more a curse than a boon."[29]

So the real question revolves around whether or not Jews employed in low-status occupations can see beyond their immediate losses and support long-term reforms. This is unlikely. Rather, as the political tenor of the peace process rises, voter fears, the force with which discrimination can be justified, increase and the impact becomes more restrictive.

Thus, on one side of the equation, Israel is by law a democracy committed to the equality of all citizens, irrespective of race, religion, or ethnicity. This commitment is manifest in the country's Declaration of Independence and in its electoral system. On the other side of the equation, Israel is by law a Jewish state committed to Zionism. As such, it provides preferential treatment to its majority religious citizens. The Israeli dilemma, then, stems from the incompatibility of these two principles. When the requisite compromise between these two principles will come about is hard to predict. Therefore the authors contend that dismantling the structure of economic discrimination cannot wait for a theoretical resolution of principles. Instead, Israel needs to move now toward ensuring equal access to opportunities, including those that are expected to be generated by the peace process.

Notes

1 The data provided in this chapter are drawn from an ongoing series of publications and projects that Noah Lewin-Epstein and Moshe Semoyanov have produced on ethnic economic inequality in Israel. What is different about this chapter and the other work they have done on this subject is that we authors are gearing their analysis toward identifying the impact of the structure of small and medium-sized enterprise (SME) sectors in Israel on people's ability or willingness to support the Arab–Israeli peace process. These include reports by Noah Lewin-Epstein and Moshe Semoyanov in *Sociological Review*, vol. 53, 1988, pp. 256– 66; *Sociological Review*, vol. 55 , 1990, pp. 107–14; *European Sociological Review*, vol. 8, 1992, pp. 39–51; *Social Forces*, vol. 68, 1989, pp. 379–96; and *Social Forces*, vol. 70, 1992, pp. 1101–19. This particular chapter was compiled collaboratively with J. W. Wright, Jr., and is based on his reconfiguration of the

data and information presented in Lewin-Epstein and Semoyanov's book *The Arab Minority in Israel's Economy: Patterns of Ethnic Inequality*, Westview Press, Boulder, Colorado, 1993, the articles listed above, and a number of unpublished papers supplied by Dr. Lewin-Epstein.

2 *The American Dilemma* was published in 1944 by Harper Brothers in New York, and remains one of the most discussed primers on the issue of economic discrimination. It was a commentary on the situation of "Negroes" in the U.S. and should be lightly applied to any other group of people. However, Myrdal, as well as Galbraith and Dahl as quoted in previous chapters, points out the inherent conflict created in essentially capitalistic economies which support democratic forms of government. As Bichler illustrates in "Political shifts in Israel, 1997 and 1992: unsuccessful electoral economics or long-range realignment," *Science and Society*, vol. 2, no. 58 (winter 1994–5), pp. 415–39, contemporary voters in Israel vote – sometimes to the exclusive disadvantage of a local minority population – based on their "perceived" economic interests, just as whites did in the U.S. in 1944. The analogy therefore applies to the Arab ethnic-minority situation in Israel in much the same way as it did (and likely still does) in the U.S. The quote presented here was taken, with slight revision, from a reprint in William Darity, Jr. (ed.), *Economics and Discrimination*, vol. 1, Edward Elgar, Brookfield, U.S., and Cheltenham, UK, 1995, pp. 131–49.

3 As quoted by J. W. Wright, Jr., in Chapter 2; Robert A. Dahl, *A Preface to Economic Democracy*, University of California Press, Los Angeles, 1991, pp. 109–10.

4 The public sector may provide an exception. Lewin-Epstein and Semoyanov presented data in 1994 which showed that the public sector offered better than average rank-advancement opportunities for Arabs. However, this applied to position advancement and did not pertain to wages or transfer into the private sector in any of these areas. "Sheltered labor markets, public sector employment, and socioeconomic returns to education of Arabs in Israel," *American Journal of Sociology*, vol. 100, pp. 622–25.

5 Numerous definitions like these are found in the two-volume 1272-page set edited by William Darity, Jr., entitled *Economics and Discrimination*, which is the most authoritative source in this field.

6 The idea that racial prejudices could become part of the labor-market cost structure was first proposed by Gary S. Becker in *The Economics of Discrimination*, University of Chicago Press, Chicago, 1957. Additional references made here include R. Bibb and William Ford, "The effects of industrial, occupational, and sex stratification on wages in blue-collar markets," *Social Forces*, vol. 55, 1977, pp. 474–96; Toby L. Parcel and Charles W. Mueller, *Ascription and Labor Markets: Race and Sex Differences in Earnings*, Academic Press, New York, 1983; Robert L. Kaufman, "A structural decomposition of black–white earnings differentials," *American Journal of Sociology*, vol. 89, 1984, pp. 585–611; E. M. Beck, Patrick M. Horan and Charles M. Tolbert, "Industrial segmentation and labor market discrimination," *Social Problems*, vol. 28, 1980, pp. 113–30; and Noah Lewin-Epstein and Moshe Semoyanov, "Local labor markets, ethnic segmentation, and income inequality," *Social Forces*, vol. 71, 1992, pp. 1101–19. J. W. Wright, Jr., added dialogue on the economic impact of religious discrimination in *Discrimination, Entrepreneurship and the Economics of Being Arab and Believing in Islam in America*, Ph.D. dissertation, Loughborough University, 1995.

7 John Kenneth Galbraith, "A question of coexistence," chapter 2 of *Economics and the Art of Controversy*, Vintage Books, New York, 1959, pp. 9, 20.

8 S. N. Eisenstadt, *Israeli society*, Weidenfeld & Nicholson, London, 1967.

9 S. Smooha, "Arabs and Jews in Israel: minority–majority group relations," *Megamot*, vol. 22, 1976, pp. 397–423 (in Hebrew). On the persistence of biased policies, see his article on "Existing and alternative policy towards the Arabs in Israel," also in Hebrew, in *Megamot*, 1980, pp. 169–206.

10 Ian Lustick, *Arabs in the Jewish State*, University of Texas Press, Austin, Texas, 1980, pp. 25–6.

11 *Ibid.*, p. 77.

12 H. Rosenfeld, "From peasantry to wage labor and residual peasantry: the transformation of an Arab village," in *Process and Pattern in Culture*, edited by R. Manners, Aldine, Chicago, 1964; and "The class situation of the Arab minority in Israel," *Comparative Studies in Society and History*, vol. 20, 1978, pp. 374–407. The quote is from p. 393.

13 E. Zureik, "The transformation of class structure among the Arabs in Israel: from peasantry to proletariat," *Journal of Palestine Studies*, vol. 6, 1976, pp. 39–66.

14 M. Hechter, *Internal Colonialism*, Routledge & Kegan Paul, London, 1979.

15 The categorizations come from Raja Khalidi, *The Arab Economy in Israel: The Dynamics of a Region's Development*, Croom Helm, London, 1988. The quotation used here came from Khalidi"s article on "The economy of Palestinian Arabs in Israel," in George Abed's collection *The Palestinian Economy*, Routledge, London, 1988, pp. 37–70.

16 Y. Peres, "Ethnic relations in Israel," *American Journal of Sociology*, vol. 92, 1971, pp. 1021–47.

17 E. Ben-Rafeal and S. Sharot, *Ethnicity, Religion and Class in Israeli Society*, Cambridge University Press, Cambridge, 1991.

18 D. Kretzmer, *The Legal Status of Arabs in Israel*, International Center for Peace in the Middle East, Tel Aviv, 1987.

19 See also Khalidi, *The Arab Economy in Israel*, and Lustick, *Arabs in the Jewish State*.

20 National Insurance Institute, *Annual Survey*, Jerusalem, 1989.

21 N. Lewin-Epstein, "Effects of residential segregation and neighborhood opportunity structure on employment of black and white youth," *Sociological Quarterly*, vol. 27, 1986, pp. 559–70; and M. Semoyanov, "Effect of community and status attainment," *Sociological Quarterly*, vol. 22, 1981, pp. 359–72.

22 J. Hendeles and A. Gripple, *Characteristics of Blue Collar Workers in Selected Industries*, Institute for Economic and Social Research, Tel Aviv, 1988.

23 B. W. Wolkinson, "Equal employment opportunities for Israeli Arab citizens," discussion paper no. 48, Golda Meir Institute for Social and Labor Research, Tel Aviv University, Tel Aviv, 1989.

24 N. Lewin-Epstein, "Labor market position and antagonism toward Arabs in Israel," *Research in Inequality and Social Conflict*, vol. 1, 1989, pp. 165–91.

25 R. W. Hodge and P. Hodge, "Occupational assimilation as a competitive process," *American Journal of Sociology*, vol. 70, 1965, pp. 249–64.

26 A. F. Taeuber, K. E. Taeuber and G. C. Cain, "Occupational assimilation and the competition process: a reanalysis," *American Journal of Sociology*, vol. 72, 1966, pp. 273–85.

27 E. Bonacich, "A theory of ethnic antagonism: the split labor market," *American Sociological Review*, vol. 37, 1972, pp. 547–59.

28 A. Tyree and M. Semoyanov, "Revisiting ethnic group discrimination and majority advantage," paper presented at the American Sociological Association meetings in Pittsburg, Pennsylvania, 1992.

29 Bichler, "Electoral economics."

5

HUMAN RIGHTS VIOLATIONS AS AN OBSTACLE TO ECONOMIC DEVELOPMENT

Restrictions on movement in the West Bank and the Gaza Strip

Fatemeh Ziai

Introduction

Throughout the Israeli occupation, reporting on human rights violations in the West Bank and the Gaza Strip has focused primarily on violent methods of repression and the denial of fundamental rights such as free expression and due process. The suppression of these rights, both by Israel as the occupying power and by the Palestinian Authority (PA) since the implementation of self-rule in May 1994, indicates a disregard for international law and for the notion of individual rights and dignity.[1] Other human rights violations, however, such as long-standing restrictions on movement, have received less attention internationally, although they have been painstakingly documented by local groups and activists. Yet these restrictions, which are inescapable for residents of the West Bank and Gaza, have had an equally profound impact on the occupied territories and their residents. In addition, the debate on obstacles to economic development in the West Bank and Gaza – which has focused on issues such as flaws in the Oslo Accords, insufficient international assistance to the PA, and corruption in the Palestinian leadership – has often ignored one of the primary impediments to economic development in the territories: continued Israeli control over the movement of individuals and goods in and out of the territories.[2]

The failure to focus on free movement may be because administrative restrictions, or even military checkpoints aimed at closing off the territories, do not appear worthy of condemnation when they follow on the heels of gruesome suicide bombings, or when compared to more graphic human rights violations such as the beating and shooting of unarmed demonstrators or the torture of detainees. Nevertheless, Israeli restrictions on movement in the West Bank and Gaza constitute violations of its obligations under international humanitarian law. Moreover, they have had a devastating impact on the economy of the occupied territories and the welfare of its population.

Since late March 1993, following a series of stabbings inside Israel, a general policy of "closure" – the term referring to Israel's sealing of the West Bank and Gaza – has been in effect in the occupied territories.[3] Indeed, this policy has been more intensely enforced in recent months than ever before. The general closure prohibits the movement of Palestinian residents and goods from or into the West Bank or Gaza, except by persons in possession of permits issued by Israel.[4] Permits are required even for those who are in Israel only in transit to other parts of the occupied territories. Different permits exist for students, medical personnel, and patients, religious worshipers, business people, day laborers, and others. Permits are usually issued for a single day, expiring at 7:00 p.m., but can also be issued for up to a maximum of three months. Different categories of permits are accompanied by their own rules: workers from the Gaza Strip, for example, must generally be married and over the age of 30 in order to be eligible for a permit; however, this rule is made temporarily stricter with each new closure.

In addition to the general closure, Israel has repeatedly imposed "total closure," preventing even those who hold valid permits from entering or leaving the West Bank and Gaza. Total closure can be imposed after security incidents, as a preventive measure when there is fear of an attack, or during Jewish holidays and other selected periods. Between the signing of the Declaration of Principles in September 1993 and late June 1996 Israel imposed over 300 days of closure, over and above the general closure, in the West Bank and Gaza.[5]

The impact of the policy of total closure was brought to light in February and March 1996, when Israel responded to four deadly suicide bombings by imposing the strictest total closure in the history of the occupation (hereinafter the spring 1996 closure). While Israelis struggled to overcome the fear and terror caused by these bombings, which had caused fifty-nine deaths, over 2 million Palestinians found themselves under a state of siege for nearly two weeks, as Israel blocked movement between the 465 towns, villages, and cities of the West Bank.[6] The interference with access to food, medical, and relief supplies, as well as the inability to reach jobs – whether within the West Bank or in East Jerusalem and Israel – led to a humanitarian and economic crisis. This unprecedented form of closure, which amounted to town arrest, was reimposed in September 1996 after the opening of a new entrance to an archeological tunnel near Islamic and Jewish holy sites in Jerusalem triggered violent clashes in the occupied territories. In both cases the eventual easing of the total closures did not end the humanitarian crisis, however, since the "general closure" was still in place.

The policy of closure does not prevent the movement only of Palestinians whose final destination is Israel. Due to the non-contiguity of the West Bank and Gaza, and Israel's 1967 annexation of East Jerusalem, the sealing of the occupied territories also prevents the movement of those who wish to pass through Israel or East Jerusalem in order to travel between the West Bank and Gaza. It also makes it very difficult to move between the north and south of the West Bank; although one route bypassing East Jerusalem does exist, it is not a practical alternative for most Palestinians since it requires making a lengthy and costly detour. This road is also often blocked off during closure. Thus Israel's policies have effectively divided the occupied territories into four distinct regions – the Gaza Strip, the northern and southern parts of the West Bank, and East Jerusalem – with access from one to another controlled by Israel. The PA has been powerless to end these pervasive intrusions into the daily lives of Palestinians; this, in turn has limited its own ability to function autonomously.

Israel as an occupying power

While the nature of the occupation may have changed, Israel remains subject to the obligations that international law imposes on an occupying power. These principles, as set forth in the 1907 Hague Convention Respecting the Laws and Customs of War on Land and its Annexed Regulations (Hague Regulations) and the 1949 Fourth Geneva Convention Relative to the Protection of Civilian Persons in Time of War (Fourth Geneva Convention) seek to protect civilians living under military occupation, and have governed Israel's actions since it first occupied the West Bank and Gaza in June 1967.[7]

The Oslo Accords, which introduced self-rule to the Gaza Strip and the West Bank as an interim measure pending a long-term agreement, created an unprecedented legal and political structure. Yet, despite redeployment and the consequent reduction of its military presence in the West Bank and Gaza, Israel has not fully withdrawn its military even from the self-rule areas, and the agreements place no restriction on the number of Israeli troops that may be present in the Gaza Strip and the West Bank. Moreover, although most Palestinian residents of the West Bank and Gaza now live under total or partial self-rule, Israel retains direct control over nearly 70 percent of the territory of the West Bank and 40 percent of the Gaza Strip.[8] Even in the self-rule areas, where the PA has responsibility for internal security, the Israeli military still retains the "overriding responsibility for security," as well as responsibility for external security and control of the borders of the self-rule areas with neighboring Jordan and Egypt.[9]

The Fourth Geneva Convention makes it clear that an interim agreement concluded between the Occupying Power and the authorities of the occupied territories cannot automatically be construed as having ended the occupation; certainly, it does not terminate the applicability of the Convention and cannot deprive protected persons of its benefits.[10] Moreover, it provides that

> the application of the present Convention shall cease one year after the general close of military operations; however, the Occupying Power shall be bound for the duration of the occupation *to the extent that such Power exercises the functions of government in such territory*.[11]

Speaking in a personal capacity at an international human rights colloquium in Gaza City in September 1994, Dr. Hans-Peter Gasser, legal advisor to the International Committee of the Red Cross (ICRC), which is charged with monitoring compliance with the Fourth Geneva Convention, stated:

> [O]bligations arising out of international humanitarian law become applicable only if and when they are relevant to an issue. Indeed, to argue for continuing applicability of international law to the situation created by the Oslo and Cairo [Gaza–Jericho] agreements does not automatically mean that humanitarian law covers all relations between Israel and the Palestinian Authority.... Israel exercises prerogatives which are de facto those of an occupying power. International humanitarian law, in particular the Fourth Geneva Convention, is therefore applicable to them.[12]

Thus, even though the PA now exercises a range of powers in the self-rule areas, the Fourth Geneva Convention is applicable to the extent that Israel takes actions, in a governmental or military capacity – whether unilateral or in collaboration with the PA – that trigger humanitarian problems which the Fourth Geneva Convention seeks to prevent during occupation. Such actions taken by Israel would automatically extend "protected" status, within the meaning of the Convention, to persons living in the self-rule areas.[13]

Joel Singer, legal advisor to the Israeli Foreign Ministry and senior legal negotiator in the talks between Israel and the Palestine Liberation Organization (PLO) talks leading to self-rule, has explicitly asserted Israel's continuing authority over the self-rule areas:

> [T]he fact that the military government in the West Bank and Gaza Strip will continue to exist is very significant. It emphasizes that, notwithstanding the transfer of a large portion of the powers and responsibilities currently exercised by Israel to Palestinian hands, the status of the West Bank and Gaza Strip will not be changed during the interim period. These areas will continue to be subject to military government. Similarly, this fact suggests that the Palestinian Council will not be independent or sovereign in nature,

but rather will be legally subordinate to the authority of the military government. In other words, operating within Israel, the military government will continue to be the source of authority for the Palestinian Council and the powers and responsibilities exercised by it in the West Bank and Gaza.[14]

An additional indication that the occupation is not over is the fact that Israel has not taken steps, pursuant to Article 77 of the Fourth Geneva Convention, to hand Palestinians detained by Israel over to the PA, as an occupying power is required to do at the close of occupation. Instead, Israel has transferred all Palestinian prisoners and detainees to facilities inside Israel. This action, in itself, violates the Fourth Geneva Convention, which requires that protected persons be detained in the occupied territory.[15]

The degree of control that Israel continues to exercise over the daily lives of Palestinians is a further indication of the continuing occupation:

> The law of occupation is also applicable to occupations in which the occupant shares power with local administering agencies. From the point of view of the law of occupation it applies regardless of the modalities of administration chosen by the occupant ... the test for effective control is not the military strength of the foreign army ... what matters is the extent of that power's effective control of civilian life *within* the occupied area.[16]

As is described below, Israel maintains significant control over the daily lives of Palestinians, primarily through the permit system, which regulates who can enter and leave the occupied territories, including the self-rule areas; the permits cover travel abroad and to schools, universities, hospitals, and jobs in East Jerusalem and elsewhere in the territories.

Israel's obligations under international law

As an occupying power, Israel has obligations, under international humanitarian law, toward the residents of the West Bank and Gaza. Specifically, according to the principles of international humanitarian law embodied in the Hague Regulations and the Fourth Geneva Convention, Israel has the duty to balance its own security needs against the obligation to ensure the welfare of the occupied population and ensure access to food, relief goods, and medical care. Pursuant to Article 43 of the Hague Regulations the occupier "shall take all steps in his power to re-establish and insure as far as possible, public order and safety, while respecting, unless absolutely prevented, the laws in force in the country." This obligation has been interpreted as follows:

The phrase "public order and safety" is an inadequate translation of "l'ordre et la vie publics," the phrase used in the French text, which is the only authentic text of the Hague Regulations. A duty to restore "l'ordre et la vie publics" reaches far beyond the mere restoration of public order and extends to the conduct of "the whole social, commercial and economic life of the country." The occupant is thus under a duty to prevent economic collapse as well as a break-down of law and order.[17]

The Israeli High Court of Justice has also recognized Israel's obligations with respect to the welfare of the Palestinian population. A 1972 opinion, for instance, stated that

alongside an occupant's right to do all that is necessary in the occu-pied territory for military purposes and the safety of its forces, is a duty imposed by international law to be concerned with the welfare of the population in the territory.[18]

This obligation is violated when the severity of restrictions on the move-ment of people and goods between and within the occupied territories bars access to hospitals, universities, and jobs, and cripples all economic activity, thus jeopardizing the livelihood and subsistence of the population.

The policy of closure also violates specific provisions of the Fourth Geneva Convention which seek to ensure the access of the population to food and medical supplies, relief goods, and health care, even in times of conflict.[19] Despite the adverse impact of its closure policy on the welfare of the population, however, Israel has not taken affirmative steps to provide for Palestinians' basic needs – such as bringing in food and other essential supplies, or permitting Palestinians to work inside Israel, thus providing them with the means to meet their basic needs independently.

Finally, both the Fourth Geneva Convention and the Hague Regulations prohibited the use of collective penalties against the occupied population.[20] Israel contravened these provisions when it imposed harsh, blanket restrictions on the movement of an entire population. These restrictions – which were in place for over three years and were often applied arbitrarily – were so broad in impact that they did not appear to be tailored to preventing individual acts of violence. Rather, they were applied against entire portions of the population, without regard to individual responsibility. These factors indicate that Israel's more recent restrictions on movement are not exclusively designed to address security concerns, but are also punitive in nature, thus amounting to collective penalties, which are proscribed under international law. Instead, any security measures adopted should be discriminate and proportional, and their necessity should be balanced against both the exigencies of the security situa-tion and the likely impact on the welfare of the population.

Use of curfews, closures, and permit restrictions

Israel has regularly restricted the free movement of Palestinians since occupying the West Bank and Gaza in 1967. During the intifada, the Palestinian uprising that began in December 1987, the use of curfews and closures to control the population of the occupied territories grew more frequent. Gaza, for example, was under curfew for 30–40 percent of the year during the first years of the intifada.[21] These measures often indiscriminately prevented Palestinian residents of the West Bank and Gaza from leaving their homes, or required them to go through a burdensome, highly bureaucratic, and often arbitrary process of obtaining a permit to enter or leave closed areas.[22]

However, aside from periods when a specific curfew or closure was imposed, residents of the occupied territories were more or less free to cross the border into occupied East Jerusalem or Israel. There were two significant exceptions. First, individuals who were considered a "security risk" were issued green identification cards and prevented from entering Israel or East Jerusalem.[23] Second, Israel introduced magnetic identification cards in Gaza in 1989, without which it was impossible for Palestinian residents to apply for permits to leave the Gaza Strip; these cards are denied to those with a record of political activism.[24]

While closures and curfews were often of short duration, there were exceptions. On January 16, 1991, during the Gulf war, Israel imposed a comprehensive curfew on the West Bank and Gaza Strip, requiring individuals to obtain permits in order to enter or pass through Israel or occupied East Jerusalem, even on their way to another part of the occupied territories. The curfew, which lasted up to seven weeks in certain areas, had a devastating economic impact. In Gaza alone, the cost of the curfew to the Palestinian economy was estimated at $84 million.[25] Equally significant, however, was the sudden upsurge in unemployment – in an area that had always known underemployment – as Palestinians employed in both Israel and Gaza were prevented from reporting for work. In many cases this turned into long-term unemployment, when thousands of workers were fired by their Israeli employers during and immediately following the Gulf war, without even the severance pay to which they were legally entitled or the ability to collect back wages.[26] Thousands of Gazans who had been illegally employed until the war – by Israeli employers who wanted to avoid paying social security or the minimum wage – also lost their jobs.[27] The cumulative effect of these closures and curfews, compounded by the severe economic crisis created by restrictions on movement during the Gulf war, caused long-term harm to the Palestinian economy.

Moreover, because closure policy is meant to prevent the entry of Palestinians who pose security threats to the Israeli population, only a limited number of Palestinian residents of the West Bank and Gaza are able to obtain permits to enter Israel or East Jerusalem, and when a total closure is imposed permits are automatically invalidated. As discussed above, the need to pass through Israel in order to travel between the occupied territories, including East Jerusalem, means that many of those who are denied permits are effectively precluded from the normal pursuit of education, work, health care, religious, commercial, and cultural interests.

In spite of the hardship that the permit policy entails for Palestinians, the process of obtaining permits is highly arbitrary and bureaucratic. Although the policy of closure and permits has existed since 1991, Israel has still not established and made public clear, consistent, written rules to govern the process. Instead, according to local human rights organizations, many rules are oral and are inconsistently interpreted by different individuals at the Israel Central Coordinating Office and its regional branches, the Coordination and Liaison Administration (CLA), and by soldiers at checkpoints.[28]

Since the implementation of self-rule, Palestinian authorities have also been involved in the permit application process. Applicants file their request with the Palestinian Authority's Civil Affairs Coordination Committee, which then submits the application to its Israeli counterpart, the Coordination and Liaison Administration. According to the Israeli rights organization Hamoked, the Center for the Defense of the Individual, "the Palestinian officials play no real role – they are like the mailman who delivers the application to the Israelis, who decide whether or not to grant the permit."[29] Still, unfortunately, the involvement of the PA adds another step to a process that is already quite bureaucratic. It also eliminates direct contact between the applicant and the decision-maker, thus removing the possibility that a sympathetic Israeli official might expedite an urgent case on the basis of a personal plea. The addition of Palestinian bureaucrats to the process has also defused accountability. When applicants whose requests have been rejected address themselves to Israeli authorities Israel's position is that the application was made to the PA and it is thus the PA that is responsible.

The glaring flaw in the process is the lack of any meaningful opportunity for appeal. No explanation is given for denial of a permit, and responses to permit requests are rarely provided in writing. According to Ahmad Faris, director-general of the PA Civil Affairs Coordination Committee in the West Bank, 70–80 percent of the applications the PA submits are refused under the umbrella of security, but no reasons are given.[30] Moreover, the Israeli official responsible for the decision is not required to sign the form, which makes follow-up difficult. Although a request for reconsideration can be submitted, applicants are not provided with an in-person hearing or any venue for substantive review of the decision.

Due to this ineffective system, the applicant's only real recourse is to the Israeli High Court of Justice. At this stage, intervention by an Israeli or other human rights organization and the implicit threat that a case will be brought before the High Court of Justice, a time-consuming prospect for Israeli authorities, will often suddenly expedite a case to which the authorities had been unresponsive, or result in the issuance of a permit to an applicant who had previously been rejected without explanation or on unspecified security grounds.[31] While Israel's eventual issuance of permits in these cases is welcome, the limited staff and resources of Israeli organizations mean that only a limited number of Palestinians are able to benefit from their help in challenging such decisions.

Palestine as an economic dependent

The general closure and the recurrent total closures have impoverished the Palestinian economy. Even prior to the March 1993 general closure (hereinafter the March 1993 closure), however, the Palestinian economy was already in a fragile state because twenty-six years of occupation had led to a high degree of dependency by the Palestinian population on trade routes, markets, and jobs controlled by Israel.

In addition, since 1967 an elaborate permit system has regulated nearly every aspect of economic activity in the occupied territories. According to the Ramallah-based human rights organization, Al-Haq:

> As early as 1967, the import, export, and internal transportation of all goods within the West Bank was made contingent upon the permit system. Restrictions were introduced controlling agriculture; military orders required permits for the transport of any agricultural good as well as the registration of all tractors, diggers, cranes, compressors, ditchers, and other construction vehicles. No tractor could be brought into the West Bank without the prior approval of the authorities. The planting of specific fruit trees and vegetables was similarly restricted. Other orders regulated currency transactions and money markets....The decline of agriculture is, in turn, directly related to the process of land acquisition by the Israeli authorities.[32]

After the intifada began in late 1987, it became nearly impossible for farmers from certain regions to obtain such permits. Agricultural productivity was further restricted by Israeli confiscations of Palestinian land and restrictions on water use.[33]

According to a study by the American Academy of Arts and Sciences, Israel's policies – particularly with respect to the industrial and agricultural sectors – have sought to create a barrier against the flow of inexpensive Palestinian goods to Israeli markets, which would otherwise undermine Israeli production and economic growth. By this analysis, the military government rarely granted permits for the establishment of industries that would compete with Israeli products. Palestinian exports to Israel were subjected to tariffs, generating an estimated $1 million annually, prior to the Gulf war.[34] Meanwhile, Israeli products freely entered Palestinian markets, without restrictions or import duties.[35]

Israel has also restricted trade and capital movements between the occupied territories and Arab countries; this has resulted in the isolation of the West Bank and Gaza from their traditional and most natural markets. Palestinian exports to and through crucial markets in Jordan, in particular, have been limited and at times cut off.[36] These and other restrictions placed on Palestinian exports abroad have required the Palestinians to market the little that is exported abroad through Israeli exporters and export agencies, at a higher cost than they would otherwise incur.[37]

Tight restrictions have impeded even the construction sector, once considered one of the most potentially profitable in the occupied territories. In an extensive study of impediments to investment in the occupied territories, the Palestinian Businessmen's Association identified a number of problem areas. The association's analysis of restrictions on construction in East Jerusalem is illustrative:

> Only 21 percent of the land that remains in Palestinian hands [in East Jerusalem] is zoned for construction.... Building height in Arab neighborhoods in East Jerusalem may not exceed two stories; [Jewish neighborhoods] are entitled to as many as eight stories.... To build a house in East Jerusalem, a detailed master plan for each parcel of land is required and the process may take two to three years, at a cost of U.S.$20,000. It takes another two years to get the actual permit to start construction.[38]

Such policies have stifled economic growth in the occupied territories and created a relationship of dependence that made it impossible for the Palestinian economy to function on its own. Since the intifada Palestinian productivity has been further hampered by widespread human rights violations, including killings, injuries, mass detentions, prolonged curfews, and closures; in addition to these Israeli actions, political strikes called by Palestinian leaders have further interfered with Palestinian productivity. Due to the shortage of viable economic opportunities in the territories, tens of thousands of Palestinians – in order to support themselves and their families – have had no other option but to seek employment in Israel.

A tradition of Palestinian labor in Israel

Palestinian economic dependency on Israel has created a situation where, for decades, tens of thousands of Palestinians have had little choice but to seek employment in Israel. Between 1970 and 1987, for example, the number of Gazans working in Israel jumped from 6000 to 80,000; another 40,000 Palestinians from the West Bank were also employed in Israel by 1987.[39] The closures and curfews imposed during the intifada, as well as the Gulf war, significantly reduced this figure. Then, following the March 1993 closure, Israel once again reduced the number of workers eligible to receive permits, this time to 65,000.[40] Prior to the spring 1996 closure the quota for workers eligible to receive permits had been further reduced, to 34,750; 17,950 permits were issued to residents of the West Bank and 16,800 to residents of the Gaza Strip.[41]

The number of permits granted to workers fluctuates with political and security developments. Several weeks after the spring 1996 closure, when permits had been canceled, Israel permitted the entry of only 7000–10,000 workers. However, even these workers were prevented from reporting to work by a closure imposed during Israel's Memorial Day and Independence Day holidays, from April 22 to April 25, 1996.[42] In early June 1996 22,000 workers from the occupied territories were issued work permits – the most significant easing of the closure since the February and March bombings.[43] Just as this number was rising, the clashes of September 1996 led to another total closure and cancellation of work permits. By mid-October the number of worker permits had risen to 35,000.[44]

Just as the weakness of the Palestinian economy has benefited the Israeli economy, so the employment of Palestinian labor has offered Israel distinct advantages. Palestinians have accepted jobs that Israelis shun, particularly in the agriculture and construction sectors, working for wages that are on average one-third lower than those of Israeli workers in roughly comparable positions.[45] They are also non-unionized and thus present few challenges to their employers.

Because the ongoing policy of closure and quotas on permits has kept tens of thousands of workers from getting to their jobs in Israel, and has led to mass unemployment among Palestinians, many workers have sought to enter Israel secretly, without permits, in the hope of finding work. This, in turn, has led to arrests of workers, who are charged with illegal entry, fined, and subject to prison sentences of up to one year. Thousands of such arrests are made each month; according to the Police Ministry, over 40,000 arrests of Palestinian workers found in Israel without permits were made in 1995.[46] According to Kav La'oved, the Workers' Hotline for the Protection of Workers' Rights in Israel, this policy of arrests

> could turn thousands of formerly legal workers in Israel into crimi-
> nals serving prison time.... After twenty-eight years of enforced
> economic dependency, Israel cannot suddenly shrug off all economic
> and social responsibility for West Bank and Gaza Palestinians, and

begin to treat workers who only yesterday built the country's infrastructure and harvested its crops – as criminals.[47]

The rise in unemployment in the West Bank and Gaza

The closure and the constant fluctuations in the number of permits granted to workers have led to significant unemployment within the West Bank and Gaza – for both those who work in Israel and those who work inside the occupied territories. As a result, more and more families have found themselves struggling to survive. More specifically, the number of Palestinians working inside Israel dropped by almost 50 percent in the first eight months after the general closure was first imposed in March 1993; in Gaza the unemployment rate rose to 55 percent during this period.[48] According to the United Nations Relief and Works Agency for Palestine Refugees in the Near East (UNRWA), Gaza alone suffered a loss of $38 million during the first two months of the closure.[49] The resulting decreases in purchasing power, savings, and consumption patterns adversely affected local markets, wages, and domestic employment, and led to halts in production. While many forms of economic activity have since resumed, the general closure has had a long-lasting impact in the occupied territories, particularly in the already poor Gaza Strip, adding to the class of permanently unemployed and causing even more families – ever dependent on Israel for income – to plunge into indebtedness or below the poverty line.

The euphoria surrounding the signing of the Declaration of Principles in 1993 and pledges of assistance to the PA have yielded few visible economic benefits in the occupied territories. As described below, onerous restrictions on movement have led to a dramatic decline in the profitability of Palestinian businesses. This has created enormous job instability and, in many cases, led to the dismissal of employees or to bankruptcies. A 25 percent increase in the cost of living since the installment of the PA in July 1994 has made Palestinians even more desperate for jobs, most of which are in Israel;[50] job growth inside the West Bank and Gaza has lagged far behind population growth.[51] At the same time, those who are locally employed are constantly prevented – due to the recurrent total closures – from getting to their jobs in other parts of the occupied territories, including East Jerusalem; during such periods they often do not receive salaries.

Before the spring 1996 closure the Palestinian Ministry of Labor estimated the unemployment rate in Gaza at 35–40 percent; others, including UNRWA, placed it as high as 55 percent.[52] In the West Bank the figure was 13 percent.[53] These figures do not include those who had work permits but were unable to reach their jobs in Israel due to regular closures. The desperation for jobs is evident in the response to job openings. For example, an announcement by the Palestinian Ministry of Education of 400 new jobs in the summer of 1994 elicited 7000 applicants. UNRWA has received similar responses to its job openings.[54]

This situation highlights the real problem: the job shortage has contributed to poverty; a 1995 study concluded that "the Palestinian family can meet its basic needs if one of its male members [has] a regular job."[55] Terje Larsen, the United Nations Special Representative for the occupied territories, estimates that every Gazan who works in Israel is able to feed ten people.[56] Following the spring 1996 closure unemployment, which had already been quite high, reached at least 60–70 percent in Gaza and 40–50 percent in the West Bank.[57] As a result, the poverty rate in Gaza rose to an estimated 25–30 percent.[58] Growing unemployment has made more families dependent on cash or food assistance. UNRWA, for example, reported an increase in requests for food aid in the months following the spring 1993 closure, which it was unable to meet due to its limited food stocks.[59]

The Palestinian Authority as an administrator

The PA, suffering daily losses from the closure, has been unable to provide adequate assistance to a needy population. This is primarily due to the substantial losses that the Palestinian economy has experienced due to closure.[60] According to the PA, daily losses are $5–6 million.[61] UN Special Representative Terje Larsen has estimated that total closure applied throughout an entire year would lead to a loss of at least $750 million, which is more than the thirty-five donor countries give annually to the PA.[62]

Losses to the Palestinian economy during closure result from a range of factors, including the interruption of economic activity and local unemployment. These losses are compounded by the increasing inability of Palestinians to work in Israel. In Gaza, for example, at least 30 percent of the gross national product (GNP) constitutes wages gained from employment in Israel.[63] At the same time, cumbersome security measures and frequent closures have served as a major impediment to the profitability and development of the private sector, which accounts for up to 85 percent of Palestinian gross domestic product (GDP). This, in turn, has led to a further decline in local employment.

Between February 25 and April 4, 1996, the PA estimated that total direct losses to the Palestinian economy from wage losses alone came to $78.3 million.[64] The total loss to the economy was estimated at $244.3 million.[65] To counteract the impact of the closure the PA regularly turns to donor countries, which, following the 1993 Declaration of Principles, pledged more than $2.5 billion over a five-year period. By the end of 1995 less than 50 percent of the $1.26 billion in commitments for 1994–5 – or $603 million – had been disbursed and only $480 million had actually translated into activities on the ground.[66] Not only has the level of interna-

140

tional assistance to the PA failed to meet expectations, but, according to the *Jerusalem Post*, "Some European envoys have privately complained that the donors feel that they are offsetting the effects of the closures instead of having the money spent on infrastructure projects."[67] For example, to combat the dramatic consequences of the spring 1996 closure donor countries were forced – as they had been with previous total closures – to divert to emergency measures and budget support contributions that would otherwise have gone to investment and development projects. This included a $23 million World Bank-administered emergency job creation program in March 1996, which created 15,000–20,000 jobs in the West Bank and Gaza, for periods ranging from ten days to three weeks. Similarly, at a January 1996 meeting donor countries noted significant progress in the reduction of Palestinian budget deficit, from $260 million to $120 million, with a projected budget deficit for 1996 of $75 million.[68] Following the spring 1996 closure, however, the deficit was projected at $180–200 million and donors expected a cash-flow crisis in the PA by June or July 1996.[69] Thus additional donor money had to be diverted to budget support.

Impediments to Palestinian investment and business

In addition to disrupting the travel of local workers to jobs inside the occupied territories, thus causing significant staff shortages, the complex and highly burdensome security measures imposed by Israel through closure impede the normal functioning and profitability of Palestinian businesses. When goods and workers are held up or blocked at borders, businesses inside the West Bank and Gaza either are unable to pay their employees or, in many cases, must shut down their operations altogether, which leads to more unemployment.

Despite the severe impact of these policies, Israel has taken few steps to reduce their harm. In particular, it has not addressed the fact that many of the haphazard, unclear, and burdensome security procedures implemented have made Palestinian trade with the outside world less competitive and logistically difficult. These factors, combined with frequent total closures when no Palestinian goods can move at all, have led to a climate of uncertainty and reduced investor confidence, as businesses find it increasingly difficult to plan or meet production and delivery schedules. In addition, many of the procedures require the payment of additional fees for Israeli middlemen, agents, and vehicles, and are thus favorable to Israeli importers and businesses, while raising costs for Palestinians.

Increased costs

Due to the closure almost all businesses have reported an increase in costs and a decrease in profitability. In many cases restrictions imposed by the closure have led to significant delays, increasing travel or delivery time by as much as a week; in one case, a 10-ton delivery to Gaza was held up at the Erez checkpoint for twenty days.[70] The need to pay for transport convoys (see below) and to load and unload merchandise at checkpoints can add another 15 percent or more to costs. In addition, although businesses are unable to operate at capacity, they are still required to pay for insurance, wages, licensing, and vehicles, all of which cut deeply into profits.[71]

The devastating impact of the closure is visible in a range of industries and businesses. A survey of the textile industry, for example, found that "[i]nterrupted delivery of goods has, since the Oslo agreement, forced the closure of 350 textile shops in Gaza, fully one-third of the textile companies in the Gaza Strip."[72] The shoe industry in Hebron has also suffered due to the lack of access to Israeli shoe wholesalers, which has put a large percentage of its 3000 laborers out of work.[73] Some companies whose deliveries are primarily to Jerusalem and Israel have come close to shutting down their operations due to the impossibility of physical delivery of the merchandise.[74] The United Arab Plastic Corporation in Jerusalem, for example, has reported a 50 percent drop in profits since the 1993 closure, which its director attributes to the inability of workers to come to Jerusalem from the West Bank and the resulting decline in production.[75] Others, such as a leading bus company in the Bethlehem area, have reported a further 60–65 percent decline in profits, below the already low levels to which they had dropped since the Gulf war. This is attributed to the fact that no Palestinian bus companies have had permits to enter Jerusalem from the West Bank, and although the buses are not running the company still has to pay taxes, insurance, and wages – or shut down altogether.[76]

The closure regularly interrupts the efficiency and productivity of even potentially productive sectors. For example, the Gazan construction sector has a daily requirement of 3000 tons of cement. Between March 25 and 31, 1996, only 6096 tons of cement were allowed into Gaza. In addition, vehicles transporting gravel from the West Bank were not permitted into Gaza between February 25 and March 27, at which point only twenty vehicles a day were allowed in, according to the Palestinian Center for Human Rights.[77] As a result, donors estimate that 23,000 Palestinians employed in the construction sector found themselves without jobs.

Restrictions on the movement of goods

The impact of restrictions on movement is exacerbated by the fact that during the occupation the West Bank and Gaza have had no port or international airport, thus requiring that a significant portion of imports and exports pass through Israel. Other than a limited number of Palestinian vehicles, only Israeli trucks may transport goods, and this adds significantly to transport expenses for Palestinians. Otherwise, Palestinian trucks can travel in convoys, escorted by Israeli vehicles, to Ashdod port in Israel to deliver or pick up goods. The trucks participating in a convoy must arrive at the Erez checkpoint by 7:00 a.m., but they are often kept waiting for eight or nine hours; as a result, by the time they reach Ashdod the port is often already closed.[78] Since there are at times only twenty Palestinian vans licensed to enter Israel in convoys, hours are spent at checkpoints while goods are unloaded, checked, and loaded. If the Israeli army delays passage the Israeli patrols accompanying the Palestinian trucks often will not wait, thus preventing delivery of the goods.[79]

Except for this limited number, no Palestinian vehicles are provided with permits to cross into Israel from Gaza, even if they are traveling only to the West Bank. In early February 1996, for example, only 600 of the 3200 trucks in Gaza were permitted to use the Karni crossing; a closure imposed on February 12 reduced this number to 200. The spring 1996 closure closed the Karni crossing altogether from February 25 until mid-March, when limited use was permitted. By late May passage had still not reached pre-March 1996 levels.[80]

Palestinians also need special permits to enter Ben Gurion airport in Israel, even if they have a permit to enter Israel. Thus Palestinian businessmen who are unable to obtain airport permits have to hire and pay Israeli agents to do their paperwork at the airport.[81]

Security procedures at crossings

Israel has imposed exhaustive clearance procedures at the Karni and Erez crossings on the Gaza–Israeli border, as well as at the bridges connecting the West Bank and Jordan. As has already been mentioned, these transit points are completely inaccessible during total closures, but even when closures are eased complex procedures have made crossing prohibitively expensive and time-consuming for many businesses. Palestinian trucks transporting goods from Gaza to the West Bank are stripped down at the border, and the merchandise is unloaded and then reloaded on the Israeli side after it has gone through a security check; similar procedures exist for the movement of goods between the West Bank and Jordan.

Even at the Karni crossing, which was specifically designed to facilitate the crossing of vehicles for commercial purposes, the security measures fail to take commercial considerations into account. Dozens of Israeli and Palestinian trucks wait back to back for hours, while goods are transferred under the supervision of the Israeli authorities.[82] Since no refrigeration or containers are made available, delays at checkpoints can often damage perishable or fragile merchandise. Truckloads of fresh produce, for example – one of the primary exports of the occupied territories – often rot after sitting in the sun for hours; merchandise can also sustain damage due to improper handling when it is moved from Palestinian to Israeli trucks. Goods are loaded and unloaded using Israeli forklifts or work crews, for which additional fees are charged. Due to the time-consuming nature of the checks and resulting delays, importers into the occupied territories must pay extra costs for storage.

The result is dependence on individual Israelis. Because permits are so difficult to obtain, companies cannot use their staff effectively. At the Electrode Factory in Gaza, for example, only two of sixty employees have been able to obtain permits.[83] Companies cannot simply send their staff, or hired drivers, to other parts of the occupied territories or to Israel to attend to daily business. Thus the head of the company, assuming that he can obtain a permit, is often the only person able to transport goods. Because of the obvious inefficiencies this can cause, Palestinian companies are required to hire Israeli companies as intermediaries, which increases their costs.[84]

Movement of businesspersons and investors

Even with respect to investors, Israel determines who can enter and leave the West Bank and the Gaza Strip. Arab investors, for example, are generally only granted one-week business visas. Israel also impedes travel by Palestinian business people and investors between the occupied territories, to Israel or abroad, for the purpose of meeting with business contacts and promoting their businesses. At the same time, Israeli products penetrate the Palestinian borders with little competition, and unimpeded by any administrative or tax barriers. According to Muhammad Qudwa, the chairman of the Palestine Chamber of Commerce:

> I have not been able to go to Tel Aviv for the last two months, and I am the chairman of the Chamber of Commerce. If permits are given to us to go to Israel, we cannot return to Erez any later than 5:00 p.m., or stay overnight in Israel or the West Bank; otherwise, our permits are automatically taken away from us. Traveling to Amman is more difficult than before. They make very scrutinizing checks on us all. It's so humiliating to go to Amman that people no longer want to go.[85]

Even those who hold valid permits can be arbitrarily denied entry to Israel. On October 24, 1995, for example, three prominent business people representing the Palestinian Businessmen's Association had a meeting in Tel Aviv with the Israeli military coordinator for the West Bank to discuss the very issue of travel impediments. At the checkpoint soldiers refused to permit them to pass, even though all three held valid permits – as well as VIP cards issued by the Israeli CLA – and were expected at a meeting.[86]

The closure and education

The policy of closure, particularly the arbitrary system for granting of permits, has also seriously interfered with education in the West Bank and Gaza, and, over time, has had a direct impact on the ability of Palestinians to contribute to and benefit from economic productivity and development. By ending or interrupting studies, and thus increasing the expense of completing a degree, these violations and interruptions come at a high cost to individuals and to Palestinian society as a whole.

Closures often prevent the access of students and staff to universities, and the students who are hit hardest by these restrictions are Gaza students who choose to pursue their studies at West Bank universities, often in order to pursue specialties that are unavailable in Gaza, such as electrical and chemical engineering, sociology, and political science. In 1995 and 1996 an estimated 1300 Gaza students enrolled in West Bank universities, but not all were granted permits.[87]

The situation at Birzeit University in the West Bank illustrates the hardship imposed on Gaza students due to restrictions on movement. In a report issued in 1995 the university estimated:

> The average Gaza student spends approximately fifteen hours waiting in line at various Israeli Civil Administration offices each time [he or she] must apply for the three necessary permits [to pass through Israel, to reside in the West Bank for three months, and to renew the permit for the fourth month of each school semester[88]]. During the first two months of the [1995] second semester, permits have been canceled twice. With each cancellation, students are forced to start from the beginning, once again.... All Birzeit students from Gaza were denied permits for the first half of the semester. Midway through the semester, Israel agreed to grant permission to about two-thirds of the students on the condition that they sign a declaration of support for the political negotiations. The remaining one-third of the Gaza students were never granted permits to attend the university. No reasons were provided to explain why so many students were denied permits.[89]

Even when a permit is granted, students must still cope with "potential refusals of any of their permits at any part of the four-tier process, arbitrary confiscations of valid permits by soldiers at checkpoints and blanket confiscations of existing permits after 'security' incidents or 'administrative' problems."[90] In addition, the canceling of permits during the academic year leaves students vulnerable to arrest.[91] Seventy days after the 1995–6 academic year had already begun Israel finally responded to the list of 350 Gaza students on whose behalf the university had requested permits;[92] 82 of

Birzeit's 102 female Gaza students and 13 of its 282 male students were granted permits, although the men received only four-day permits.[93] For the 1996–7 academic year, which began on September 9, no Birzeit students from Gaza had received permits by late October. As a result of such problems, the university must constantly schedule make-up classes and tutoring for students who miss significant portions of the academic year.[94]

According to the Palestinian Council for Higher Education:

> Harassment of students who happen to come from Gaza illustrates well the backward premise of "guilty until proven innocent" that has characterized Israel's recent pursuit of security objectives.... As all students must undergo a rigorous security check prior to being issued permits in the first place and are subsequently required to travel between the West Bank and Gaza in groups coordinated by the Regional Affairs Office in Gaza, the targeting of these students cannot be considered a legitimate security concern and must be seen as arbitrary and punitive.[95]

The impact of the spring 1996 closure

During the spring 1996 closure almost 90 percent of Birzeit's students, faculty, and staff who come from outside of Birzeit village were unable to get to the university. Although Israel did not formally shut down Birzeit University, this effectively closed down the university's operations for eleven days. Israel did formally close the University of Hebron, with a student body of 1700, and the Hebron Polytechnic Institute, with a student body of 900, as well as the Abu Dis College of Science and Technology, with a student body of 1050, and the College for Islamic Da'wa and Religious Affairs, with a student body of 520, the latter two at Al-Quds University.[96] For the first time, the Israeli army imposed six-month, rather than the customary three-month, closure orders on these universities. The closure orders for the two universities located in Hebron were renewed in the fall of 1996.

In all, an estimated 71,000 students at all educational levels were affected by the spring 1996 closure, and a number of universities and primary and secondary schools in the West Bank were forced to close temporarily.[97] According to UNRWA, many UN-run elementary schools in villages and camps had to be closed altogether, while others operated with only 50 percent of their staff.[98]

On March 11, during the spring 1996 closure, the Israeli army also ordered all Gaza students at West Bank universities, including those holding valid student permits, to return immediately to the Gaza Strip. Those who did not comply would, according to the then chief commander for the West Bank, Major-General Ilan Biran, "face all possible consequences."[99] At dawn on March 28, 1996, the Israeli authorities raided student dormitories and houses at Birzeit, at times arresting every resident of a building; 280 – almost 10 percent of the university's student body – were arrested and detained. The students were blindfolded, and some were beaten and otherwise abused during a day of interrogation. That evening, all but seventeen were released – an indication of the arbitrary nature of the arrests. By May 1996 another ten had been released without charges.[100] This raid was reminiscent of the intifada, when studies were regularly interrupted by raids, arbitrary arrest, and detention, and an average of 150 Birzeit students were detained or imprisoned every year.[101]

Conclusion

Israel's policy of general closure has had a profound impact on the Palestinian population of the West Bank and Gaza Strip. Regular total closures have blocked access to food, relief, and medical supplies, as well as medical treatment. In addition, due to the high correlation between the existence of commercial activity in the occupied territories and the ability of the population to meet its basic daily needs, onerous restrictions on the movement of goods have caused a serious decline in business profitability and wages, and a rise in local unemployment. At the same time, Israel has dramatically cut back on the number of Palestinians permitted to work in Israel. These factors have not only further impoverished the Palestinian population and economy, but also posed serious obstacles to economic development in the West Bank and Gaza.

It is Israel's "obligations" that are in question. States have no obligation under international law to *create* an optimal investment or economic environment in occupied territories. Furthermore, like every sovereign nation, Israel has the right to regulate the entry into its territory of foreigners seeking employment.

However, under international humanitarian law Israel is bound, as an occupying power, to ensure the welfare of the population. Thus when its security policies make it difficult or impossible for Palestinian residents of the West Bank and Gaza to meet their basic needs independently Israel bears responsibility for ensuring that these needs are otherwise met. This duty is heightened in view of the fact that the current economic stagnation and dependence on the Israeli economy are direct outgrowths of the long-term military occupation, and only exacerbated by the policy of closure. Until the occupation ends or the economic dependency is considerably reduced, this history imposes on Israel the obligation to allow Palestinian day laborers to work inside Israel or to provide relief to the tens of thousands of workers who have been accused of no wrongdoing but have lost their jobs due to over three years of closure, and whose families face destitution as a result.[102]

The rise in poverty in the West Bank and Gaza due to closures has increased the number of individuals and families requiring assistance. As a result, contributions to the PA by the international donor community have often had to be diverted from investment and development projects to emergency job creation or relief programs. Yet, although it has urged measures to mitigate the impact of closures, the international community has failed to condemn the arbitrary and punitive nature of the restrictions imposed.

This critique does not preclude Israel from taking measures to secure the safety of its citizens. Israel's security concerns are real and substantial. The government of Israel has the right – indeed, the duty – to protect its citizens against attacks or the threat of attacks. However, the measures it takes must conform to principles of international humanitarian law. Both Israel and the international community have an obligation to subject any security measures implemented by Israel to greater scrutiny in order to ensure that they comply with international law. Israel's policies must reconcile security needs with the rights and welfare of the Palestinian population, and stop subjecting the entire Palestinian population of the occupied territories to collective punishment and suffering for the crimes of a few.

Notes

1 The PA, which is also referred to as the Palestine National Authority, is the interim self-governing authority for Palestinians in the occupied territories. It is led by President Yasser Arafat and the Palestinian Council, whose members were elected in January, 1996.
2 The Oslo Accords refer to the Declaration of Principles on Interim Self-Government Arrangements, signed by Israel and the Palestine Liberation Organization (PLO) in Washington, DC, on September 13, 1993 (hereinafter the Declaration of Principles), the Agreement on Gaza and the Jericho Area, signed by Israel and the PLO in Cairo, Egypt, on May 4, 1994 (hereinafter the Gaza–Jericho Agreement), and the Israeli–Palestinian Interim Agreement on the West Bank and Gaza Strip, signed by Israel and the PLO in Washington, DC, in September, 1995 (hereinafter Oslo II).
3 The territory known as the West Bank includes East Jerusalem, which was annexed by Israel in 1967. This annexation has not been recognized by the international community, which considers East Jerusalem to be occupied territory under international law. However, since Israel has applied different legal and administrative structures to East Jerusalem and the West Bank, a distinction is often made between the two areas. For the purposes of this chapter, references to the West Bank do not include East Jerusalem, unless otherwise stated.
4 Israel has used the policy of closure in the West Bank and Gaza with varying degrees of frequency since the military occupation first began in 1967. The March 1993 closure, which is still in place, has lasted the longest.
5 Shomron News Service, citing a June 24, 1996, report by Peace Watch, based on Israeli Defense Forces figures.
6 In 1995 the population of the West Bank (excluding East Jerusalem) was 1,333,000 and the population of the Gaza Strip was 934,000. Palestinian Bureau of Statistics, *Demographic Survey 1995*, June 2, 1996.

7 There has been a consensus within the international community, including the United States and the United Nations Security Council, that the Fourth Geneva Convention applies to Israel's military occupation of the West Bank and Gaza. Israel has rejected the applicability of the Fourth Geneva Convention, while pledging to uphold its "humanitarian" provisions on a de facto basis. Israel does, however, consider the Hague Regulations, which are part of customary international law, to be binding. For a discussion of the applicability of the Fourth Geneva Convention to the occupied territories and Israel's position on this issue, see Richard A. Falk and Burns H. Weston, "The relevance of international law to Israeli and Palestinian rights in the West Bank and Gaza," in Emma Playfair (ed.) *International Law and the Administration of Occupied Territories*, Clarendon Press, Oxford, 1992.

8 Approximately one-third of the Palestinian population of the West Bank lives under total self-rule, and 68 percent lives under partial self-rule. In the Gaza Strip nearly 100 percent of the Palestinian population lives under total self-rule (Foreign Ministry of Israel, as cited by the Embassy of Israel, Washington, DC).

9 See Oslo II, Art. XIII, para. 2(a), and Art. XII, para. 1.

10 Fourth Geneva Convention, Art. 47.

11 *Ibid.*, Art. 6.

12 Hans-Peter Gasser, "On the applicability of the Fourth Geneva Convention after the Declaration of Principles and the Cairo Agreement," paper presented at the International Human Rights Colloquium, Gaza City, September 10–12, 1994.

13 The ICRC is still present in the self-rule areas, pursuant to a 1 September, 1996, Memorandum of Understanding entered into with the PLO. However, "the ICRC's presence and activities in the Autonomous Areas are not linked to the Geneva Conventions. They are not 'treaty-based' activities." Rather, they are an example of the ICRC "offer[ing] its services in situations not covered by the Convention, if needs of a humanitarian nature so require" (*ibid.*).

14 Joel Singer, "The Declaration of Principles on interim self-government arrangements," *Justice*, International Association of Jewish Lawyers and Jurists, February 4 1994, p. 6.

15 Fourth Geneva Convention, Art. 76.

16 The quote was taken from a paper by Eyal Benvenisti's entitled "The present status of the occupied territories," in which he concludes that Israel does not control civil life in the occupied territories. He may be contacted through the Faculty of Law at the Hebrew University of Jerusalem to get a copy of that paper. Readers should also see his similar definitions provided in "The status of the Palestinian Authority," in Eugene Cotran and Chibli Mallat (eds) *The Arab–Israeli Accords: Legal Perspectives*, London: Kluwer International, 1996, pp. 47–66.

17 Christopher Greenwood, "The administration of the occupied territories in international law," in Playfair (ed.) *International Law and the Administration of Occupied Territories*, p. 246.

18 H.C. 337/71, *The Christian Society for the Holy Places v. Minister of Defense et al.*, 26(1) Piskei Din 574 (1972).

19 See Fourth Geneva Convention, Arts. 55, 59, 16, and 17, respectively.

20 See Fourth Geneva Convention, Art. 33, and Hague Regulations, Art. 50.

21 Sarah Roy, *The Gaza Strip: The Political Economy of De-development*, Institute for Palestine Studies, Washington, DC, 1995, p. 296.

22 See Arts. 89 and 90, respectively, of Israeli Military Order #378, as cited in "Punishing a nation: Human rights violations during the Palestinian uprising, December 1987–1988," *Al-Haq: Law in the Service of Man*, Al-Haq, Ramallah, December, 1988, pp. 260, 277.

23 Green identification cards were issued to former administrative detainees and ex-prisoners convicted by a military court, as well as to individuals who had been detained and released without charge. See "A nation under siege, annual report on human rights in the occupied territories, 1989," *Al-Haq: Law in the Service of Man*, Al-Haq, Ramallah, 1990, p. 328.

24 Physicians for Human Rights – Israel (hereinafter PHR – Israel), *Annual Report 1994*, Tel Aviv, p. 18. All references in this chapter to Physicians for Human Rights' or PHR are to the independent Israeli sister organization of Physicians for Human Rights–U.S.

25 Roy, *The Gaza Strip*, p. 310. The loss of direct aid from Gulf countries and remittances from Palestinians living in the Gulf to their family members in the occupied territories also dealt a severe blow to the occupied territories.

26 *Ibid.*

27 Amira Hass, "Gaza's workers and the Palestinian Authority," *Middle East Report*, May–June/July–August, 1995, p. 26.

28 The Coordination and Liaison Administration was formerly the Civil Administration, and is sometimes referred to here by that name.

29 Interview with Hamoked, East Jerusalem, February 29, 1996.

30 Interview in Ramallah, West Bank, March 2, 1996.

31 Based on interviews conducted with Hamoked and PHR – Israel, February–March, 1996.

32 "A nation under siege," *Al-Haq*, p. 409.

33 Richard Toshiyuki Drury and Robert C. Winn, *Plowshares and Swords: The Economics of Occupation in the West Bank*, Beacon Press, Boston, Massachusetts, 1992, p. 35. See also American Academy of Arts and Sciences, *Transition to Palestinian Self-government: Practical Steps Toward Israeli–Palestinian Peace*, report of a study group convened by the American Academy of Arts and Sciences (AAAS) (hereinafter the report of the AAAS), AAAS and Indiana University Press, Cambridge, Massachusetts, and Bloomington, Illinois, 1992, p. 104.

34 Patrick Clawson and Howard Rosen, *The Economic Consequences of Peace for Israel, the Palestinians and Jordan*, policy paper no. 25, the Washington Institute for Near East Policy, as cited in the report of the AAAS, p. 107.

35 *Ibid.*, pp. 105, 107.

36 *Ibid.*, pp. 38–9.

37 Muna Jawhary, *The Palestinian–Israeli Trade Agreements: Searching for Fair Revenue-sharing*, Palestine Economic Research Institute (MAS), Jerusalem, December, 1995, p. ix.

38 Palestinian Businessmen's Association, *Impediments to Investment in East Jerusalem*, autumn, 1995, pp. 4–5.

39 Interview with Dr. Sarah Roy, Boston, Massachusetts, May 17, 1996.

40 Graham Usher, "Palestinian trade unions and the struggle for independence," *Middle East Report*, May–June/July–August, 1995, p. 21

41 Kav La'oved – Workers' Hotline for the Protection of Workers' Rights, "Employment of Palestinian workers in Israel," *Newsletter*, October, 1995. The quotas are occasionally altered. On December 9, 1995, for instance, Israel announced that 9500 additional laborers would be permitted to enter Israel from the West Bank and Gaza (*Reuters*, December 9, 1995). It should also be

noted that tens of thousands of illegal Palestinian workers annually have managed to penetrate Israel and find jobs without permits.

42 *Reuters*, April 22, 1996.
43 Consulate-General of Israel, *Israel Line*, New York, June 5, 1996.
44 *Ibid.*, October 11, 1996.
45 Usher, "Palestinian trade unions and the struggle for independence," p. 20.
46 Policy letter from Ido Guttman, Reconnaissance Unit of Police Ministry, January 29, 1996.
47 Kav La'oved, "Mass arrests of Palestinian workers without permits," *Newsletter*, October, 1995, pp. 2–3.
48 Roy, *The Gaza Strip*, p. 3.
49 *Ibid.*
50 Usher, "Palestinian trade unions and the struggle for independence," p. 21.
51 Hass, "Gaza's workers and the Palestinian Authority," pp. 26–7, n. 8.
52 *Ibid.*, p. 26.
53 Palestinian Central Bureau of Statistics, *Labor Force Survey*, September/October, 1995 round.
54 Hass, "Gaza's workers and the Palestinian Authority," p. 26.
55 Radwan A. Shaban and Samia M. Al-Botmeh, *Poverty in the West Bank and Gaza*, Palestine Research and Economic Policy Research Institute (MAS), Jerusalem, November, 1995, p. xxxi. According to the study, "as a lower bound estimate ... 20 percent of the population of Gaza is poor."
56 David Makovsky, "While Peres ponders ending open borders," *Jerusalem Post*, March 1, 1996, p. 7.
57 American Near East Refugee Aid, *Middle East Trip Report*, April 8–27, 1996 (hereinafter the ANERA report), p. 6.
58 Dr. Sarah Roy, talk at the Center for Policy Analysis on Palestine, Washington, DC, May 15, 1996.
59 Interview with Bill Lee, chief of the UNRWA Liaison Office, New York, May 24, 1996.
60 An additional problem which has not been well documented but is growing more serious is the fact that many Palestinian state enterprises have become monopolies, which has resulted in the distortion of prices for essential commodities such as flour, sugar, petroleum, steel, and tobacco. Many of these monopolies are run by individuals who hold senior positions within the PA or are simply close to President Arafat. This issue was raised by Dr. Sarah Roy during her talk at the Center for Policy Analysis on Palestine.
61 Interview with Samir Huleileh, PA deputy minister of economics, trade, and industry, in *Palestine Report*, March 15, 1996.
62 Makovsky, "While Peres ponders ending open borders," p. 7.
63 Usher, "Palestinian trade unions and the struggle for independence," p. 20.
64 Palestinian Bureau of Statistics, as cited by Dr. Sarah Roy during a talk at the Center for Policy Analysis on Palestine.
65 *Ibid.*
66 Joachim Zaucker, Andrew Griffel, and Peter Gubser, *Toward Middle East Peace and Development*, InterAction Occasional Paper, December, 1995, pp. 8–9.
67 Makovsky, "While Peres ponders ending open borders," p. 7.
68 Roy, talk at the Center for Policy Analysis on Palestine.
69 ANERA report, p. 6.
70 Interviews with Fuad Dweik of the United Arab Plastic Corporation in Jerusalem and Kamal Hassouneh, director of the Electrode Factory, in

Palestinian Businessmen's Association, "Impediments facing Palestinian busi-nessmen in their different regions" ("Impediments"), pp. 1, 4, 5.

Mohammed Yaziji of the Union of Industrialists of the Gaza Strip also describes the additional expenses and delays that he now encounters: "Usually I cannot leave Gaza because of the strict closure. If I get a permit to enter Israel, I can use two different procedures. I can rent an Israeli taxi which takes me to and from Erez. This will cost U.S.$150. Or if a Gazan car or taxi has a permit to enter Israel I can go with him. But at Erez they make all Palestinian cars stop. The security check for the car or taxi takes about half an hour. With all the other security checks, it takes about two to four hours at Erez." *Ibid.*

71 Telephone interview with Majid Abu Daqa, Director of the Abu Daqa Sewing Company in Gaza, 13 March, 1996.
72 Palestinian Businessmen's Association, *Impediments to Investment in Palestine*, autumn, 1995, p. 4.
73 ANERA report, p. 7.
74 Khaled Asaileh, director of the company Asaileh for Trade, as quoted in Palestinian Businessmen's Association, *Impediments to Investment in Palestine*, p. 5.
75 *Ibid.*, p. 1.
76 Telephone interview with Ali Hassasna, director of a bus company, Bethlehem, March 6, 1996.
77 Palestinian Center for Human Rights, *Closure Update no. 5*, Gaza City, April 3, 1996, p. 4.
78 Palestinian Businessmen's Association, *Impediments from Gaza*, autumn, 1995, p. 1.
79 Telephone interview with Majid Abu Daqa, director of the Abu Daqa Sewing Company in Gaza, March 13, 1996.
80 Arieh O'Sullivan, "Yanai: IDF troops at crossing failed to detect bomber," *Jerusalem Post*, March 11, 1996, p. 2.
81 Telephone interview with Nabil Buwab, a director of APICO, a flower exporting business, in Gaza, March 13, 1996.
82 Trucks carrying medical supplies must go through the same procedures. According to PHR – Israel, "The trucks unload at the Erez Industrial Zone [in Israel]...and only after a special permit is extended are the Gazan trucks allowed to enter the area and reload the drugs and medical equipment. This 'back-to-back' method leads to a triple-digit increase in the rate of shipment and can delay, sometimes for days, the transfer of foods, medicines or urgent materials such as oxygen that may be running low. In some cases, the long wait in the sun has led to drug spoilage" (PHR – Israel, *Annual Report 1994*, p. 22).
83 *Ibid.*
84 Palestinian Businessmen's Association, *Impediments to Investment in Palestine*, p. 4. According to Hassan Badran, director of the Badran Factory for Fashion and General Trade, "This gives privileges to the Israeli companies; it lets them take advantage of our company, and to impose costs on us by force, which we have no choice but to accept."
85 *Ibid.*, p. 5.
86 *Ibid,*. p. 5.
87 Nigel Parry, "Problems facing Gazan students in the West Bank," *Middle East International*, March 31, 1995, and Human Rights Actions Program (HRAP), Birzeit University, West Bank.
88 In addition to these three permits, Gaza students must be in possession of a valid magnetic identification card.

89 "High toll of human rights violations continues," *Birzeit Human Rights Record: A Report on Human Rights at Birzeit University*, no. 14, June, 1994–March, 1995.

90 Nigel Parry, "Birzeit University takes initiative on Gaza permits," *Jerusalem Times*, September 22, 1995.

91 See, for example, Birzeit University, *Academic Freedom First; Gaza Students Campaign*, September 22, 1995.

92 Eight Gazan professors also taught at Birzeit during this period and needed to obtain permits.

93 "Academic Freedom First: Gaza Students Campaign," November 29, 1995.

94 Birzeit University press release, October 11, 1995. For years, Birzeit had also called on Israel to issue permit rejections in writing. Israeli authorities finally complied in January, 1995.

95 "Israeli siege paralyzes university," *Birzeit Human Rights Record*, no. 16, August, 1995–March, 1996, p. 5.

96 B'Tselem – the Israeli Information Center for Human Rights in the Occupied Territories, *Without Limits*, Jerusalem, April, 1996.

97 Land and Water Establishment, *Update on the Human Rights Situation in the West Bank*, Jerusalem, March 13, 1996.

98 Interview with UNWRA in East Jerusalem, March 10, 1996.

99 Arieh O'Sullivan and Jon Immanuel, "IDF orders expulsion of all Gaza Students from West Bank," *Jerusalem Post*, March 12, 1996, p. 1.

100 Human Rights Action Program (HRAP), Birzeit University. See also "One-tenth of our university is missing," preliminary report from Birzeit University, March 30, 1996. See also Human Rights Watch/Middle East, *Israel and Palestinian Authority Engaging in Arbitrary Arrest, Denial of Due Process and Torture in Response to Suicide Bombings: U.S. Criticized for Failure to Condemn*, April 3, 1996.

101 HRAP, Birzeit University.

102 According to a 1994 Israeli defense establishment study (cited in *Ha'aretz*, July 7, 1994, as reported in FBIS) and press reports following the spring 1996 bombings, not a single attack within Israel has been committed by a Palestinian holding a work permit.

6

EMBEDDING SOCIAL STRUCTURE IN TECHNOLOGICAL INFRASTRUCTURE

Constructing regional social capital for a sustainable peace in the Middle East

Shaul M. Gabbay and Amy J. Stein[1]

Introduction

New emerging markets increasingly provide opportunities in burgeoning economies. At the same time, many countries are encouraging intra-regional commercial cooperation as a means of reducing supply and production inefficiencies. Today it is the nations which are slow to liberalize their economies and sluggish about reaching regional cooperation agreements which are feeling the effects of global competition most intensely. Indeed, nations intent on economic isolation are being left behind in global trade and are facing exacerbated commercial and financial problems.[2] In areas where constrictive economic policies are coupled with political instability, social disarray and dysfunctional competition become significant threats. This is clearly the case in the Levant, where a tradition of hostility has up to now prevented regional cooperation. However, through the development of trade interdependencies in this region the relevant economies could be strengthened and political stability promoted. Indeed, if pursued correctly, increased commercial cooperation between Israel and its Arab neighbors could propel the entire region into the level of economic status that other emerging markets enjoy; it could create favourite investment climates.

Unfortunately, limited trade compatibility and cultural homogeneity remain two outstanding factors that policy-makers have yet fully to connect when analyzing failures in the Middle East peace process. Even before the current peace process began, numerous attempts to build a Middle East common market had failed.[3] This paper investigates several explanations for these past failures, and proposes an alternative structure for regional commercial and economic integration that could help avoid future failures.

Current and theoretical contexts

A decade ago Ben-Shahar wrote about economic cooperation in the Middle East that "[i]t is hardly conceivable that the countries of the Middle East will in the foreseeable future be able to overcome the obstacles to establishing highly advanced forms of integration and the institutions necessary for them."[4] Several global events have since affected the Middle East. Most notable are, on a global scale, the disintegration of the USSR[5] and, on a regional scale, the Gulf war.[6] Since these events, countries in the Middle East have been engaged in negotiations aimed at building a comprehensive Arab–Israeli peace. To date Israel has signed peace treaties with Egypt and Jordan, and a Declaration of Principles with the Palestinians. Today, with the perpetuation of terrorist activity in Israel and Arab fears of Israeli economic hegemony, coupled with Israeli regional military superiority, the peace process is characterized by a high degree of skepticism. We have also seen moves toward building interdependencies via economic summits like those in Casablanca in 1994, Amman in 1995, and Cairo in 1996 – although, as Wright points out in the Introduction, the Doha Summit in 1997 met with some success and elicited benign results.

This general movement should be seen in a positive light, especially given that the building of regional cooperative blocs is not part of a broader tradition in the Arab Middle East. This is particularly true in the area of infrastructure development. However, there are projects presently being undertaken in the Egypt–Jordan–Israeli triangle that may facilitate the building of positive (i.e. efficient) economic dependencies. If successful, these could serve as models for regional participation projects. The authors see building infrastructure as a stepping stone to building a lasting peace.

More specifically, we view regional participation projects, especially those involving infrastructure development, as providing new forums in which to form productive social, as well as merchant, relationships between Arabs and Israeli business. As these commercial relationships grow, so does the potential for reaching cooperative agreements in other areas of the economy. In this chapter the authors attempt to illustrate why this idea has potential by building on social and economic interdependency theories. First, they set out theoretical contexts through which joint construction projects currently underway can be analyzed. Second, they describe potential projects which, if realized, could create sustaining mechanisms in a peace-oriented economy. Finally, they discuss the political climate and determine how it may effect the implementation of joint participation infrastructure projects. And, while conflict over border issues exists in the Middle East from the Maghreb (North Africa) to the Mashreq (Iraq, in the East), the authors feel that the antagonisms that traditionally made strategic alliances impossible can be limited through sharing infrastructure systems.[7]

The argument is best framed within two lines of theoretical inquiry, the first positing that economic interdependencies create positive social relations, the second asserting that the building of trust between adversaries leads to social capital constructions/mobilizations that can be used for creating peace in troubled regions.

Economic interdependence theory sees regional economic alliances as extensions of national recognition that one's neighbors produce goods that are "complementary" to one's own, and that such complements could serve as a basis for building mutual "comparative advantages."[8] Trade blocs usually begin with preferential trade agreements[9] which eliminate barriers between them and jointly strengthen them vis-à-vis non-member states. Common markets are developed when cooperation extends into areas that define the movement of factor inputs between states, i.e. coordinating fiscal and monetary policies.[10] Such arrangements are often accompanied by more flexible policies on labor mobility and capital transfers/repatriations (or other resource endowments).[11]

While the Middle East shares a certain degree of commodity complementarity, the salient feature of the region deterring the emergence of a meaningful economic alliance has been its long history of mistrust, political conflict, and war. In fact, for the most part the (Arab) Middle East is divided into two markets with different needs: the populous resource-poor markets, where demand is insatiable and capacity expansion is restricted by the availability of funds, and the sparsely populated resource-rich countries, which have seen their development plans hit by the low oil prices of past years. Makdisi, in an analysis of the Middle East Common Market of the late 1960s and early 1970s, notes that trade between those participant economies actually diminished in that period.[12] Nations that share little obvious commodity complementarity and perceive neighbors as hostile (or even simply unfriendly) entities have little reason to gear trade toward each other.[13]

Take, for example, the case of the Middle East in the 1970s and 1980s. With rising oil prices and the emergence of the petrochemical industry in the Arab Gulf States, laborers from impoverished Arab countries with high unemployment rates migrated to financially well-endowed economies lacking labor for service and technology industries in skilled, semi-skilled, and unskilled positions. Despite a successful history of labor and capital mobility in the Middle East, the crisis of the Iraqi invasion of Kuwait subsequently displaced Arab (mostly Palestinian and Jordanian) workers.[14]

Another glimpse at how we perceive such cooperation could have looked in the Middle East can be obtained from the following example reflecting the effect of factor input of resource mobility. Before Egypt found such vast resources of natural gas one could have considered a nontraditional answer to input-factor mobility, or the reverse of labor mobility: resource mobility. Instead of mobilizing Egyptian masses able to work in the Gulf, where oil and natural gas were abundant, the population could have stayed at home and a Gulf–Egyptian joint venture could have been created in which resources would arrive in the population centers via pipeline to provide the basis for a substantial petrochemical operation. Instead of moving the labor source to the resource, one could move the resource to the labor source. This would have allowed the employment of both natural and labor resources without destroying the social fabric of the societies from which, instead, the young, able men – a vital component of society – were absent for most of the 1970s and 1980s.

In addition to the obvious benefits of creating an association where factor inputs could be freely exchanged to create an increase in efficiency, the authors postulate that such a bloc, if adhered to by member states, could present a formidable force and gain relative world strength in its geopolitical and economic positioning vis-à-vis other world forces.[15] Extrapolating from examples elsewhere in the world where similar factors have come together, it can be seen that, given that the Middle East possesses a third of the world's natural gas resources and that the cost of extracting them from underground is lower than in other regions, and that cheap semi-skilled and skilled sources of labor are also highly abundant there, when combined with adequate financial backing all this would (and does already) produce cheaper petrochemical products than are available anywhere else in the world. Significantly lower-priced and higher-quality products over various vital industries in which such factors come together throughout the Middle East region would have a direct effect on the Middle East's strength in economic matters, just as the economies of certain Asian countries have been propelled to new importance via their success in manufacturing.

Moreover, policy-makers are coming to understand that they need to update antiquated production facilities to the level of those in other nations in order to provide for increasing demand for energy due to their countries' swelling populations. Those that supply others with natural resources must do so to remain economically competitive. Facing a crunch of financial capital due to a decrease in economic rents available from oil profits, they are forced either to privatize state-owned industry or to seek private sources of funding. While in the past foreign financing was inconceivable, several models of foreign financing pursued in the region today include build, operate, and transfer (BOT), and build, own, and operate (BOO). Traditionally these resource-rich nations have sought to maintain a distance from foreign dominance, and therefore it is conceivable that regional development would be a welcome alternative to a more global route to development. Additionally, regional joint ventures may also be viewed as more attractive due to the lower costs that accrue. In fact, the authors see these nations mixing various solutions to answer their development needs.

Since infrastructural projects are the first (and therefore the most developed) that would be affected by this shift, we have chosen two to illustrate the merits of cooperation. The discussion of infrastructural joint ventures is particularly rich for several reasons. First, while they provide material for understanding the sustenance of peace, they also draw from the Middle East's relative advantage with respect to the rest of the world – natural resources in energy production. Joint ventures and cooperation in other sectors like trade, finance, and tourism are presumed to follow infrastructural development.[16] Second, while the importance of small and medium-sized business cooperation is of extreme importance, cooperation on large infrastructural projects requires a relatively small number of actors at the governmental level. Therefore, this chapter focuses on only one of the two dimensions of cooperation – the macro infrastructural projects – where the relevant actors are nations and business interest groups. The second important dimension – the micro level of small and medium-sized private entrepreneurship – is beyond the scope of this chapter.[17] Third, infrastructural projects require long-term and relatively high investment, which enhances both a long-term commitment to cooperation by each of the actors and the signaling process to other actors about this long-term commitment. The higher the investment required, the higher the costs of defection.

This economic explanation provides the rationale as to what attracts an individual state to participate in the structure, which we will describe in detail later. However, suffice it to say that it simply allows a nation's resources to go further and comes down simply to good economic sense.

Next we examine the factors that ensure that these nations will not defect from such arrangements and how they can be sustained over time.

Social capital theory

Economics provides the incentive for nations to consider cost-saving benefits to infrastructural interdependence; however, it may not provide what is necessary to overcome historical tensions to the extent that nations will not defect from a cooperative arrangement. Even so, the construction of "social closure" can provide the "glue" to keep such an arrangement intact.

As noted earlier, as a region the Middle East is characterized by low levels of trust. This need not be the case forever. The projects discussed here show how trust can be built over time as economic incentives for joining a system become clear. The key is constructing incentive structures with higher benefits for common social closure based on cooperation rather than egoistic behavior. We argue that, over time, the incentive to cooperate increasingly exceeds the incentive to defect for all actors in the system. As the projects advance further, interdependencies will increase the price differential for defecting and cooperating. At each time increment the incentive structure will increasingly favor cooperation over defection.

"Social capital" is defined as social structural arrangements which facilitate the attainment of goals.[18] "Social structure" refers to the network arrangements between a set of relevant actors. Usually the reference is to individuals as actors; however, the argument is extended here to include actors as nations and therefore to the "social capital" of a region.[19] One of the arrangements which facilitates the attainment of goals is "social closure." This is particularly the case when the goal is the creation of trust and sanctioning mechanisms against defection and threats against the survival of the system. "Social closure" refers to a closed network of actors in which relationships tend to be monitored by other members within the network.[20]

For the purposes of "social closure," it is useful to consider relationships in a triad; that is, for each two actors a third actor exists who observes every interaction, and is not only a balancing mechanism for the continuity of the entire relationship, but will most certainly be affected in future interactions with any of the given two. It is therefore in each actor's best interest to maintain a monitoring role when the other two actors are involved in any given transaction. It is also in that actor's best interest to ensure that the stated objectives of the relationship are upheld. In effect, each member acts as a sanctioning mechanism for each combination of two. Trust and trustworthiness, and the emergence of norms between two (a dyad) are more likely to occur in a closed structure where each has a relationship with a third (a triad – where another party monitors and sanctions the relationship) than in an open one.[21] The fact that the two are aware of the third, who is watching, creates an additional incentive for each of them to cooperate rather than defect from a given transaction. Social closure can also inhibit any negative actions of actors in the network against other members. Such incentives and inhibitions would not exist in the absence of "closure."

As suggested by Coleman, "[c]losure of the social structure is important not only for the existence of effective norms but also for another form of social capital: the trustworthiness of social structures that allows the proliferation of obligations and expectations."[22] Closure creates a public good which is an advantage for each actor. A further strengthening of trust lies in the dyadic strength of ties, which are related to the frequency of interaction that is created in a closed network. The stronger the ties between each pair, the higher the levels of trust and sanctioning capabilities. For example, Uzzi suggests that "embedded ties" are characterized by personal relationships, trust, rich information exchange, and joint problem-solving.[23] At the firm level, several studies have illustrated the higher propensity for cooperation based on the more common alliances that existed in the past.[24] The creation of "tie strength" is also related to the level of interdependence and the frequency of interaction. The higher the frequency of interaction, the stronger the tie. The emergence of this form of closure could create trust mechanisms between peace process players but, more importantly, once implemented could inhibit the violation of shared norms ("defection"). In this chapter we argue that a sharing of energy resources will facilitate the interdependence of countries in the region, which is based on two complementary joint projects. The first is the electricity grid, which will create a form of closure and facilitate the emergence of trust. It requires constant negotiations whereby prices and quantities will be set and reset on a daily basis. An increase in the frequency of interaction will increase the stakes and set the stage for true economic interdependence. The second project – the gas pipeline – will again create and/or further social closure. The fact that these infrastructural projects create dependency closure furthers the incentive for cooperation over time, thus creating regional social capital. Here we take the creation of regional social capital to be based on the embeddedness of actors of the region – on being locked not only by sanctioning relationships but also by actual regional infrastructural interdependencies. These will, over time, create the "social glue" for future cooperation. Moreover, as argued above, this will create an ever-increasing incentive for cooperation and an ever-decreasing likelihood of defection at each given time increment.

Projects for social-capital cooperation

Middle East electricity grid

The first project to be discussed, the Middle East electricity grid (and its various off-shoots), illustrates the notion of "social closure" in the region. After describing this project we will conclude by using "technological closure" as the basis upon which an even greater level of trust can emerge. We will first demonstrate how actors' incentives to participate in the project are derived from an economic rationale, but once they become participants in the joint venture not only will they benefit from cost reductions in the generation and transmission of their electricity (economically), but they will also have created a forum for continued dialogue, cooperation, and negotiations that will lead to a sustainable peace. It will do so because a situation will be created in which the economic costs of defecting will be higher than those of remaining a cooperative member.

The Middle East electricity grid project is fully based on the notion of these nations' complementarity in electricity needs. The first phase of the $623 million project is to link four Mashreq countries (Syria, Jordan,

160

Egypt, and later Iraq) to a common electricity grid with Turkey.[25] Later phases include connecting other countries to the Mashreq grid and linking it to the Maghreb (Morocco, Algeria, and Tunisia) grid, hooking up the two grids, and extending the project to other places such as Europe and Turkey.

Another plan for an electricity grid project as an off-shoot of the Mashreq project is the inclusion of Israel in a mini-grid to link the existing system of the three border towns of Eilat (Israel), Taba (Egypt),[26] and Aqaba (Jordan), which has been "operative" since the fall of 1995.[27] These towns are remotely situated with respect to their main population, and power generation is costly in such sparsely populated areas. Sharing costs by linking lines and coordinating energy flows drives down the costs of power generation. In fact, Vebudplan – an Austrian firm advising both Jordan and Israel on the plan – estimates $300–500 million savings for Israel's power industry by delaying construction of a large power plant. Such estimates are likely to be found elsewhere in the region as well.[28] Although this project is small in scope compared with the Mashreq grid plan,[29] it has a fundamental impact on it. Israel, currently connected to Egypt and Jordan, provides a connection to Egypt and Jordan's other partners. Inevitably, countries still officially at war with Israel (Syria and Iraq) will be connected the moment they "plug in" to the system. And once they actually do, the above discussion on interdependence applies to them as well.

The rationale behind erecting a regional electricity grid takes into account that policy-makers and engineers for each country must agree on how many power-generating stations will satisfy the demand for electricity in their respective countries. Although each country estimates the base power requirements (a fixed amount), it still needs to cover the generation of power for peak times, which tends to vary depending on each country's need in particular seasons and times of day. For example, since the people of the Middle East are of different religious backgrounds and celebrate their holy day on different days (Christians on Sunday in the case of parts of Turkey and Lebanon, Jews on Saturday in Israel,[30] and Muslims on Friday in Syria and Jordan), the industry will be most productive at complementary times of the week.[31] Moreover, due to the variation in geographic location, the hottest (thus most energy-consuming) time of the year varies throughout – diversifying countries' electricity needs even more so.

Electricity grids allow countries to share the costs of erecting and operating power stations that will be used only during their (minimal or) peak times. This allows countries to buy from the base load of other countries while they are experiencing their peak times and other countries are experiencing their periods of excess, which in turn results in countries needing to finance only their own base requirements while sharing the costs of generating and transmitting electricity for their peak loads.[32] Intra-party conflict in the short run is irrelevant, in the sense that no member country knows exactly which party receives its excess or which country its peak demand electricity is provided by.

While admittedly oversimplifying for the sake of illustration, we will discuss the case of Jordan. Let us say that based on its power needs Jordan must erect seven power stations to cover its base requirements. However, it must actually put up eight or nine stations because it has to cover its peak-time needs. (As indicated, peak times usually occur during the hottest month(s), when homeowners use air conditioning, and during the hours of the week and at times of year when industry is most productive.) In the current situation Jordan would have to absorb the entire cost of planning and construction of the one or two more stations to serve its peak need. With the creation of a regional grid network, Jordan and its neighbors can share the cost of erecting a power-generating/transmission station, and all can be supplied enough energy to satisfy their peak requirements for only a portion of the cost of doing it solo – particular arrangements become a matter of technical coordination and ongoing negotiation. However, we offer the following for consideration with regard to such arrangements:

- Conveniently, the Middle East enjoys various cheap sources of electricity. Because of Turkey's dams (and production of hydroelectricity), fewer power stations have to be built, which eventually brings down the costs of implementing the entire system.
- Logistically, there must be a control center in each country and upgraded lines compatible with the other countries' lines.[33] Countries must sign an agreement as to the terms of electricity exchange.
- Each country must also be responsible for financing the capital investment of base power stations and upgrades in power lines, while the Arab Fund for Economic and Social Development (AFESD) could finance the control centers and transformers.[34]
- In addition, countries letting electricity pass through their territory profit from this. For example, if Egypt requests electricity the source of which is in Turkey, Syria and Jordan enjoy profit.
- Countries do not commit to buying and selling, but rather to flow amounts. They buy fuel at market prices. This prevents a situation where, for example, Jordan can constrain Egypt to buying only from Jordan and will not allow Syrian energy through because of a Jordanian–Egyptian dispute. Again, most of the time countries will not know where energy specifically originates, as it could come from several places depending on need and availability.
- The regional electricity grid arrangement reduces the need to import excessive amounts of fuel.
- As mentioned above, the grid reduces the expenses of constructing costly and inefficiently used power plants, and it increases reliability

within the system because if a problem arises within the system it can be bypassed and electricity can arrive from another network member.

- Finally, since it requires a constant negotiating process[35] the grid paves the way for repeated interaction between operators in various nations. Accordingly, it eliminates the situation whereby any member country would go to war against any other member because they are all dependent on each other for meeting their respective energy needs.

Further to the last point, at the moment, without taking into account the effect of regional cooperation, Israel's growth in population and in gross domestic product (GDP) will produce a 7 percent per year growth in electricity.[36] It is also expected that by the year 2010 the aggregate of electricity needs for the Arab states will grow by 297 percent.[37] Thus for countries facing such estimations of growth and concurrently striving to cut domestic spending the notion of sharing the costs of power generation and transmission must be highly attractive and worthy of serious consideration. Moreover, this expected growth also means that peak loads will grow as well, which means more power to the central "bank" of the proposed grid system, and a further increase in intra-regional interdependence.[38] While each country forfeits its excess energy in non-peak times, all countries essentially empower a central "super-entity" to monitor the flow of energy. This arrangement institutionalizes cooperation in the dimension of fundamental energy need.

Natural gas pipelines

Besides shared electricity transmission, natural gas transfer through various proposed pipeline projects serves as another potential joint venture for Middle East economic cooperation. The energy grid discussion highlighted "technology closure" in the creation of a super-entity as the basis for social closure implying the formation of trust. Adherence to the grid is stimulated by economic good sense and ensured by efficiencies strengthened by interdependence. Pipeline projects, on the other hand, are different in nature. They gain their strength from the macro perspective of solving regional economic dilemmas like "lopsided development," as addressed earlier in the discussion of moving resources to population centers instead of relying on labor mobility, as has occurred in past decades. With the complete mobility of factor inputs in the Middle East, production will not be constrained as it is at present. By appropriately matching the region's profound natural resources to its population centers (ranging from unskilled to highly technologically skilled workers) the Middle East, as a region, stands a chance of propelling itself as a competitor into the twenty-first century.

Sociologically, these projects employ another form of closure, which is based on cooperation, again because it provides a forum for the frequency of interaction based on the growing energy needs of member developing nations and the final destination nations. The success of an interdependent grid system will set the stage for regional pipelines because it is slated to be implemented first and because, as is explained later, pipelines are more vulnerable to attack,[39] which concerns policy-makers.

At the moment various oil pipelines exist in the Middle East. However, these two proposed energy projects enforce a level of cooperation that exceeds oil-pipeline cooperation. They are more comprehensive because they are planned to extend ultimately to final consumers in the target markets of Asia and Europe.

Increased investigation of natural gas pipelines and the opportunity they provide for nations with a history of minimal past interaction has been stimulated as a result of complementary events: while energy demand in the Middle East and neighboring regions is growing, the centers growing most rapidly are not located where the vast reserves of cheap unexploited reserves are.[40] In this section, after a brief description of the natural gas industry and a look at the growing energy demand, the two most promising projects for fostering regional cooperation will be discussed. A brief discussion of the obstacles to these projects then follows.

Natural gas in the Middle East

Because natural gas is becoming the fuel of choice of the twenty-first century, and because the populations and productivity of the Middle East are growing, it is important to consider the growth of the natural gas industry and examine its potential relevance to the region. With growing environmental concerns, natural gas is gaining in attractiveness relative to coal and oil, particularly in power generation and as a domestic fuel. According to the Oxford Institute for Energy Studies, carbon dioxide (CO_2), the culprit of global warming, can be reduced by 40 percent through the use of natural gas as opposed to coal, and by 25 percent opposed to oil. Thermally, burning gas is more efficient; while one unit emits less CO_2 and covers a greater energy requirement than other fuels, it is more controllable and can more easily cover the amount of energy desired while reducing waste. Furthermore, delivery can be automatic, with no need for delivery trucks, which only add to congestion and give off their own exhaust fumes.[41]

Besides its positive environmental attributes, gas can be used as a fuel in electricity generation for commercial and residential purposes, and in feed-stock in the petrochemical and chemical industries; where relevant, it also serves as a fuel for re-injection into oil reservoirs to maintain formation pressure and enhance the rate of oil recovery.

Unlike crude oil, economics of natural gas developments are driven by location advantage, project economics, and proven reserves.[42] Although it was not always the favored commodity, the Middle East possesses a relative advantage in natural gas production compared to other regions. With natural gas reserves estimated at 45,000 billion cubic meters (bcm), this region represents roughly 30 percent of the world's total reserves. In contrast to its reserves, the Middle East's gas production is limited and underutilized, accounting for only 8 percent of world production. Discovered simultaneously with oil in the Middle East, natural gas was not initially perceived as being as valuable as oil. Even though technology designed to exploit its fuel-making properties was well established in the U.S. and Europe, the Middle East, with such vast quantities, barely supplied these growing energy markets at the industry's outset. Middle East gas production increased in twenty-three years (1970–95) from 85 bcm to 315 bcm.[43]

In the 1970s and early 1980s, since technology did not present a way to exploit distant gas reserves, in order further to exploit the vast oil reserves of the region oil companies would flare the fields to burn off natural gas, which stood in the way of what they perceived as the more valuable commodity – oil. After a massive increase in oil production in the 1980s, experts started to recognize the region's finite quantities of supply. In the 1980s researchers started developing technologies to transport vast quantities of natural gas to distant populations.

Although it is seemingly attractive, the lack of enthusiasm for natural gas production and marketing in the Middle East stems from five main factors:

- Some countries' large endowment of oil reserves inhibited interest in new commodity development.
- Capital expenditures and transport costs are prohibitively high (three to five times the price of oil transport, driving up the cost to $4 and $5.5/Mbtu (million British thermal unit) in Europe and Japan and the Far East compared to international oil prices of $2.5–$3/Mbtu and $3.5–$4/Mbtu, respectively).
- A long lead-time is required (four to five years) between the planning and construction of pipelines and/or liquefaction plants being completed and gas "coming on line." Long-term contracts of twenty to twenty-five years must be tendered at the outset of production.[44]
- The region is considered politically unstable, which presents a potential threat to pipeline gas (as opposed to liquefied natural gas (LNG)), which must traverse miles of exposed and vulnerable tracts of land.[45]
- Since natural gas is usually consumed where it is produced, the low population density of the areas where the largest reserves are concentrated makes commercial market development difficult.

Recently, escpecially since the Asian financial crisis, forecasters in Europe and Japan, the Middle East's two most potentially lucrative markets, have predicted the upcoming stagnation of Dutch and Indonesian natural gas reserves.[46] This gives a natural incentive to companies and governments active in natural gas development to explore opportunities in untapped resources in other regions – namely, the Middle East. They are now actively looking to boost sources of hard currency with gas exports. Moreover, the region's productive capacity is growing at rates quick enough to justify local production, as discussed in the previous section.

Motivations and obstacles for pipeline projects

Although roughly fifteen proposed projects that would depend on some form of regional cooperation to supply natural gas to Europe and Asia are under study, only two have been chosen for analysis here: the Egypt–Israel–Jordan–Palestine Peace Pipeline and the Trunkline Loop over the Middle East countries. The Peace Pipeline has been chosen because it is the furthest along of the proposed projects and therefore the most realistic, and because of its "radical" nature; [47] as with the electricity grid, it is a plan that includes Israel in its regional design. Until recently, this sort of arrangement would have been impossible despite the Egyptian–Israeli "cold" peace (except for oil sales). The Trunkline Loop has been chosen because it will provide the Middle East with the most comprehensive form of regional cooperation and coordination to which it has committed to date.

The following points about costs should be noted: at an estimated rate of $500,000 per pipeline transmission mile, if all fifteen projects were considered (equaling a total of 26,908 miles) total installed costs would amount to $13 billion; projects over difficult terrain cost $1.2 million per mile; 150 miles is the average length; while the Peace Pipeline is considered of modest size, the Trunkline Loop is one of the largest projects discussed.[48]

Like other countries worldwide, Israel has considered the possibility of operating electrical power plants with natural gas because it is one of the cleanest commercial fuels[49] and because Israel is interested in diversifying its energy resources.[50] Egypt has natural gas in the Gulf of Suez, the Sinai Peninsula, its Western Desert, and offshore in the Mediterranean. The economic rationale in support of constructing such a pipeline and the closeness of the project's implementation have been recognized by numerous authorities. Ben-Shahar et al. note that the idea of constructing a pipeline such as the Peace Pipeline is based on two complementary features: while Egypt has an increasing surplus of gas, Israel's requirements are satisfied completely by imports; and supplying natural gas via a pipeline is less costly than supplying it in liquefied form.[51] As Ismail Mohyedin puts it:

> Putting in liquefaction is a long-term process and it's expensive.
> The margin you are going to make is probably no greater if the

money is spent over 10 years to export to Europe or five years to the Near East. You are not going to make any more money.

The vice-president of Amoco, Sidney Greer, notes that Israel is intended to be the hub of a system that will also incorporate Jordan and the Palestinian Authority (PA). The next part of the plan is for Egypt and Israel to share in the delivery of a 2 bcm-plus per year natural gas supply. As for financing, the most likely form will be a combination of investment bank and commercial financing.[52] Ultimately, besides supplying gas to Egypt's neighbors, the intention is to transfer it to Europe via Lebanon, and Turkey. At least in the short and medium term, the Peace Pipeline serves as a chance for Egyptians, Israelis, Jordanians, and Palestinians to negotiate, and facilitates frequent interaction leading to sustained cooperation in the long run.

We recognize that this plan, despite its advanced stage, still faces obstacles. On the one hand, according to Dr. Abdel Malek Jabber of the Palestinian Energy Resource Center, despite Palestinian aims not to depend solely on the Israelis for basic needs, the route of the pipeline is still in question and is perceived by all parties concerned as a potential security risk. Although unable to divulge pricing information, he claims that the Israelis are interested in the pipeline going overground from Sinai through Israel toward the north, with various trunk-lines connecting the PA at key points and various branch-lines connecting different Israeli industrial parks. On the other hand, the PA has suggested that the pipeline should travel through the Gaza Strip to Ashkelon in Israel and on towards the north in Israel. A third option would be to place the pipeline offshore in the Mediterranean as a means of resolving this conflict. However, doing so would drive up the costs of the entire project. In addition, the Egyptians could bring their gas to one common point between themselves, the Israelis, and the Palestinians, and let the Palestinians and Israelis construct their own pipeline facilities to accommodate their own populations. The costs of this plan will inevitably be the highest, but since both Israelis and Palestinians are, first and foremost, preoccupied with security concerns it seems the most likely.

The 'trunkline loop' proposal also has its proponents. The basic concept underlying this project is the loop-route design of the gas collection and distribution system, which will provide access to multiple sources of gas existing all over the region, and insure higher security and greater stability of long-term gas supply to consumers. Due to its vast reserves, the Middle East could become one of the largest exporters of gas to Asia and Europe. United Nations Industrial Development Organization (UNIDO) and the Chiyoda Corporation of Japan undertook a feasibility study of the plan in 1994. The Trunkline Loop would pass through eight Middle Eastern countries, and in the future it would be expected to be connected to other countries not included in the initial stage. Financing is expected to be secured by soft loans to be repaid over a fifty-year period. At various points, LNG liquefaction plants would be erected to make Middle East gas more readily available for export to the main consumption areas, but connecting the Trunkline Loop to the North African Pipeline may be more advantageous and is being considered as well.

The immediate benefits of the Trunkline Loop project would be numerous. It could replace the need for increasing the LNG stockpile in Japan. Moreover, it could also strengthen the cooperation among Middle Eastern countries, and lead to mutually beneficial utilization of gas resources and long-term export commitments. It could also promote the industrial development of each member country by providing secured access to natural gas, mainly as a means of energy supply. Of course, it would benefit gas-producing countries through income generated by the service, but it would also benefit them by increasing crude-oil export potential through the replacement of domestic oil consumption by gas. It will certainly provide higher security, and a more stable and longer-lasting supply to gas-importing countries. And, as natural gas is known to do, it will improve the environmental conditions.[53]

However, in most pipeline projects the most significant challenges are political or "security"-oriented in nature. On the one hand, governments must trust each other implicitly to fulfill their contracts. On the other hand, in the past, due to wars and various border conflicts, like the Gulf war, leaders in this region in particular are highly suspicious of each other. In both the projects discussed a low level of trust exists amongst the proposed participants: in the case of the Peace Pipeline this is illustrated by the Israeli/Palestinian reservations; and in the proposed Trunkline Loop it is demonstrated by the exclusion of Iraq and Kuwait in the UNIDO/Chiyoda Trunkline Loop study. Until this situation changes, or unless alternative mechanisms can be created, the likely implementation of either of these projects is questionable.

In addition to institutionalized mistrust, uncertainties still exist as sabotage of overground pipelines threatens the safety and profitability of these projects. However − again as stressed throughout − the results of such projects, among other things, would be to foster sustained cooperation amongst the participants, encourage industrialization, and provide areas with secured and growing markets in the region so they could redirect exports for other resources and provide a cheaper solution to export markets for natural gas; overall, this would create more stability within the region.

This chapter began by noting that various experts on Middle East policy are pursuing the peace process with high levels of skepticism. This section attempts to provide the bridge that links the reality of the described projects (which in some instances are underway and in others require up to twenty-five years of investment in order to realize profits − a difficult proposition in such a tumultuous region) to the political realities that tend to attract never-ending attention from the media. This will provide the framework to understand how both the short- and long-term prospects of the peace process may be affected by these projects, and vise versa. This section notes the main political events that have shaped the current reality of the peace process: the assassination of the Israeli prime minister, Yitzhak Rabin; the tit-for-tat acts of terrorism between Israelis and Palestinians that occurred during 1996 and 1997; the election of Israel's new prime minister, Benjamin Netanyahu, and the Arab nations' reaction to it; the aftermath of Israel opening the archeological tunnel in the Old City of Jerusalem; the Hebron agreement; subsequent Israeli withdrawals from Palestinian terri-tory; and the decision by Israel to build at Har Homa/Jabal Abu Ghneim. The primary focus here is the relationship between the Israelis and Palestinians, rather than inter-Arab or inter-Islamic agreements. The section employs a primary, secondary, and tertiary analysis of the actors in the region.

Of course, each Arab nation has its particular issues against Israel and vice versa. For example, the relationship between Israel and Egypt is entirely separate from that of Israel and Jordan, although both are "at peace with Israel" and opposed to the Israeli occupation of Palestinian territory. While the Egyptian–Israeli peace has lasted for nearly twenty years, it has remained "cold" and slightly antagonistic. On the other hand, the Jordanian–Israeli peace has been characterized by high levels of trust. This is evidenced in a variety of ways, the latest being King Hussein's recent and successful inter-vention in the Hebron withdrawal negotiations. However, many of the antagonisms that exist between Israel and Arab nations, despite the specific and "neighborly" differences,[54] completely hinge upon the resolution of tensions between Israel and the Palestinians.

The secondary analysis discusses the effects of this relationship on other neighboring nations. Direct negotiations between Syria and Israel are also important, but will prove to have less impact on the inter-workings of the energy grid and on the Peace Pipeline than Israel's relationship with other "tertiary" parties – other Arab nations and other parties investing in the region as a whole.

Finally, a tertiary analysis will include the rest of the region and other actors heavily involved in the region, like the private Western firms doing big business there, in the United States, and in the European Union.

Analysis and conclusions

Primary analysis: Israeli and the Palestinians

Although the Palestinians and Israelis are pitted against each other around the negotiating table and often on the streets, they share two fears that have a tendency to grip their nations and motivate individuals to take extreme measures. Unfortunately, such measures have a negative impact on the peace process by temporarily derailing it until the "victim" nation puts itself back together and the pain subsides.

One of these issues of commonality is that each side is convinced that the other continues to act in ways that are contrary to or violate the spirit of the agreements between them. Examples of these violations are Palestinian noncompliance with respect to what Netanyahu deems "reciprocity" to the Oslo Accords, and Netanyahu's decision to open the archeological tunnel in September of 1996 and the Israeli government's decision to build a Jewish neighborhood in Arab East Jerusalem – both acts which were very much opposed by Palestinians.

The point here is *not* whether either side is actually breaking the agreement; both claim the other is. What becomes important is whether each nation's action or inaction is "perceived" by the other side to be "true" to the spirit of the process. Such perceptions and impressions are much more relevant – indeed, critical – to the building or destroying of trust. They provide the foundation upon which future negotiations will take place.[55] The fact that public opinion is influenced so negatively in all of the above instances threatens the integrity of the progress and the possibility of a lasting peace. In essence, the objective reality of either side's interpretation of incidents is not important. What influences trust is the "perception" of positive interactions between the two sides. The more positive the interactions, the stronger the foundation of regional social capital. However, such violations will eventually be felt in terms of the details to be negotiated with respect to the proposed cooperative energy projects, like dates of withdrawals. In the case of the aforementioned infrastructure projects, a perpetual perception of mistrust on side issues will bog down negotiations about central issues, such as prices and quantities of electricity in the grid system.

The second fear that Israelis and Palestinians share – actually other Arab nations face them too, but are not as directly affected by them – is what happens if the other side's extremists gain too much influence or continue to act out against their own nation. This fear has been prompted by events like the bombing of civilian buses and public markets, and the worry that the assassination of Rabin and the election of Netanyahu would end the prospects for peace. The entire question of what might happen if extremists in either nation – or in any nation in the region – take a significant role in government frightens all moderates in the region. Perhaps reality as it is today will disappear and a jihad will start tomorrow, or perhaps settlers will start to deport Palestinians to Lebanon or Jordan. Neither perception is entirely unfounded, since groups who claim jihad and the overthrow of Israel have become more popular and mainstream,[56] and since Israel deported Hamas activists and exiled them to Lebanon during the time of a Labour (more peace-oriented) government.

While it is important to consider the validity of these fears, analyzing them fully is beyond the scope of this chapter. Some have suggested, however, that as extremists become mainstream they tend to bring a new flavor of pragmatism rather than ideology to their struggles.[57] Thus if pragmatists hold the balance of power – even when they are inspired by ideology – achieving primary goals would take precedence over giving in to extremism. Thus the question becomes what impact a binding agreement like an electricity grid would have on the Israeli–Palestinian relationship. Would interdependence on natural gas enhance the peace process?

While progress is habitually undermined by violations of trust it is hard to imagine how the proposed projects would not lead to catastrophe. For this reason, until some of these inflammations subside it would probably be best not to engage in direct and constant negotiations over energy supply with the Palestinians,[58] but rather to allow the process to continue and let each entity live in tandem and independently after the process of withdrawal is concluded. This is not a prescription for the future of Israeli–Palestinian relations, but a way of calming the tensions that arise as a result of the interim status. Eventually, after trust has been established due to a period of non-violation of the spirit of the process, interdependencies can be fostered, as they have been or are being between other nations and Israel.

In the likely event that autonomy negotiations proceed while the Arab nations continue to upgrade their electricity lines and plans for pipeline projects get underway, when it actually comes time for Israel to negotiate quantities and prices for electricity the Palestinians will probably have been maintaining their own energy policy for some time. This will enable them to participate as any other actor in all energy-transmission discussions and will give them the chance to come as an equal partner to the multinational negotiating table. Governments and private companies engaged in natural gas pipeline projects are in agreement that because of the nature of the projects under discussion it would be better, for now, to establish mutually exclusive lines from the source of the resource directly to the Israelis and Palestinians. In this way, each entity can protect its own supply of gas instead of worrying about the very real possibility of sabotage.

Secondary analysis: Israel and its neighbors

The relationship between Israel and its neighbors, as mentioned earlier, is complex in that each neighbor has individual interactions with Israel – such as border disputes – but is also quite influenced by Israel's relationship with the Palestinians. Since part of the peace process addresses individual disputes, the peace process and the projects discussed earlier act as a sanctioning mechanism to ensure that the Israeli–Palestinian accords run as smoothly as possible. It is important to note that, while both Jordan and

171

Egypt are "peaceful" neighbors, Syria and Lebanon are not. In fact, in the region's recent history Israel has been embroiled in various exchanges of fire in southern Lebanon. Meanwhile, the Syrians hold incredible power over Lebanon, so sometimes although Israelis exchange fire with Palestinians in southern Lebanon (and sometimes harm Lebanese civilians) it is unclear where the seeds of the conflict lie. While stability prevails on the Syria–Israel border, southern Lebanon has become the vehicle for expressing dissatisfaction between the two nations. The military maneuvers in 1997 of both the Israelis and the Hezbollah are an example of this.

Despite these conflicts between Syria and Lebanon, on the one hand, and Israel, on the other, for all the reasons given above regarding the economic benefits of adhering to regional joint ventures it is economically in the best interests of both Syria and Lebanon to engage in cooperation rather than undermine it. Moreover, the level of influence they (especially Syria) can exert over Israel will increase dramatically if the Syrians sanction Israel's actions. For example, recently this sanctioning mechanism (of Arab influence over Israel) has succeeded in two instances. After Israeli elections in 1996, Arab nations feared the peace process had been stalled for good, since Netanyahu exclaimed several times during his election campaign that he would not meet with the PA's widely accepted chairman, Yasser Arafat. Until the delayed Hebron discussions got underway, Mubarak threatened to cancel the high-profile Middle East Economic Summit scheduled for October in Cairo, the third of its kind in three years. Similarly, as mentioned earlier, King Hussein of Jordan was able to exert influence over the final stages of the stalled and thorny Hebron agreement as well. Each instance demonstrates how being engaged in peace allows one to wield more influence than staying out of an agreement or away from a summit.

The two projects discussed above will undoubtedly follow the course of regional politics, as described in the social theory section of this chapter. Both projects will enhance relations between Israel and neighboring countries, as long as they are part of the arrangement/project and not outside of it. Such projects will also serve to put pressure on the smoothing of relations between Israelis and Palestinians, as we saw with regard to Egypt and Jordan's roles in initiating and finalizing the Hebron agreement.

Tertiary analysis: other Arab states and foreigners

The establishment of cooperation on the first two levels will have the largest impact on the third level of participation. Most of these actors, although they maintain differing individual stances with regard to the peace process, are in favor of it as long as it provides economic expansion, and as long as the primary and secondary nations' goals are met. These nations – provided their allies are satisfied – assist the process of sanctioning described earlier. For example, without full peace the Omani government set up a diplomatic office and an economic trade mission in Tel Aviv. However, once Israel violated the spirit of the peace process by opening the tunnel in the fall of 1996 Oman pulled its staff from the premises and has not operated since. If Israel deems Oman's reserves of natural gas vital to its scheme to diversify energy resources, eventually it will be influenced by such actions. Another example of providing a sanctioning mechanism in terms of trade is Saudi Arabia. The Saudis are perhaps the most hostile tertiary player toward Israel. Nevertheless, in the recent past they have lifted various clauses of the Arab boycott against Israel due to progress in the peace negotiations. It is widely presumed, however, that they will not go as far as the Omanis in establishing formal diplomatic and trade relations until the Palestinian conflict subsides and until Syria urges them to do so.

A final example of the influence third parties to the conflict have is demonstrated in the relationship with foreign entities like the U.S. and the European Union, and the various interests they represent in the region. While the media makes certain we hear of political tensions whenever another event occurs, what gets left out is the behind-the-scenes progress being made towards long-term arrangements. However, with regard to economic peace projects such as those discussed above, in a second research trip to the region the authors found a twist to the usual media fare. On the surface they were met with a closed attitude to discussing peace projects. This was an attitude opposite to that of one year earlier, when business people and government officials opened doors and were ready to discuss the plans and projects made possible by the "impending" peace. Although figureheads were more reluctant to meet, the International Power Press still talks about the imminent reality of these projects. It is inconceivable that the press is covering up a stalling in plans in order to preserve faith in these projects. Rather, it is more realistic to assume that, while public figures complain about lack of progress on the political level, real progress is being made at the infrastructural and economic levels. We must keep in mind that the projects described above require precision, detail, time, heavy investment (including private foreign investment), and the security that the plans will come to fruition. Thus it may be that real progress toward a sustainable peace is still afoot. If such projects are still "in the works," as it seems they are, then, as posited earlier, they can provide the essential economic and social structure for a real and lasting peace in the region to be negotiated and expanded.

Conclusion

This chapter has examined various infrastructural projects slated for future implementation in the theoretical context of social capital and economic interdependence. It has also attempted to show that, while economic efficiencies attract actor nations to the fold, the creation of social closure provides the conditions to strengthen ties and build regional social capital. In this regard it is noteworthy that since the data were originally collected one of the energy grids has been implemented between Aqaba and Eilat,[59] and in other countries transmission lines are being upgraded so future linkages will prove successful. Now that one of the projects has been implemented, evaluating the grid's effectiveness in the context of this analysis could enhance this research.

The other main grid project is almost ready for implementation, but Syria is sluggishly upgrading its power lines. The authors speculate that in the face of the two-city grid's implementation Syria would prefer to "plug in" only after it comes to some final conclusion to defining its relationship with Israel. Since Syria would be effectively sharing its energy with its current enemy, Israel, via Aqaba, it may perceive the situation as one not to rush into. It is reasonable to believe that these systems will operate in unison, however, in coming years.

The various pipeline projects also have different time-frames. The Egypt–Israel–Palestine project is scheduled to come on line by the end of 1998. Of course, negotiations could delay the date, but all parties are presently working toward this end. Whether or not it will extend to Turkey, as originally intended, will depend on the success of the peace process and, to some extent, the success of other infrastructural joint ventures, namely the energy grids. As for the Trunkline Loop, planning is in the early stages, and much will depend on political resolutions and the success of preliminary projects.

Infrastructural projects serve – as do environmental projects – as a convenient basis for cooperation between nations, primarily because they usually require large financial outlays and can, with little extra cost, serve a region instead of a single country. As sharing costs becomes more and more attractive, engaging in sustained interaction creates a basis of mutual understanding. It can also act as a springboard for other types of economic interaction, such as tourism, finance, and ultimately trade. Further research into joint ventures in these sectors is recommended.[60] At the micro level of medium-sized and small private business enterprises, a similar policy of further enhancing social closure would go in the same direction. The more linkages, and the more closure and interdependence, the greater the incentive for cooperation and the higher the cost of defection. Regional social capital could and should be constructed both at the macro level of actors, such as states and large multinationals and domestic conglomerates, and at the micro level of actors, such as small and medium-sized business, as well as individuals.

It is crucial to note that, in and of themselves, closed social structural forms do not constitute social capital; they do so only if they benefit actors – in this case the nations of the Middle East. That is, social capital is based on social structures which facilitate the goals and interests of the participants. It is this match between the interests of particular actors and a particular social structural form that makes social capital an asset.[61] Additionally, frequency of interaction is always positive, but can also be negative, based on conflict. Here the authors suggest that the building of trust, which is crucial to the Middle East peace process, must be based on positive interactions, such as those suggested in this chapter. Moreover, the monitoring and sanctioning aspects of closed relationship structures discussed in this chapter have already manifested themselves on several recent occasions, such as the concessions made by Israel after a failed assassination in Jordan.

This chapter has also examined long-term trends and only marginally reflects current events. In a broader sense, however, current events in the Middle East may ultimately have an impact on the willingness of the Arab nations to become part of an infrastructural scheme with Israel. However, the authors argue that through such infrastructural arrangements not only will economic development be stimulated – which even in the face of opposition movements can still occur – but the high price to be paid by defecting parties, and the monitoring and sanctioning aspects arising from such arrangements, may be just the answer they are seeking to ensure that all parties live up to not only their economic agreements, but their political ones as well.

Unfortunately, an issue that remains beyond the scope of this chapter is best framed by the question of what happens when cooperative arrangements are made between countries whose economies are growing at disproportionate rates. To examine this, one would have to refer to the literature on other regional trade pacts and examine what happens to more sluggish economies when they form economic unions with more aggressive economies. Of course, it would be necessary to frame it correctly within the sector of complementarity. This chapter did not discuss trade complementarity, but complementarities in factors of production. Most of the existing literature, however, describes trade complementarities.

This chapter began by noting the high level of skepticism shared by regional experts and average people on the streets. However, an example could be taken from the post-Second World War European goal of progressing through partial integration to an interdependence that would eventually make "any war between France and Germany not only unthinkable, but materially impossible,"[62] which modestly (or perhaps not so modestly) began with the Treaty of Paris in 1951; this treaty established the European Coal and Steel Community, a free-trade area between six countries which, only five years earlier, had been engaged as enemies against each other in the second of two world wars, and it eventually led to the establishment of the European Union of today. Of course, suggesting that a Middle East common market will result from the types of projects discussed here is still unwarranted, but, then again, no one imagined that France and Germany would come so far as to be on the verge of adopting a single European monetary unit and a common central bank.

Notes

1 Direct all correspondence to Shaul Gabbay, William Davidson Faculty of Industrial Engineering and Management, Technion, Haifa, 32000, Israel. An earlier version of this paper was presented at the Sunbelt Conference in South Carolina in 1996. The authors wish to thank Rashid Khalidi, J. Wright, and Marvin Zonis for valuable comments on earlier versions of this paper. The study was made possible by a visiting position at the University of Illinois at Chicago to Gabbay and a CIBER grant from the University of Chicago, as well as a visiting position at the Arab Fund for Economic and Social Development (AFSED) to Stein.
2 Rodney Wilson, "The economic relations of the Middle East: toward Europe or within the region?," *Middle East Journal*, vol. 48, 1994, pp. 268–7.
3 R. Owen, *Power and Politics in the Making of the Modern Middle East*, Routledge, New York, 1992.
4 H. Ben-Shahar, G. Fishelson and S. Hirsch, *Economic Cooperation and Middle East Peace*, Weidenfeld & Nicolson, London, 1989, p. 26.
5 The USSR's disintegration served as the impetus to change the previous "world order," in which various Middle East "players" had formally been closely allied with the USSR and depended on that superpower economically and militarily. The disintegration has created the situation whereby those former dependents are now faced with new economic and military constraints vis-à-vis their geopolitical and economic position (S. P. Huntington, "The clash of civilizations?," *Foreign Affairs Reader*, summer, 1993).
6 The Gulf war had a profound effect on the psyche of Arabs of the Middle East as a result of the Iraqi occupation of Kuwait and the subsequent pitting of Arabs against Arabs in a united front led by the U.S. (B. Tibi and D. Tschirgi, *Perspective on the Gulf Crisis*, Cairo Papers in Social Science, vol. 14, 1991, pp. 1–95.)
7 The data for this research is based on fieldwork in the Middle East, which included archival data collection and structured and unstructured interviews with policy-makers in the region on regional economic integration and past attempts at Middle East economic integration, as well as various pertinent questions central to understanding the current economic situation of the region (like labor migration and mobility, industrialization, and the oil, natural gas, and petrochemical industries). The aim of the fieldwork was to get a first-hand and updated look at the possibilities toward regional economic cooperation. The fieldwork included Kuwait, Qatar, Jordan, Egypt, Israel, and the occupied territories of the West Bank and the Gaza Strip.
8 Daniel Ricardo in Piero Sraffa (ed.) *On the Principles of Political Economy and Taxation*, Cambridge University Press, 1981.
9 They are also known as "customs unions."
10 Factor inputs include land, labor, and capital, the building blocks of economics.
11 J. R. Markusen, J. R. Kaempfer, W. H. Maskus and E. Keith, *International Trade: Theory and Evidence*, McGraw-Hill, New York, 1995.
12 The membership of this common market was inter-Arab. Today, proponents of Middle East economic integration fall into two camps: inter-Islamic or inter-

Arabic; and regional, which include Israel and Turkey. Although there are merits to discussing the first, this paper focuses more heavily on the later aspect of integration.

13 Even among Arab nations, which tend to act formally as allies, trust and economic interdependence have historically been viewed with suspicion.

14 G. Feiler, *Labor Migration in the Middle East Following the Iraqi Invasion of Kuwait*, Israel/Palestine Center for Research and Information, Jerusalem, 1993.

15 The most striking example of this type of arrangement was first evidenced by the 1973 attempt on the part of OPEC (oil-producing and exporting countries with the world's largest reserves, which incidentally included several key Middle Eastern nations) to form a cartel to determine the price of oil and set quotas for oil production, then the world's most important commodity natural resource. The disruption of OPEC's success in maintaining high oil prices was the result of one member nation's (Saudi Arabia) shift to a policy of putting its individual goals ahead of those of the cartel. The authors argue that in future attempts at policy coordination it must be made clear to the countries involved that the costs associated with defection from agreed arrangements are higher than the benefits, and that greater benefits can be derived from adhering to the process. OPEC did not create a strong enough mechanism to insure the interdependence of all its member states, since in reviewing its options Saudi Arabia perceived its aspirations to be better served by defection (R. S. Pyndick and D. L. Rubinfeld, *Microeconomics*, Prentice-Hall, New Jersey, 1992).

16 See Walter Hallstein, *United Europe: Challenge and Opportunity*, Harvard University Press, Cambridge, Massachusetts, 1962, p. 10, on Robert Schumann's proposal to establish the European Coal and Steel Community, which would eventually make "any war between France and Germany not only unthinkable but materially impossible."

17 For an analysis of the micro level of small and medium-sized cooperation projects, see S. Mishal, M. Semoyanov and S. M. Gabbay, *Economic Entrepreneurship in an Era of Peace*, the Chaim Herzog Center for Middle East Studies & Diplomacy, Ben Gurion University, Israel, 1997.

18 J. S. Coleman, *Foundation of Social Theory*, Belknap Press of Harvard University, Cambridge, Massachusetts, 1990; Burt, 1992; S. M. Gabbay, *Social Capital in the Creation of Financial Capital*, Stipes, Champaign, Illinois, 1997.

19 See R. T. A. J. Leenders and S. M. Gabbay (eds.) *Corporate Social Capital: and Liability,* Kluwer Academic Press, Boston, 1999, for elaboration on the social capital of corporations.

20 Coleman, *Foundation of Social Theory*.

21 Coleman gives several examples of this social closure, which is advantageous in situations where cooperation is required. The cooperative dimension is the premise behind parents cooperating to constrain their children to study, it is the driving force behind the merchants in an Egyptian marketplace, and it is what makes communication among Korean students possible (*ibid.*).

22 Coleman, *Foundation of Social Theory*, S107–S108.

23 B. D. Uzzi, "Social structure and competition in interfirm networks: the paradox of embeddedness," *Administrative Science Quarterly*, vol. 42, 1996, pp. 35–67, uses embedded ties as those which encompass these different dimensions, including trust. Here his work is used at the dyad level, although, as he points out, third parties create trust between two. This aspect is mentioned in the next section.

24 R. Gulati, "Does familiarity breed trust? The implications of repeated ties for contractual choices in alliances," *Academy of Management Journal*, vol. 38, 1995, pp. 85–112; R. T. A. J. Leenders, *Structure and Influence: Statistical Models for the Dynamics of Actor Attributes, Network Structure and their Interdependence*, Thesis Publishers, Amsterdam, 1995.

25 "World's developing regions spark for pipeline construction," *Oil & Gas Journal*, 5 February, 1996.

26 Taba was dropped from the interconnection, as Egypt has no plans for development there and it is not experiencing a growth in population. Its electricity requirements are met by the existing system.

27 Although lines have been set up, there has been no actual sharing of transmission. Locals tend to perceive the linking as an act of goodwill between the nations rather than a necessary economic policy. Only once the region is directly affected by real growth and plans to expand power-generating stations are discussed will it be possible to evaluate the efficiencies created and the level of cooperation fostered.

28 "Israel's first private power plant 10 MW gas fired unit goes on-line," *Independent Power Report*, 12 August, 1994.

29 According to the Arab Press Service Organization, if Israel signs a treaty with Syria it will be linked to the Mashreq grid as well.

30 This five-country grid does not initially include Israel; Israel is used here only to draw out regional energy complementarities to illustrate the point. The grid project in which Israel is involved is discussed below.

31 Although Israel is relatively smaller in population, its immense industrial capacity exceeds the demand for power of its largest power-consuming neighboring country, Egypt, which induces regional complementarity (Ben-Shahar *et al.*, *Economic Cooperation and Middle East Peace*).

32 Actual data on countries' peak and base loads could not be collected for the purpose of this study, except in the few cases where the country willingly publicizes such information in its Energy Ministry's yearly bulletin. While comparative data have been collected and analyzed by private firms, foundations, and government agencies considering investment in these projects, such information is regarded by the above as secret and is not made available for publication. Estimates of power capacity until 2000 are 50,000 MW, worth $30–40 billion in investment.

33 400 kW has been agreed upon.

34 AFESD underwrites the project costs for Arab participant countries only. Turkey has had to find other sources of funding.

35 Demand is expected to change constantly.

36 Israel Ministry of Energy, Kuwait 1995.

37 AFESD report, Government of Israel Publications, Jerusalem, 1994.

38 This brings up the question of how a disproportionate development – and thus growth – within the region would affect interdependence and trust.

39 While energy towers can be tampered with, pipelines pose the threat of emitting noxious gases into the air until they can be repaired. Such emissions, if located near a population center, will have debilitating effects on people, whereas severed electricity lines have no detrimental effect on a nearby population.

40 Although natural gas is often transported via pipeline, in politically unstable environments where sabotage threatens the viability of transport, reserves located near commercial, industrial, and residential users are favored for development.

41 Robert Mabro, "OPEC and the price of oil," *Energy Journal* 13(2): 1–17, 1992.

42 *Oil & Gas Journal*, January 1, 1994.

43 With aggregate Arab consumption in 1992 of 109.93 billion cubic meters (OPEC data bank and Cedigaz Survey).

44 Ichizo Aoki and Yoshitsugi Kikkawa, "Technical efforts focus on cutting LNG plant costs," *Oil and Gas Journal* 93: 43–7, 1995.

45 British Petroleum and Gas, memo, London 1995.

46 Aoki and Kikkawa.

47 Egyptian Trans Gas Company (ETGC), owned by Amoco and Agip, and William Press, a British gas distribution company, are negotiating to secure gas from this pipeline .

48 *Gas World International*, December, 1994.

49 Government of Israel, Ministry of Finance and Ministry of Foreign Affairs, Government of Israel Publications, Jerusalem.

50 Ben-Shahar *et al.*, *Economic Cooperation and Middle East Peace*, p. 89.

51 *Ibid.*, p. 96.

52 F. A. Felder and S. T. Jones, "Natural Gas pipelines: roadmap to reform," *Public Utilities Fortnightly* 133(1): 34–7, 1995.

53 The surveying team (mentioned above) was most challenged by the task of harmonizing and matching proposed countries' individual gas development goals and overcoming historical conservatism regarding gas transactions between countries. Finally, the team could not arrange an interview with high-level officials of Saudi Arabia, the country possessing one of the largest reserves of natural gas (and incidentally not putting much effort into developing its natural gas industry).

54 Just as Egypt and Jordan maintain disparate relationships with Israel that revolve around various and not always similar issues, so do Syria and Lebanon.

55 Israelis and Palestinians alike tend to delegitimize the other's position, and label the consternation in public opinion a fabrication and simply a chance for the leadership of the other party to manipulate public opinion. This serves to further the state of mistrust on a pragmatic basis.

56 Y. Sadowski, *Egypt's Islamic Movement: A New Political and Economic Force*, the Brookings Institution, Washington, DC, 1988.

57 When it comes down to it, most Palestinians would rather rally for a state than adhere to principles of Islamic jihad, which distinguishes them from the extremist entities in Egypt (Sadowski, *Egypt's Islamic Movement*).

58 In no way is this intended to suggest that negotiations about the autonomy of Palestinian energy production should cease. They need to continue so that eventually, once the Palestinians have established their own policy, they will be able to enter cooperative negotiations to reduce inefficiencies in production too. However, in that these negotiations are not bilateral but multilateral in the context of the projects described, it would be advantageous for the Palestinians to try to gain the same savings as the others.

59 In the second examination of the projects the authors found that, while connected, the Israel–Jordan first energy grid link is inoperative. Experts indicate that each country currently still meets peak needs separately. Until the population and thus the demand for power grows, the grid will remain inoperative.

60 Mishal *et al.*, *Economic Entrepreneurship in an Era of Peace*.

61 S. M. Gabbay and Y. Sato, "Revisiting social capital through images of social structure," paper presented at the American Sociological Association meetings, Washington, DC, 1996; S. M. Gabbay. and E. Zuckerman, "Social capital and opportunity in corporate R&D: the effect of brokerage on mobility expectations," *Social Science Research*, 1998.
62 Hallstein, *United Europe*, p. 10.

Part III

BORDER AGENDAS

7

LEBANON, SYRIA, AND THE MIDDLE EAST PEACE PROCESS

Reconstructing viable economies

Imad Harb

Introduction

After a devastating civil war that lasted over fifteen years, Lebanon seems to be on the road to social peace, political reconciliation, and economic rebuilding. Power has returned to the constitutional organs of government, the unity and integrity of the country have once again been assured, authority over vital installations such as airports and seaports has been reasserted, and militias have been disarmed, to name only a few accomplishments. With ambitious plans for reconstructing the infrastructure of a strong and competitive economy that has traditionally depended on a dominant services and financial sector, the present government has seized the opportunity of communal peace to chart a course that should steer the country toward playing a central role in the future, the "new" Middle East.

The current drive for Middle East peace cannot be separated from the economic picture most likely to be drawn for the region now and in the beginning of the next century. Despite the tough negotiating going on between Israel and Syria over peace, security, and the Golan Heights, it is only a matter of time before the agreements between Israel and Egypt, the Palestine Liberation Organization (PLO), and Jordan will be followed by others with Syria and Lebanon. Such agreements are only preludes to the establishment of a large, open market in the Levant whose relations are going to be governed by the dictates of economic and political power. Such dictates are predetermined by the current configurations of the economic underpinnings of the polities that will eventually enter such a large market, either as producers and dominant players or as consumers and subsidiary participants. It is in this light that the reawakening of the Lebanese economy must be seen. In its restructuring and reconstruction, Lebanon is working against time to position itself as one of the producers and dominant players: its financial sector is being reorganized; its factories are being rebuilt to supply both internal and external markets; its agriculture is undergoing a technological transformation; and its bureaucracy is being reorganized to direct the future activities.

This chapter will analyze the current economic climate in Lebanon and ongoing efforts to revitalize the economy after the civil war in preparation for the new century. It will emphasize the efforts being undertaken by both the private and public sectors to reestablish Beirut as a business center and the country as a preeminent player in regional growth. Such an analysis, however, cannot be made in isolation from the immediate regional considerations. First, Syria still plays a central role in Lebanon, and its fortunes are greatly affected by the direction and scope of Lebanese reconstruction and revival. Second, Israel still occupies a significant part of Lebanon's national territory and maintains and equips de facto forces to do its bidding as supreme power in the region. Third, there are still over 300,000 Palestinian refugees whose economic, political, and social conditions are dire, to say the least, and whose fate remains uncertain in the future Middle East but will clearly affect Lebanon's politics and economy. Thus the chapter will contain an evaluation of the effects of these regional considerations on Lebanon's reconstruction and future role in the Middle East. Finally, the essay will conclude with a general evaluation of the prospects of Lebanon's economy as it approaches negotiations which may lead to an eventual peaceful settlement. But, first, it is essential to write a brief overview of the historical development and character of the Lebanese economy and its controlling class structures and political sectors. This overview will provide the background for a comparison of pre- and post-civil war conditions so that the current reconstruction may be understood in the proper light.

Lebanon's internal political economy

The exact details of the origins of the economy of post-independence Lebanon are beyond the scope of this chapter. Suffice it to say here that this economy took root in the middle decades of the nineteenth century, when feudalism in its geographic core – the area known as Mount Lebanon – was effectively defeated by the rise of both a cash-crop economy dependent on silkworm production, and a mercantile class based in Beirut and controlling internal and external trade. Mount Lebanon at the time was part of the Ottoman empire, and its communities – especially the Maronite Christians and the Druze – were continually fighting to assert economic and political control. In reality, this sectarian conflict was a direct result of the changes taking place in the socioeconomic foundations of feudalism. The economist Paul Saba writes of the conflicts:

[I]n broad terms the whole of the upheaval in the middle decades of the nineteenth century must be regarded in the first instance as a political and economic struggle involving, on the one side, the feudal ruling class, and on the other, the class of oppressed and exploited peasants, the Maronite Church and its dependencies, and an emerging class of merchants, money lenders, and better-to-do villagers and peasant landowners.[1]

This economy was consolidated during the later part of the nineteenth century when Mount Lebanon was placed under an administrative arrangement (called the *mutasarrifiyyah*)[2] that actually stripped away the remaining vestiges of feudalism and consecrated a nascent capitalist economy whose pillars were trade and services. Many of the feudal lords who lost out in the fight against the new economy found employment in the new political arrangement and, as it later transpired, became the nucleus of modern Lebanon's political elites.[3] Thus a new class of entrepreneurs was born within feudalism and traders in Beirut became the nucleus of a commercial-financial bourgeoisie that came to control the economy.

As a political and geographic entity, today's Lebanon is a French creation. After the defeat of the Ottoman empire in the Second World War, France and Britain placed the areas of the Eastern Mediterranean under their own control, and in 1921 the League of Nations approved a French mandate system for Syria and Lebanon and a British one for Palestine and Iraq.[4] In 1920 the French high commissioner established Greater Lebanon by adding to Mount Lebanon areas to the south, west, north, and east. The new areas provided the necessary depth for a dependent services economy that became inextricably linked with the French and international economies. From 1920 to 1943, when Lebanon won independence, the French controlled the infrastructure, investment, and large economic enterprises such as Beirut Harbor, the railroads, tobacco production, banks, and radio. In 1939 French investments in Lebanon were estimated at a total of 851 million French francs (Ffr.), of which Ffr.729 million was in the banking sector.[5] Carolyn Gates writes that the relationship between the country's economy and that of France depended on an exchange of "manufactured wares in return for agricultural goods, raw materials, and semi-finished goods 'in a closed economic circuit designed to exclude foreign traders and shipping.'"[6] In the end, what Lebanon inherited from the French mandate was a dependent capitalist economy controlled by a bourgeoisie centered in Beirut and relying on services and banking instead of an agricultural and industrial base.

Thus the post-independence Lebanese economy became a capitalist one with a dominant services and trade sector. What helped it most as a services and trade economy was the state of war between the Arab countries and Israel (a war Lebanon never actually entered) and the political upheaval that beset the Arab countries after independence in the 1940s and 1950s. The Arab–Israeli conflict and the attendant Arab economic boycott of Israel gave Lebanon a central role in transit trade between west and east. Land routes from Beirut to as far as Iraq and the Arabian Gulf increased customs and fee collections, and aided many trading companies and communities. On the other hand, the political turmoil of the Arab republican regimes (manifested in *coups d'état*) and the nationalization of businesses and banks drove their middle classes either to emigrate or secretly to deposit their wealth in Lebanese banks for investment. In addition, the cosmopolitan character of Beirut and the country in general, its social freedoms, its natural beauty, and the temperate climate brought Arab and non-Arab tourists with their hard currency and international connections. By the 1950s government planners had already set the institutional and constitutional framework for a dependent services, trade, and tourism economy.[7]

Also interesting is the configuration of the relationship between the controllers of such an economy – the commercial-financial bourgeoisie – and the political system. Owing to its colonial and dependent character, this class had been politically weak and incapable of establishing an independent capitalist state. Instead, it shirked its "historic" responsibility to establish such a state and relegated the mission of running the country to traditional elites rooted in the sectarian makeup of Lebanese society. The sociologist Samir Khalaf writes that because of its political weakness it could not "promote its cultural hegemony and establish a secular nationalism," or "create the necessary autonomy for the state to control or manage the contradictions inherent in the transition to capitalism."[8] The Lebanese Marxist theoretician Mahdi 'Amel posits further that this bourgeoisie actually benefited from communal sectarianism and encouraged sectarian politics.[9] In abdicating from its mission of establishing a traditional capitalist state, the Lebanese commercial-financial bourgeoisie has helped to create a sectarian-capitalist state in which the ostensible leaders, the traditional elites, have preserved the "organization" of production while supporting legislation aimed at enhancing a market economy, in which the bourgeoisie operated unhindered by the limitations of feudal "relations" of production.

Finally, the general features of Lebanon's economy from independence to 1975 (the year of the start of its long civil war) have been, *inter alia*, the relative unimportance of the public sector; the sanctity of private property and free enterprise; the preponderance of services and trade; and inequality in income.[10] Before 1975 Lebanon had become the financial and commercial center of the Levant. In 1975 agriculture accounted for 50 percent of the employed workforce and contributed only 9 percent of gross national product (GNP); industry employed 20 percent and contributed 17 percent of GNP; and services, trade, and finance employed 30 percent and contributed 74 percent of GNP.[11] Alongside this bright picture of services and trade there lurked the inevitable indications of poverty and social inequalities. By 1975 the political system, controlled by traditional sectarian elites, could no longer contain the social unrest; neither could the commercial-financial bourgeoisie make the necessary adjustments because it lacked the political strength of an independent class. When the civil war began in April of that year neither group could stop the carnage, which lasted until 1990, when the Taif Agreement was finally ratified by Lebanon's parliament.[12]

The 1989 Taif Agreement[13]

The Taif, Saudi Arabia, Agreement was signed on October 22, 1989, and created the Lebanese Second Republic. What it originally signified was that the Lebanese could not themselves devise their own salvation and that the war was guaranteed to continue so long as there remained any Lebanese capable of mustering a militia or faction. In a sense, Taif came as a response to the Lebanese people's admitted failure to find a solution, as well as to the Arab world and world community's tiredness of the Lebanese question. Finally, Lebanese Muslim and Christian politicians and Saudi and Syrian intermediaries met in Taif for a grueling three weeks during which they hammered out an agreement that basically reaffirmed the original nature of the political system as a sectarian arrangement between Christians and Muslims. Specifically, it promulgated political reforms that:

- redistributed some powers from the Christian Maronite president to the Sunni Muslim prime minister and the Shiite Muslim speaker of parliament;
- split parliamentary representation equally between Muslims and Christians (instead of the established 6:5 ratio in favor of the Christians);
- reaffirmed Lebanon's Arab identity and special relationship with Syria;
- abolished political sectarianism in government appointments except for top-level positions.

In essence, the Taif Agreement reiterated what the Constitutional Document of February 1976 had attempted to institute when, under Syrian pressure, the Christian rightists accepted a redistribution of political power that was rejected by the leftist and progressive alliance.

Taif was finally adopted by the parliament on November 5, 1989, and incorporated in an amended Constitution in September of 1990. The parliamentary elections of 1992 and 1996 were sure steps that have provided the institutional prerequisites for continued civil peace – although many in Lebanese Christian and Muslim opposition groups claimed they were unfair and led to the dominance of the prime minister, Rafiq al-Hariri, in Lebanese politics. The elections in the summer of 1996 brought only token opposition to the parliament, allowing Hariri and his team to forge ahead with their plans for post-civil war reconstruction – the centerpiece of which is a thriving commercial, banking, and services economy.

Post-civil war reconstruction

The civil war of 1975–90 was a cataclysmic event in the history of Lebanese politics and economics. Politically, the country's old confessional[14] arrangement collapsed, producing extreme positions and intense communal competition without the requisite strong regulating institutions and mechanisms. Originally, the war began when the system could no longer accommodate the disparate groups and ideologies or redress the inequities inherent in sectarian politics and the laissez-faire economy. Later, when the war raged on into the late 1970s and the 1980s, the state became weaker and was unable to stop the hostilities, while the opportunities for compromise failed to find willing and capable centripetal forces (such as political parties or personalities) and were thus squandered. The Lebanese recognized that the 1943 National Pact had become a liability; however, those who had previously opposed it could not really kill it, while those who supported it did not dare change it lest they should lose their privileges. By the end of Amin Jmayyil's presidential term, in September of 1988, the political environment had become so polarized and uncertain that many speculated that Lebanon could no longer exist as a unified entity and openly advocated partition along confessional lines. The climax came with the ascent of General Michel Aoun, army commander during Jmayyil's term, to the position of prime minister[15] and the creation of two centers of official power, one with the incumbent prime minister, Salim al-Hoss, and another with Aoun. This arrangement was untenable and some decisive action needed to be taken, especially after Aoun declared war on all militias and the Syrians, a war that completed the vicious cycles of violence that had gripped the country since 1975.

Economically, productive, and sustainable economic activities in agriculture, industry, tourism, and services were devastated in the fifteen years of war. What sustained the population was government spending (civil service salaries and some projects continued), private-sector activity (especially banking), expatriate remittances (between 500,000 and 700,000 Lebanese worked in the Gulf countries alone), illegal militia activities (especially the seizure of government port facilities and drugs), and real-estate and financial speculation. Agriculture lost its workers to emigration and militias, industrial plants were decimated (especially during the 1982 Israeli invasion), and tourism lost its clients because of the security situation. In addition, the social situation became bleak, with over a million displaced persons and internal refugees, hundreds of thousands of dead, wounded, and maimed, and de facto partition of the country along religious and sectarian lines.

New outlook and plans

With the institutionalization of the Taif reforms and the eventual defeat of General Michel Aoun in October, 1990, Lebanon seemed finally to have found its way out of the morass. A Herculean task awaited the government, the private sector, and the Lebanese people. The rebuilding plan, Horizon 2002, is a ten-year, $30 billion development plan that depends on government expenditures, international assistance and loans, and private-sector investment.[16] Initially, an emergency recovery program ($2.8 billion) was instituted to alleviate the immediate economic and social problems faced after the war.[17] The effectiveness of these plans has been influenced most by Israeli military aggressions. While some of the most damaging of these will be referred to later, it is worth noting that actions in southern Lebanon have continued throughout Netanyahu's term in power in Israel.

Reconstruction in Lebanon today depends on the capabilities, activities, and successes of the state's Council for Development and Reconstruction (CDR), originally set up in 1977, and the real-estate firm Solidere, which was established by Rafiq al-Hariri (the billionaire prime minister) and his many Lebanese and Arab friends. CDR is a very well-respected agency under the capable directorship of two prominent economic managers, al-Fadl Shalak and Butrus Labaki, who are determined to restore international private-sector and official confidence in the Lebanese economy and institutions. Their task is daunting and can be summarized by the short phrase "rebuilding a country." Between short-term and long-term priorities, their plans include:[18]

- rehabilitating and developing electrical utilities, water supplies, and telecommunications (local and overseas);
- restoring the transport sector, which has been neglected for over sixteen years;
- reconstructing the ever-important Beirut International Airport and Beirut Harbor;
- redeveloping agriculture, irrigation, and rural light industry;
- rebuilding what was once, before the civil war, a nascent and capable export-oriented industrial sector.

Corporations have a stake as well. Solidere is the real-estate company in charge of rebuilding downtown Beirut and transforming its ruins into a new economic wonder. This task is estimated to cost $3.5 billion and includes the creation of a 395-acre commercial-financial district, the restoration of 3000 years of antiquities and archeological finds, and the construction of hotels, theaters, entertainment parks, libraries, government buildings, and underground parking facilities and metro stations.[19] Solidere is a public company capitalized at $2.4 billion, with shares traded on the revitalized Beirut stock exchange (bourse) by Lebanese and Arabs only. It was set up by Hariri and initially created a lot of resentment and opposition because it expropriated lands in the downtown area, and unilaterally assessed property values and converted them to shares to be distributed among the original owners.[20] Today Solidere is a very successful company, and construction work on its plans is afoot. Indeed, Solidere is among the ten largest firms in the region.[21] However, the perception of the company as a private tool in the hands of the rich prime minister still smacks of a conflict of interests, although individual share ownership is limited to 10 percent of the total and at least 51 percent of the total must be owned by Lebanese. In fact, the Lebanese have ambivalent feelings about the issue: Hariri is credibly believed to be the best prime minister the country has had since independence and is felt to be more able than anyone else to control the country's fate.[22]

While Solidere can finance its activities from the sale of its shares (financing stands at $310 million a year for ten years), the CDR will have to raise its money from government revenues and international assistance. Of concern at the start of the rebuilding program was the ability of the country to absorb funds, and the potential of long-term inflationary pressures that would compound the economic and social problems inherited from the war. With the current pace of reconstruction and improvements, the fears about inflation have not yet materialized, although they always might. In 1993 inflation fell below 10 percent for the first time in many years (8.9 percent),[23] and it remained low in 1994.[24] However, a snag had developed in the hoped-for supply of international funding, owing to the slowdown in the world economy, the need for funds by Eastern European countries, and, most importantly, the near lack of aid from the Gulf countries after the 1991 Gulf war and the decline in oil revenues. Of $3 billion needed by the end of 1995 for the reconstruction program, only $1.9 billion arrived ($1.5 billion in loans and $400 million in grants).[25] Consequently, large budget deficits are being posted, and the fear that aid money will continue merely to trickle in might eventually arrest the whole process. At the end of 1995 the budget deficit was $1.71 billion (15 percent of gross domestic product (GDP) of $11.4 billion)[26] and had largely been financed by Treasury bills bearing interest rates of 17–20 percent. (In 1994 the actual deficit was about $1.8 billion.)[27] In 1995 imports rose to $7.3 billion and exports to $824 million, leaving a large balance-of-payments deficit that was made up by net capital inflows which actually showed a surplus of $256 million.[28]

The Lebanese central bank (Banque du Liban) is in charge of regulating the money supply and banking activities, and protecting the national currency (it has stabilized since 1993). While maintaining a comfortable gold reserve ($4.6 billion), it has refrained from printing unprotected money and has resorted to issuing Treasury bills to finance the public debt, which stood at $8.3 billion in May of 1996, of which foreign debt accounted for $1.35 billion.[29] This large amount of domestic and foreign debt has its drawbacks in that it is a burden on public spending. Debt service in 1996 is expected to reach $1.6 billion.[30] The outlook, however, remains optimistic and banks (about seventy at the last count) show no signs of a lack of confidence in their general outlook.

Redeveloping the agricultural and industrial sectors is also a government priority. The ten-year plan allocates $435 million for agriculture and establishes a $120 million bank for industrial development.[31] Strategic industrial zones will be set up and economic activity in rural areas will be augmented with light industry. Moreover, reviving the tourism sector promises great rewards. Plans for Beirut and other areas mix the pleasure industry with the business atmosphere, a traditional Lebanese economic emphasis.

The infrastructure and telecommunications sectors are also receiving their due attention for economic and political reasons. During the war these sectors suffered from lack of government investment and neglect. Restoring them means more public confidence in the overall programs and in the government's intention to alleviate the social strain. Beirut International Airport, Beirut Harbor (with its four basins and a possible fifth), the Beirut-Damascus Highway, solid-waste disposal and water and electricity plants, and road networks are getting their share. Beirut International Airport and Beirut Harbor have been allocated $350 million and $200 million, respectively,[32] while the others are being auctioned off to foreign and local firms. In telecommunications, repairs and improvements have begun. One million telephone lines are being installed at a cost of $500 million. European firms developed the whole network: Siemens of Germany, Alcatel of France, and Ericsson of Sweden.[33]

The conspicuous absence of U.S. firms from the lucrative reconstruction projects can be blamed on the American government's travel ban on Americans and restrictions on American business activity in Lebanon, both of which have deprived large U.S. companies of the opportunity to compete with European firms, although U.S. exports to the country totaled $555 million in 1994.[34] This ban was lifted in 1997, but the impact had already been made – Lebanon's fragmented economy is not in a position to compete well for international direct investment.

In sum, Lebanon is a huge construction and development site. From plans for downtown Beirut to those for developing agriculture and industry, the government seems to be set on recovering the country from the doldrums of fifteen years of civil war and outside intervention, and on reestablishing Lebanon as a preeminent business center. However, such ambitious plans still involve risks inherent in reconstruction itself, as well as in the future business atmosphere inside Lebanon and in the region at large. Any major impediments to the process of funding the rebuilding plans might help derail the optimistic analyses. Obviously, Hariri's cabinet and the country's business community are enthusiastic about long-term prospects. Such prospects, however, are not affected solely by issues related to Lebanon, but are significantly influenced by regional considerations involving Syria, Israel, and the Palestinians.

Lebanon and the region's political economy

Netanyahu's combative approach to negotiating with Syria has been defined by military aggression in southern Lebanon. This keeps Syrian and Lebanese forces on double alert. Indeed, to enter into a Middle East peace settlement and participate in post-settlement economic activities, Lebanon must contend with its two immediate neighbors, Syria and Israel, and with a resident Arab community, the Palestinians, that has been central to internal and external politics since 1948.

Syria

Syrian forces have maintained effective control over much of the country since 1976 and Syrian foreign policy has accorded the Lebanese civil war and its resolution much time, energy, and effort. Any analysis of a future role that Lebanon might play in Middle East relations must include what has since 1976 become a symbiotic relationship between the two countries.

The histories of Lebanon and Syria are similar in many respects, although the actual workings and circumstances of the two countries have effected dissimilarities in social development, economic status, and political orientation. After gaining independence from the French in 1943, the Lebanese ruling elites maintained "confessional political allocations" as a political system that provided for communal peace but necessitated a measure of democratic politics based on compromise and ad hoc agreements between powerful leaders. The Syrian immediate post-independence period was unstable, and no political and economic leadership could maintain control over the competing interests in the country. Consequently, military *coups d'état* became the order of the day in the late 1940s, and the 1950s and 1960s. The relationship with Lebanon continued to be important, even though it experienced fluctuations between closeness and ambivalence. One thing was sure, however, and that was that Lebanon could never totally free itself of the necessity of considering Syria's reaction to any policy initiatives or internal problems.

The eruption of the Lebanese civil war in 1975 was immediately made a Syrian affair by both Lebanese and Syrian officials, politicians, and political parties. After all, Syria had always been extremely interested in internal

Lebanese matters since they affected Syria and the region as a whole so closely. To the Lebanese leftists, Syria had been what Lebanon could never be: a bastion of Arabism, an Arab-socialist state (although many thought Syrian socialism imperfect), and a bulwark against Zionism and Israeli policies. To the rightists, it had been a necessary evil; it was militarily powerful *vis-à-vis* Lebanon, it was a large market for many manufactured goods, and, when necessary, Syria was able to pressure the armed Palestinians in the country. On the other hand, Lebanon was to Syria the prosperous little brother who needed protection from Israel, provided employment opportunities for hundreds of thousands of Syrian laborers, imported agricultural goods from Syria, and represented a general sphere of influence.

For ten months after the start of the Lebanese civil war (from April 1975 to February 1976) Syrian mediators worked very hard to find a peaceful solution acceptable to all parties. They were most interested in maintaining the communal and confessional equilibrium which had (until the early 1970s) helped peaceful coexistence in Lebanon. From the beginning their mediation efforts concentrated on giving the Muslim-leftist alliance more political power; but the Christian-rightist camp vetoed their efforts. At the beginning of 1976 the rightists were on the defensive and risked losing everything. The Syrians thus convinced them to accept the Constitutional Document of February 1976, which split political power equitably between the Muslims and Christians. When the Muslim-leftist alliance (helped by the Palestinians) rejected the document and continued its offensive the Syrians were force to intervene militarily. Their intervention actually saved Christian position and privileges in the country. President Hafez al-Asad proclaimed at the time that Syria's military intervention preempted an Israeli invasion to "save the Christians."

During the late 1970s and throughout the 1980s Syrian influence in internal Lebanese affairs was obvious. In retrospect – and despite widespread resentment toward Syria's role and power, and the Syrian military's tactics and involvement in illegal activities in Lebanon – the presence of Syrian forces has thwarted the partition of the Lebanese entity into sectarian statelets, has checked Israeli policies and designs, and, lastly, has brought peace by brokering (together with the Saudis) the 1989 Taif Agreement. Today Lebanese–Syrian relations depend on a high degree of coordination, and Lebanese politicians (even the Christians) have come to accept the fact that Syria's interests in Lebanon must be safeguarded, even if that means some loss of the country's sovereignty and independence.

In May 1991 Lebanese–Syrian relations were consecrated by the signing of a Treaty of Brotherhood, Cooperation, and Coordination that includes politics, economics, security and defense, education, science, and other fields.[35] The treaty established a Higher Council composed of the presidents, prime ministers, deputy prime ministers, and speakers of parliament of the two countries, and meets once a year. Paul Salem writes that the

Higher Council constitutes an effort to establish a loose confederation between the two countries, with Syria as the dominant partner. He further explains that the two agreements basically supersede the Taif Agreement as it relates to the issue of the redeployment of Syrian forces in Lebanon.[36] On the other hand, the argument that Syria's military presence in Lebanon could provide the necessary balance of power against potential Israeli plans of subversion cannot be discounted. Furthermore, economic agreements were also signed between the two countries in 1993 that would consecrate a complementarity of production and interests. These include agreements on agriculture, labor, health, the movement of persons and goods, employment and residence, customs, and, most importantly, a common market.[37]

It is particularly significant that such agreements have been signed between two countries with historically divergent economies established at independence in the 1940s. While the Lebanese economy is one of free enterprise, dominated by trade and services, the Syrian economy has been centrally planned and directed, with an emphasis on the public sector, agricultural production, and industrialization, even though efforts have been made since the late 1970s to change it to a mixed economy inclined toward the free-market model.[38] The post-civil war reconstruction program in Lebanon emphasizes common Lebanese–Syrian interests. Syrian agricultural products can be utilized in joint industrial projects; Syrian oil and natural gas can help the development of a large electrical grid; and Lebanese expertise in services, tourism, and banking can greatly benefit the Syrian economy.[39] It is likely that any potential long-term lucrative rewards will depend on the ability of the Syrian economy and political system to adapt to accommodate Lebanon's economic openness and priorities. What is certain is that the Syrian government sees an unprecedented opportunity to alleviate the hardships that have plagued its economy since the early 1980s, and the signing of the political and economic agreements with Lebanon is the best proof of efforts to do just that.[40] If Lebanon hopes to be a major economic player after any future Middle East peace settlement it must rely on Syria's ability and willingness to be the protective sister it claims it can be, especially if future economic relations are going to be dominated by an industrially and militarily powerful Israel. On the other hand, if Syria hopes to enter the future Middle East economy on its terms it must allow a great deal of Lebanese economic and political independence, and adroitly exploit the opportunities created by the Lebanese window.

Israel

No long-term plans for reconstructing Lebanon can survive if the issue of Israel's occupation of part of south Lebanon is not resolved. Indeed, the continuation of bombings in 1998 proves that Israeli aggression is not only continual and imminent, but also expansionist.

Israel maintains a "security zone" that was originally established after the Israeli invasion of 1978 (Operation Litani) and expanded after the Israeli invasion of 1982 (Operation Peace for Galilee). The security zone is no more than a directly colonized area in which Israeli goods are sold, and from which cheap agricultural and industrial laborers are recruited. The zone is also a base of operations for continued Israeli military attacks against unoccupied territories to the north, for disrupting Lebanese government activities in the south, and for exerting pressures to forestall the reestablishment of political and social peace in Lebanon.

Southern Lebanon has always figured prominently in Israeli policies. In the 1950s the Israeli political establishment was serious about assisting the establishment of a Christian-dominated Lebanon or a partitioned Lebanon with a strong Christian enclave. Moshe Sharett, Israel's prime minister in 1954, reports in his diary that Moshe Dayan (later defense and foreign minister), with David Ben Gurion's approval, proposed that Israel should bribe a Christian Lebanese army officer (even a major) to declare himself savior of the Christians. Israel would invade the country and annex the south up to the Litani river.[41] These plans were shelved for various reasons. In 1978 Israel got its opportunity, after the invasion, in the person of a major in the Lebanese army, Sa'd Haddad, who was its proxy until his death in 1981. He was succeeded by Antoine Lahd, a retired Lebanese army general, who continues to lead the South Lebanon Army, a militia of 2500 recruits paid and equipped by the Israelis.

By occupying southern Lebanon, Israel can now bargain for the waters of the Litani river. By 2000 Israel's water deficit will reach 800 million cubic meters (mcm) and the Litani provides about 900 mcm.[42] Israel claims that the Litani should be included in a three-river water system that feeds the Jordan valley: the Hasbani, the Awali, and the Litani rivers.[43] Geographically, only the Hasbani can actually feed the Jordan valley since the Litani and Awali originate and run off within Lebanese territory. Obviously, water is one important consideration in Israeli policy and the final status of southern Lebanon will necessarily deal with Lebanon's waters.

United Nations Security Council Resolutions 425, 426, 508, and 509 call on Israel to withdraw from southern Lebanon. Israel refuses to abide by the resolutions. On May 17, 1983, after basically installing a rightist Phalanges government in Beirut, Israel signed a "peace treaty" with Lebanon that guaranteed Israeli hegemony over the south. The treaty was rejected by Syria and its Lebanese allies, and was immediately abrogated by the Lebanese parliament.[44] Today United Nations peacekeeping forces (UNIFIL) monitor the situation in south Lebanon, but they cannot do much to stop continued Israeli attacks against civilians and agricultural land. Obviously, Lebanon considers Israel's occupation a hindrance to peace between the two countries, and resistance forces (especially leftists and

Hezbollah fighters) continue to launch military attacks against both Israeli and South Lebanon Army forces.

Each year since the peace talks began the Israeli government has pursued armed interventions into Lebanon. In August, 1997, the Musa'ad was actually beaten (or at least exposed) in a South Lebanon Army offensive. However, before that, Israel's Operation Grapes of Wrath in April of 1996 was a clear reminder of the position of strength from which it deals with the Lebanese government. For two weeks Lebanon was placed under siege and close to 500,000 persons were displaced from the south because of indiscriminate Israeli shelling from land, sea, and air. Over 150 Lebanese civilians died (104 were massacred at the Fijian UNIFIL contingent at Qana alone). Power stations all over the country were destroyed, roads cut, and harbors shelled. Estimates put the damage at $500 million.[45] Israel knows it has the upper hand militarily in any duel with the Lebanese government, while the Lebanese government can only hold on to the Syrian presence in the country as a counterweight. Lebanon also knows that only economically can it compete with Israel in a future Middle East economic market. In essence, Israel's military operations against Lebanon can be seen in the light of Lebanon's reconstruction. As open economies, the Lebanese and Israeli economies might be at loggerheads if no amicable solution is found.

The Palestinian refugees

The job of reconstituting political Lebanon and reconstructing its society and economy cannot proceed without a serious debate on the issue of the resident Palestinians, whose status within Lebanon is intricately linked with the prospects of a Lebanese–Israeli peace settlement. As an internal matter, the Lebanese authorities and policy-makers see the Palestinian presence in the country as an economic, political, and sectarian issue. As an external matter, they treat it as unfinished business open to discussion with, first, Israel as originally responsible for the Palestinian refugee problem and, second, the Arab countries as "co-sponsors" of the destiny of the refugees in Lebanon, Syria, and Jordan. The Oslo Accords and later agreements between the Palestinian Authority (PA) and Israel have unfortunately probably sealed their fate in Lebanon. While the PA is most concerned about refugees living in the West Bank and Gaza, discussions about an Israeli–Palestinian peace have left the issue of refugees in Lebanon, Syria, and Jordan unresolved.

Officially and constitutionally, Lebanon rejects the resettlement (*tawteen*) of its resident Palestinians, which is explicitly stated in the Taif Agreement. The official government position was clearly stated by the foreign minister, Faris Buwayz: Lebanon adamantly refuses resettlement because of its geographic size, small area for development and investment, and its social structure.[46] Although accurate figures are unavailable, the Palestinians are estimated to number around 320,000–400,000, with about half living in twelve camps and the rest distributed all over the country.[47] Most importantly, these refugees came to Lebanon from the Galilee in northern Palestine as a result of the 1948 Arab–Israeli war, and for all intents and purposes cannot be repatriated to their homes and villages.[48] Herein lies the Lebanese government's apprehension about the fate of the Palestinians.

The current status of the Palestinian refugees in Lebanon is reminiscent of their status before the rise of the PLO as an independent organization. In the 1950s and 1960s refugee camps were under the direct control of the Lebanese army and internal security forces. In 1969, and after clashes between government forces and Palestinian resistance fighters bent on asserting independent Palestinian action, the Cairo Agreement was signed; under this agreement the PLO gained control of the camps and some independent bases in southern Lebanon. In the early 1970s, after the expulsion of the Palestinian resistance movement from Jordan, the PLO (with its different factions) became a powerful organization and Lebanon became its base of operations, a situation the Lebanese rightists dubbed "a state within a state." During the civil war and up to the Israeli invasion of 1982 the PLO basically ruled the streets of West Beirut, and transgressions of Lebanese sovereignty (or what was left of it) brought the organization much criticism, even from its friends. Its expulsion from Beirut in 1982 and subsequent splits within Palestinian ranks weakened its position vis-à-vis Arab governments. Furthermore, the rise of the rightist Phalanges Party to Lebanon's presidency, the Sabra and Shatila massacres following the 1982 invasion, and the continued assaults on independent Palestinian action, both within and outside of Lebanon, meant that the Palestinians had collectively become weak targets. In 1987 the Lebanese parliament abrogated the Cairo Agreement and reasserted government control over the camps.

In a sobering reassessment of the question of the Palestinians in Lebanon, Rashid Khalidi writes that the Palestinians had "erred grievously" over the years and corrective action was necessary for future relations.[49] Unfortunately, however, in post-Taif Lebanon and the ongoing reconstruction of the country, repairing Palestinian–Lebanese relations does not seem to be a priority for the Lebanese government's, and the PA is today more interested in what happens on the West Bank and in the Gaza Strip than it is in Lebanon's Palestinian refugees. Sayigh writes that both PLO and United Nations Relief and Works Agency (UNRWA) funding for refugees has declined.[50] Moreover, to the south, Jordan is reluctant to admit more refugees because of the unfair employment situations it faces.[51] Thus Palestinians who in Lebanon are excluded from social and public services, and barred from opening clinics, pharmacies, and laboratories and from rebuilding destroyed homes remain stranded in an threatened Israeli war zone, where they are denied civic, employment, and residency rights.[52]

In current Lebanese political and economic matters the emphasis is on plans for reconstruction. Both government officials and public opinion consider the Palestinian presence to be no more than an obligation and, unfortunately, do not think the well-being of the Palestinians should be a priority. However, and despite the ambivalence and the priorities, resolution of the problems of a community of disenfranchised refugees cannot be avoided if Lebanon is to have the internal peace it has deserved for so long. The Palestinians cannot simply be incarcerated in their camps; nor can they be fully integrated in society without social, political, and economic disruptions. On the one hand, the Lebanese Muslims, traditionally the backbone of support for the refugees, cannot propose resettlement, even for the sake of their protégés, for they would be sacrificing their gains after Taif. On the other hand, the Lebanese Christians (whose support for a successful reconstruction effort is essential) consider Lebanon to be socially too Islamicized (Muslims are about two-thirds of the population) to integrate yet another predominantly Muslim community if resettlement is remotely probable. Thus official Lebanon awaits the final settlement of the Middle East conflict and hopes for a satisfactory resolution of the status of its refugees.

Conclusion

From the foregoing analysis of the reconstruction efforts after fifteen years of civil war it is obvious that the current political establishment is bent on joining the Middle East peace process from a position of strength. Reviving the economy and reestablishing Beirut as a financial–commercial center in the eastern Mediterranean seems the best way to accomplish this. As the country gears up for the inevitable, the following observations seem to be most salient.

Internally, the country needs to continue vigorously with its reconstruction program. In spite of new bombings in 1997–8, Lebanon has maintained rapid growth. However, all sectors have not benefited equally and the government must be careful to address the social problems associated with rebuilding the country and revving up its economic machine to meet the challenges of the future Middle East, especially in the face of the extraordinary number of unemployed refugees who are unofficially resettling in its southern regions. The Lebanese economy must diversify its activities and production. The old emphasis on trade, banking, and services must be tempered to include a planned program for strengthening and modernizing agriculture and industry. The future Middle East market will require (as it does now) agricultural and industrial products in addition to services and loans. Furthermore, Lebanese capitalists – if they are to succeed vis-à-vis others, especially Israelis – must, first, be supported by strong government incentives and, second, be able to meet the challenges that lie ahead. It appears that the fissured relations between the Lebanese political system and the country's bourgeoisie have finally been resolved in favor of a full-blown capitalist state (with some sectarian undertones) headed by a billionaire and sanctioned by the economic elites.

Regionally, and out of necessity, Lebanon should enter the future Middle East market as Syria's friend and ally. The Lebanese–Syrian market alone has about 15 million consumers and can provide a powerful northern flank of the wider market. Although the economies of the two countries are not compatible, the economic agreements signed can bridge large gaps between them. Complementarities in agriculture, industry, water, oil, electricity, labor, education, and transport facilities are important. What is lacking is a much larger degree of Lebanese independent political and economic action that would allow Lebanon's entrepreneurs and financiers to strike the necessary balance between investment and production, two necessary elements of economic success. In addition, the Palestinian refugees in Lebanon (and in Syria as well) must be allowed to be involved as players in the Lebanese–Syrian political-economy, especially if the PA continues to sidestep its responsibility to resolve their dilemma. They can provide another segment of the required pool of laborers and consumers. Their legal status can easily be addressed by granting them work permits and residency rights, at least provisionally, until the larger issue of Palestinian refugee rights can be addressed and resolved on a regional basis.

On the positive side, the opportunities of peace in the Middle East present the region with unimaginable rewards. There surely is a chance for cooperation and development, investment and growth, and complementarities and large markets. However, the obstacles are very difficult to surmount. From the political issues of Israeli occupation of land, expulsion of Palestinians, lack of democratic development, and disrespect for human and national rights, to economic considerations of dependency, lack of funds for development, cut-throat competition, and neglect of the poor and needy, the process is fraught with pitfalls. It is important for the Middle East to recognize that good economic relations must be based on mutual respect and equal opportunity. Israel must not insist on zero-sum outcomes, i.e. it must not be allowed to become the Hong Kong of the region to the detriment of all others. Such an outcome would reignite the antagonism and hostility that have characterized the area since the beginning of the twentieth century.

Finally, Lebanon must be allowed to continue on the road toward full recovery. Obviously much depends on its plans for reconstruction, development, and growth. All indicators point to the fact that a political decision has been made at least to let the recent past fade into the far recesses of memory. The emphasis is currently on the tasks of recovering Lebanon and preparing it for the challenges of an integrated Middle East economy. It is actually not so farfetched to state that if the political will to remake the country exists Lebanon will be one of the players at the table of major economic decisions for the future Middle East.

Notes

1 P. Saba, "The creation of the Lebanese economy: economic growth in the 19th and 20th centuries," in R. Owen (ed.) *Essays on the Crisis in Lebanon*, Ithaca Press, London, 1976, p. 12. An excellent account of the events of the mid-nineteenth century and their aftermath can be found in Leila Fawaz, *An Occasion for War: Civil Conflict in Lebanon and Damascus in 1860*, I. B. Tauris, London, 1994. Also see, Antun 'Aqiqi, *Lebanon in the Last Years of Feudalism: A Contemporary Account*, translated by Malcolm Kerr, the American University of Beirut, Beirut, Lebanon, 1959.

2 *Al-mutasarrifiyyah* (governorate) was an agreement worked out between the Ottomans and the European powers according to which a Christian, non-Lebanese governor, or *mutasarrif*, would be appointed and assisted by a twelve-member Council of Representatives of the resident population (two each: Maronites, Druze, Greek Orthodox, Greek Catholics, Sunni Muslims, and Shia Muslims). This arrangement worked until 1914, when the Young Turks established a direct military administration which isolated the region until the Ottomans were defeated in the First World War.

3 Samir Khalaf, *Persistence and Change in 19th Century Lebanon: A Sociological Essay*, the American University of Beirut, Beirut, Lebanon, 1979, p. 109.

4 During the war France and England signed a series of secret agreements, such as the San Remo and Sykes–Picot Agreements, which basically decided the future of the conquered Ottoman territories. Needless to say, these agreements contradicted British assurances to Sharif Hussein of the Hijaz about the establishment of a unified Arab state between the Arabian Peninsula and the Fertile Crescent.

5 'Ali Shami, *Tatawwur at-tabaqah al-'amilah fi al-ra'smaliyyah al-Lubnaniyyah al-mu'asirah* [The development of the working class within contemporary Lebanese capitalism], dar al-Farabi, Beirut, Lebanon, 1981, p. 41.

5 Carolyn Gates, *The Historical Role of Political Economy in the Development of Modern Lebanon*, Center for Lebanese Studies, Oxford, 1989, p. 12.

6 Tariffs and customs duties were limited in 1948; the economic union with Syria was abolished in 1950; controls on foreign exchange were lifted in 1952; and banking secrecy was institutionalized in 1955.

7 Khalaf, *Persistence and Change in 19th Century Lebanon*, p. 224.

8 Mahdi 'Amel (Muhammad Hamdan), *Bahth fi asbab al-harb al-ahliyyah fi Lubnan* [A study of the causes of Lebanon's civil war], dar al-Farabi, Beirut, Lebanon, 1979, pp. 226–7.

9 Elias Saba, "Prospects for Lebanon's economy," in Nadim Shehadi and Bridget Harney (eds.) *Politics and the Economy in Lebanon*, Center for Lebanese Studies, Oxford, 1989, pp. 1–6.

10 International Bank for Reconstruction and Development, table in B. J. Odeh, *Lebanon: Dynamics of Conflict*, Zed Books, London, 1985, p. 77.

11 Paul Saba, "The creation of the Lebanese economy," p. 12.

12 The civil war was actually begun as a "preemptive" counter-revolution by the Christian-rightist camp, which interpreted the social unrest as a prelude to the impending revolution of the underclass. Of course, there were many complicating factors, including the Palestinians in the country, Syria's role, Israeli interference, and the general slowdown in the economy.

13 A full translation of the text is in Dilip Hiro, *Lebanon: Fire and Embers*, St. Martin's Press, New York, 1992, pp. 231–40, app. 3.
14 Confessionalism can be simply defined as a political arrangement by which government posts are distributed among the different religious communities according to predetermined formulas based on population numbers.
15 According to the Lebanese Constitution, if no presidential elections can be held the incumbent president can appoint a Maronite Christian as prime minister. Aoun was a Maronite and friend of Jmayyil's. Moreover, Jmayyil himself was widely believed to have subverted the elections so that he could create a constitutional void and appoint Aoun to replace him.
16 *ARAMCO World*, vol. 45, no. 1, January/February, 1994, p. 18.
17 *Ibid.*
18 *Euromoney*, supplement, April, 1992, p. 4.
19 *ARAMCO World*, p. 19.
20 Paul Salem, "The wounded republic: Lebanon's struggle for recovery," *Arab Studies Quarterly*, vol. 16, no. 4, fall, 1994, p. 59.
21 For a list, see Rodney Wilson, "Will the peace process bring portfolio investments into the Middle East?," in J. W. Wright, Jr. (ed.), *Economic and Political Impediments to Middle East Peace: Critical Questions and Alternative Scenarios*, Macmilllan, London, 1998.
22 The prime minister sold back to the government his shares in the official Lebanese Television Company. In 1991 his purchase of the shares saved the company from bankruptcy.
23 *Wall Street Journal*, March 29, 1994. See also *United Nations Yearbook, 1993*, vol. 47, Martinus Nijhoff Publishers, Boston, Massachusetts, p. 645.
24 *Middle East Economic Digest* (MEED), March 17, 1995, p. 5. During the war years inflation was as high as 140 percent. The low inflation figures have, however, been achieved at the expense of wages in both the public and private sectors. The minimum wage is low at 300,000 Lebanese pounds (about $192) per month and unofficial estimates put the number of those below the poverty line at one-third of the population.
25 The main sources have been the World Bank, the European Economic Community, Saudi Arabia, Kuwait, the Arab Fund for Economic and Social Development, and Italy. Japan has not yet joined the list of donors but is expected to do so since it has reopened its embassy in Beirut (See *ibid.*).
26 *MEED*, September 6, 1996, p. 3.
27 *MEED*, February 3, 1995, p. 24.
28 *Ibid.* Lebanon has always had a positive balance of payments due to transfers from services and tourism as well as remittances from expatriate Lebanese, which in 1993 and 1994 alone amounted to $10 billion (*MEED*, February 24, 1995, p. 40).
29 *MEED*, August 2, 1996, p. 20.
30 *MEED*, September 6, 1996, p. 3.
31 *ARAMCO World*, p. 24.
32 *ARAMCO World*, p. 28.
33 *MEED*, March 17, 1995, p. 4.
34 "Lebanese government statistics," *al-Safir* newspaper, Beirut, 3 April, 1995, cited in *MEED*, April 21, 1995, p. 25.
35 See the full translation of the text in Hiro, *Lebanon: Fire and Embers*, pp. 241–5, app. 4.
36 Salem, "The wounded republic," p. 51.

37 Simone Ghazi Tinaoui, "An analysis of the Syrian–Lebanese economic cooperation agreements," *Beirut Review*, vol. 4, no. 8, fall, 1994, pp. 101–11.
38 The Syrian Ba'ath party is agrarian-based and has pursued an Arab-socialist economic strategy since the Ba'ath takeover of the country in the 1960s. In 1988 the government devalued the Syrian lira by 70 percent to attract hard currency and opened up several thousands of hectares of arable land to private investment (Tinaoui, "An analysis of the Syrian–Lebanese economic cooperation agreements," p. 98).
39 *ARAMCO World*, p. 24.
40 Early 1990s relations with Lebanon have actually benefited the Syrian economy. GDP rose by 6 percent in 1993, and agricultural production by 4.8 percent (*United Nations Yearbook, 1993*, pp. 645–6).
41 Moshe Sharett's diary for May 16, 1954, p. 996, cited in Livia Rokach, *Israel's Sacred Terrorism*, the Association of Arab American University Graduates, information paper no. 23, Belmont, Massachusetts, 1982, p. 29.
42 T. Naff and R. C. Matson, *Water in the Middle East: Conflict or Cooperation*, Westview Press, Boulder, Colorado, 1984, cited in H. A. Amery and A. A. Kubursi, "The Litani river basin: the politics and economics of water," *Beirut Review*, vol. 3, no. 3, spring, 1993, p. 102.
43 Fida Nasrallah, *The Questions of South Lebanon*, Center for Lebanese Studies, Oxford, 1992, pp. 9–10.
44 See the text in Nasrallah, *The Questions of South Lebanon*, pp. 63–9.
45 *MEED*, 23 August, 1996, p. 24.
46 Interview with *al-Safir* newspaper, 18 April, 1994. See the translated and abridged text in *Journal of Palestine Studies*, vol. 24, no. 1, autumn, 1994, pp. 130–1.
47 Rosemary Sayigh, "Palestinians in Lebanon: harsh present, uncertain future," *Journal of Palestine Studies*, vol. 25, no. 1, autumn, 1995, pp. 46, fn. 20, 53. See also Nawaf Salam, "Between repatriation and resettlement: Palestinian refugees in Lebanon," *Journal of Palestine Studies*, vol. 24, no. 1, autumn, 1994, p. 20. Her Majesty Queen Noor also makes this point in her introduction to *Economic and Political Impediments to Middle East Peace: Critical Questions and Alternative Scenarios*.
48 The Israeli Knesset resolved in 1961 that Palestinian refugees in the Arab countries cannot be repatriated and must be resettled where they reside.
49 Rashid Khalidi, "The Palestinians in Lebanon," in Halim Barakat (ed.), *Toward a Viable Lebanon*, Croom Helm, London, 1988, p. 139.
50 Sayigh, "Palestinians in Lebanon," p. 38.
51 See Chapter 2.
52 *Ibid.*

8

INTERNAL AND EXTERNAL CONSTRAINTS ON SAUDI ARABIAN ECONOMIC GROWTH

The role of defense expenditures and remittances

Robert E. Looney

Introduction

After nearly twenty-five years of relatively high oil revenues, Saudi Arabia and the other economies of the Gulf States remain overwhelmingly dominated by revenues from this source. In addition, while considerable industrial diversification into non-oil sectors has been achieved, the results have largely been below expectations. Consequently, it is not apparent that the non-oil sectors can sustain growth and development without a steady infusion of government expenditures.[1] Specifically, lower oil prices have resulted in falling state revenues and consequent reduced spending on infrastructure and industry. This, in turn, has exacerbated social unrest. At the same time, increased military spending by Iran and Iraq is also forcing the country to expand its allocations to the military.

On a more fundamental level, it might be argued that beginning in the mid-1980s the decline in oil revenues and their increased instability affected the path of development. For example, Ghamdi presents strong evidence that Saudi government consumption and investment expenditures experienced instability that was positively related to the instability of total revenue.[2] However, the effect was more marked for development expenditure, which supports the view that revenue instability did have an impact on the country's goals of development.

While it does not question this assertion, the research below focuses on a somewhat different issue. That is, has the actual mechanism underlying economic growth in the kingdom fundamentally changed or has the old model simply run into a period of diminishing returns?

Overview

During the oil-boom years Saudi Arabia and the other Gulf Cooperation Council (GCC) states' economies were characterized by:

- a lack of binding budgetary constraints, which, in turn, reduced and sometimes even eliminated the need to set spending priorities and allocate scarce economic resources;
- financial resources so large that even with a highly skewed income distribution all sectors of society saw some measure of improvement in their standard of living;
- a situation in which unemployment was unimaginable, since governments showed a seemingly infinite capacity to hire both citizens and foreigners in public jobs.[3]

The oil boom created a lasting legacy, which is now stifling growth and development in the region. It created a parallel escape from politics in which ruling elites rarely faced the need to share power, renew their legitimacy and credibility, or tolerate any meaningful public debate on major economic, social, or political issues such as oil and budgetary policy. It also brought about a system which had neither taxation nor representation. And perhaps the greatest burden imposed by the oil-boom years was an illusion that the oil bonanza would last indefinitely.

All this has resulted in governments being slow to adapt to the new reality of lower revenues. For example, many of the Gulf governments have run chronic deficits averaging well in excess of 5 percent of gross domestic product (GDP), and reaching 15 percent in Saudi Arabia; and budget shortfalls have been almost entirely reflected in the external accounts, leading to large current-account deficits. In addition, external and domestic deficits were initially financed by drawing down the substantial foreign resources accumulated during the 1970s and early 1980s. In fact, with the exception of the United Arab Emirates (UAE), most Gulf countries depleted their assets and turned to borrowing, and, in doing so, for the first time exposed their economies and economic policies to serious international scrutiny. Most of these governments have finally responded by reducing spending; Saudi Arabia has made major reductions in expenditure and increased many fees for services.

Current problems

The Saudi population is growing rapidly. According to UN projections, population growth will average 3.5 percent per annum until 2002. Some 60 percent of the population is less than 24 years old, and the 15–24 age group is the fastest-growing in the country. Even economic growth of 3.8 percent per annum, as is expected under the new five-year plan, will barely generate enough jobs for a labor force expanding at these rates. In addition, some fear that employment levels could actually fall because of technological advances and increasingly capital-intensive investment. This would leave a rising number of young nationals chasing even fewer jobs.

Government finance

Public-sector employment has become a means of disguising unemployment, and government jobs are still seen as having high status. Unemployment is also a serious problem. Nevertheless, low oil prices have put increased strain on Saudi government finances. With wages and salaries accounting for almost 50 percent of government spending, rationalization has become unavoidable. However, this is unlikely to mean redundancies. Instead, the government will rely on natural attrition, in combination with a freeze on new recruitment, to cut its wage bill.

Dependency

Bringing in expatriate workers has been a major factor in Saudi Arabia's economic development. The government now feels that the economic and fiscal costs are growing too fast and without commensurate benefits. Foreign workers are a major burden on the state's finances – like everyone else in Saudi Arabia, they are not liable for income or sales tax. However, they do enjoy free government services, in particular free health care. In addition, foreign workers in the kingdom sent home almost $16 billion in earnings in 1993, thereby contributing to a current-account deficit of $14.2 billion (equivalent to around 15 percent of GDP).

The authorities recognize that preventive action is needed if these problems are not to worsen. Thus the new development plan sets out measures to increase job opportunities for Saudi nationals. This may mean restrictions on the recruitment of expatriates into skilled and semi-skilled jobs. The government may also publish "targets" for private-sector companies, while tying government financing to progress on Saudiization. These measures are hardly draconian, and it is clear that pressure on the government to create jobs is less severe than in neighboring countries, where unemployment is more of a problem. Saudi Arabia will therefore persist in its cautious approach to "localization" – the minister of health said recently that it would take at least forty-seven years to get Saudis into only 62 percent of jobs in the Saudi Arabia health sector.

Saudi Arabian growth patterns

Another way of identifying some of the problems currently facing the Saudi authorities is by examining the changes in several key macroeconomic relationships during the 1980s and into the 1990s. The following points provide a brief overview of these relationships:

- Government investment as a share of non-oil GDP has declined dramatically since 1979, a pattern that also appears to be associated with the government's fiscal deficits.
- On the other hand, private investment has retained a stable share of non-oil GDP, although it is experiencing a slight downward trend.
- The fiscal-deficit share of non-oil GDP peaked in 1987, and after that date stabilized somewhat with regard to its share of non-oil GDP.
- As has its investment, the public sector's consumption has declined with regard to its share of non-oil GDP.
- Also as has investment, government consumption has shown a slight tendency in recent years to increase its share of non-oil GDP.
- Private consumption has also experienced a gradual decline with regard to non-oil GDP. This expenditure category appears to be stabilizing at slightly over 60 percent of non-oil GDP.
- As with consumption and investment, both private- and public-sector expenditures have fallen with regard to the country's non-oil GDP.
- The decline in private-sector expenditures has been more stable, with public-sector expenditures experiencing much greater fluctuation.
- The decline in public-sector expenditures (as indicated by its trend) has also been somewhat sharper than in the case of private expenditures.
- GDP associated with the oil sector has shown the greatest fluctuation of all, falling below non-oil GDP for the first time in 1983. Since that date oil GDP seems to be stabilizing at somewhere between 40 and 60 percent of non-oil GDP.
- Private consumption has consistently accounted for a higher share of GDP than government consumption. However, in recent years this gap has narrowed somewhat.
- On the other hand, government investment and private investment have changed places in accounting for the greatest share of GDP. Up to1985 government investment had the larger share, private investment had the larger share during most of the rest of the 1980s, with government again taking the larger share in the 1990s.
- Regime expenditure's share of GDP has experienced a downward trend, although this has been reversed in the last several years.
- During the last several years public expenditures have accounted for a larger share of GDP than that associated with private expenditures.

- Of the aggregates examined here, investment has shown the most stability in terms of its share of GDP.
- Capital formation has averaged around 20 percent of GDP and has experienced a very slight downward trend since 1979.
- Consumption has been volatile, although it appears to be stabilizing at around 75 percent of GDP.

While these patterns are valuable in describing certain changes that are taking place in Saudi Arabia, they are of less use in identifying whether the country's economic mechanisms have undergone fundamental alteration. The unanswered question is whether the links between government expenditure, the private sector, and the non-oil economy have changed in a way that alters the effectiveness of the regime's ability to manage the economy.

Causal links

To answer this question one must satisfactorily address the issue of causation. In this regard, several statistical tests using regression analysis for this purpose are gaining wider acceptance. The original and most widely used causality test was developed by Granger.[4] According to this test, some economic variable such as government investment causes (say) growth in non-oil GDP if rates of expansion in non-oil GDP can be predicted more accurately by past values of government investment than by past rates of growth in non-oil GDP. To be certain that causality runs from government investment to non-oil GDP, past values of government investment must also be more accurate than past values of non-oil GDP in predicting the observed rates of growth in state investment over time.

The results of Granger causality tests depend critically on the choice of lag length. If the chosen lag length is less than the true lag length, the omission of relevant lags can cause bias. If the chosen lag is greater than the true lag length, the inclusion of irrelevant lags causes estimates to be inefficient. While it is possible to choose lag lengths based on preliminary partial autocorrelation methods, there is no a priori reason to assume equal lag lengths for all types of economic activity. To overcome the difficulties noted above, the authors used the Hsaio[5] method to identify the optimal lags.[6]

In our example of government investment and non-oil GDP, several patterns are possible:

1   *Government investment causes non-oil GDP* when the prediction error for non-oil GDP decreases when government investment is included in the growth equation. In addition, when non-oil GDP is added to the manufacturing equation the final prediction error should increase.

2 *Non-oil GDP growth causes growth in government investment* when the prediction error for non-oil GDP increases when government investment is added to the regression equation for non-oil GDP, and is reduced when non-oil GDP is added to the regression equation for government investment.

3 *Feedback* occurs when the final prediction error decreases when government investment is added to the non-oil GDP equation, and the final prediction error decreases when non-oil GDP growth is added to the government investment equation.

4 *No relationship* exists when the final prediction error increases both when government investment is added to the non-oil GDP growth equation and when non-oil GDP growth is added to the government investment growth equation.

The data used for the causality tests cover the period 1970–92 (the last year for which comparable data were available); they were from the Saudi Arabian Monetary Agency Annual Reports and were deflated by the non-oil GDP deflator. Causality relationships were examined for the following pairs of variables:

- *Private investment* and (1) non-infrastructural investment, (2) infrastructure investment, (3) defense expenditures, (4) government consumption, (5) private consumption, and (6) non-oil GDP.
- *Non-oil GDP* and (1) non-infrastructural investment, (2) infrastructure investment, (3) defense expenditures, (4) government consumption, and (5) private consumption.

Prior to the actual causality analysis, several tests were performed to determine whether any of the pair of variables had undergone a structural shift during the period examined (1970–92). For most sets of variables a distinct shift in their relationship occurred between 1980 and 1982. The causality tests were therefore performed using the subgroupings 1970–82 and 1980–92.

Summing up, the main questions of interest are as follows:

- What macroeconomic linkages characterize the Saudi economy?
- To what extent have government expenditures provided a positive stimulus to the private sector?
- Have these linkages changed over time?
- Is the private sector evolving in such a way that it may be ready to replace oil-based government expenditure as the engine of growth?
- Is the linkage between public expenditure and private investment strengthening or weakening?
- What are the major implications for future government policy?

Results

The analysis found a number of interesting relationships for both sets of subperiods. It was found that several patterns characterize the first period (1970–82). Most important for longer run growth is the link between private investment and non-oil GDP. During this period private investment had a positive impact on non-oil GDP. This relationship was not particularly strong, but it did indicate that the private sector's activities were flowing into productive ventures. During this first period it was also found that private investment itself was mainly stimulated by defense expenditures, non-infrastructural investment. Government consumption and infrastructural investment provided considerably less of a stimulus to private investment. In addition, non-oil GDP received its strongest stimulus from government consumption during this period, followed by defense expenditures. Ironically infrastructural investment had a negative impact on the growth in non-oil GDP. In addition, several distinct changes took place during this time. First, and most important, was the severing of the link between private investment and non-oil GDP. Second, non-oil GDP was no longer simulated by defense expenditures or government consumption. Third, the only macro variable that had a statistically significant link with non-oil GDP was non-infrastructural investment, and this link was rather weak. Fourth, private investment's link with defense expenditures weakened during this period, but was still positive. In contrast, the stimulus provided by government consumption strengthened during this period. On the other hand, the earlier stimulus provided by non-infrastructural investment shifted to a negative impact. Another major change from the earlier period was the shift from private-sector investment affecting private consumption to that of private consumption providing a stimulus to private investment.

A comprehensive explanation of the causes for the apparent shifts in Saudi Arabia's growth mechanism is beyond the scope of this study. However, recent developments in statistical analysis have resulted in the development of new methods (largely cointegration analysis) for identifying the manner in which variables interact over long and short periods.[7] Several of these patterns are suggestive of possible factors that may be affecting the country's growth mechanism. The following sections apply this methodology to two areas often cited as being responsible for many of the kingdom's current economic difficulties, excessive defense expenditures, and the acceleration of remittance payments.

Defense expenditures

Defense expenditures in the kingdom account for around one-third of the government's budgetary allocations. While there is no doubt that the country can afford a high level of defense expenditures, the issue here is whether these allocations come at the expense of economic services, and, if so, whether they reduce the budgetary shares of economic allocations, infrastructure, and the like to the point where imbalances occur. That is, given the country's ongoing needs for infrastructure and other necessary economic services, have defense expenditures skewed the budgetary process away from productivity-enhancing activities?

Budgetary patterns

The main trends in the country's budgetary shares (see Table 8.1) are as follows:

- There has been a slight increase in the share of the budget allocated to defense. This share increased from slightly over one-quarter of the budget in 1979 to a little over one-third by 1995. It should be noted that this increase has not been linear, but rather reached a peak of over 35 percent in 1988, only to fall to around 31 percent in 1993 and to 33.02 percent in 1995.
- The major expansion in budgetary shares has gone to human resources. This category represented 8.46 percent of the budget in 1979, increasing to nearly 18 percent by 1995.
- Transport and communications have seen their budgetary shares eroded over the years. These allocations accounted for 12.69 percent of the budget in 1980, falling to slightly over 4 percent by 1995. This decline has been fairly constant over time, perhaps reflecting the completion of the major post-oil-boom wave of capital expenditure projects.
- Health expenditures do not show a discernible trend, although they have increased somewhat, from 4.55 percent in 1979 to 6.78 percent in 1995. As with defense expenditures, a peak occurred in the late 1980s, with health reaching 7.65 percent of the budget in 1988.
- Economic resources have declined over time. For the period under consideration, they reached a high of 8.54 percent of the budget in 1980. Since that date they have dropped steadily, reaching 2.57 percent by 1995.
- Infrastructure follows a pattern similar to that of economic resources. A high of 4.68 percent was reached in 1980. Subsequently, the share has fallen, reaching 0.93 percent in 1995.
- Municipal services have also declined over time, although again the trend has not been strictly linear. Starting at 5.88 percent of the budget in 1979, allocations to the municipalities increased to 8.82 percent in 1981. Since that time there has been a generally downward trend, with the budgetary share reaching 3.26 percent by 1995.
- Government lending has fallen dramatically over time. In 1979 this category received 11.46 percent of the budget. By 1995 the share allo-

cated for this activity was only 0.32 percent of the budget. The decline in this activity was most rapid in the 1980s, with budgetary shares falling to 0.42 percent by 1988.

- The share of resources allocated for local subsidies has fluctuated over time, with a high of around 4.65 percent in 1993 and a low of 2.02 percent in 1980.
- Administration has seen its share increase over time. From a low of 14.23 percent in 1982, allocations to this activity reached 29.54 percent in 1993, only to fall to 26.48 by 1995.

Previous studies

On the surface, budgetary tradeoffs between defense and allocations to socioeconomic programs would seem to be straightforward. That is, a given budgetary increase in military expenditures will crowd out an equivalent amount of all other spending and these programs will be reduced according to their proportion of the total. However, recent research has shown this view of the budgetary process to be simplistic and not in conformance with the manner in which governments often choose to prioritize expenditures.[8]

A related issue, and one of significant relevance for the Saudi authorities facing austerity programs, is the manner in which austerity-driven budgetary cuts are allocated. Anecdotal evidence suggests that officials often follow rather ad hoc rules for making large contractions in a short time, cutting new rather than ongoing projects, new rather than existing employment, and materials and travel expenses rather than personnel; and favoring ministries that are politically powerful or reducing those that expanded most rapidly in the past.

In the classic study of relative vulnerability to budgetary cuts, Hicks and Kubisch examined thirty-seven cases of budgetary reduction. These were defined as occurring in countries where real expenditure declined in one or more years. Hicks and Kubisch's main findings indicated that the countries examined experienced an average decline of 13 percent in real government expenditure. Associated with this decline was a contraction of only 5 percent in the social sectors (producing a vulnerability index of 0.4). By contrast, the index was 0.6 for the administrative/defense sectors and over 1 percent for production and infrastructure. In short, the various social sectors were less vulnerable to cuts than defense and administration, which in turn were considerably less vulnerable than production and infrastructure.[9] This finding was contrary to the prevailing view of the time.

The fact that social sectors and defense were both relatively protected suggests that there were high political costs associated with reducing them. Countries appeared to have been more willing to cut spending on infrastructure and production, which, of course, is likely to have adverse

Table 8.1 Saudi Arabia: budgetary shares (%), 1979–95

Year	Defense	Human resources	Transport and communications	Health	Economic resources
1979	26.12	8.46	11.31	4.55	6.89
1980	27.27	8.94	12.69	4.88	8.54
1981	27.70	8.81	11.86	4.60	7.61
1982	29.64	10.10	10.38	5.43	7.03
1983	29.06	10.67	9.60	5.23	5.08
1984	30.73	11.70	8.53	6.21	4.82
1985	31.98	12.27	7.25	6.45	4.54
1986	32.86	13.41	7.06	6.67	4.36
1987	33.97	14.84	6.83	6.95	4.14
1988	35.47	16.56	6.72	7.65	4.17
1989	34.04	17.09	6.06	7.57	3.59
1990	34.27	15.56	4.84	6.81	2.55
1991	34.27	15.56	4.84	6.81	2.55
1992	31.81	17.59	4.67	7.52	2.55
1993	31.32	16.31	4.16	6.92	2.57
1994	33.47	18.27	4.28	7.04	2.68
1995	33.02	17.95	4.08	6.78	2.57

Year	Infrastructure	Municipal services	Government lending	Local subsidies	Administration
1979	3.13	5.88	11.46	4.16	18.04
1980	4.68	7.81	7.71	2.02	15.45
1981	4.74	8.82	8.34	3.05	14.47
1982	3.73	8.37	7.46	3.56	14.23
1983	3.68	7.33	7.69	3.49	18.16
1984	3.78	6.56	6.73	4.05	16.90
1985	3.46	5.95	4.65	4.17	19.29
1986	3.12	5.56	3.58	4.03	19.34
1987	2.69	5.08	2.25	3.85	19.40
1988	2.51	4.97	0.42	3.77	17.75
1989	1.99	3.87	0.01	3.47	22.32
1990	1.36	3.30	0.59	2.79	27.92
1991	1.36	3.30	0.59	2.79	27.92
1992	1.15	3.27	0.36	3.92	27.16
1993	1.05	3.11	0.36	4.65	29.54
1994	0.90	3.27	0.33	4.36	25.33
1995	0.93	3.26	0.32	4.61	26.48

Source: Saudi Arabian Monetary Agency Annual Report, July, 1996.

implications for longer-term growth but few early direct and immediate costs.

Summing up these findings, Hicks and Kubisch found that when faced with difficult choices in reducing public expenditures governments consider a wide range of factors, including political and economic costs, present versus future consumption, and the potential impact on employment, distribution, and welfare. Their empirical results suggest that when governments in developing countries implement austerity programs they do not apply across-the-board reductions in expenditures. Generally, capital expenditures are reduced more than recurrent expenditure. Within both capital and current budgets, the social and administrative/defense sector appears to be relatively protected, while infrastructure and production absorb disproportionately larger reductions. That the social sector does not appear to be highly vulnerable to expenditure reductions in times of austerity was the novel finding of that study.

Throughout most of the 1980s and into the 1990s Saudi Arabia experienced a period of relative fiscal austerity. Falling oil revenues forced a number of significant budgetary cutbacks. Of particular interest is the manner in which the authorities set priorities. Did expenditure on certain categories vary systematically with unanticipated changes in revenue? If so, which sectors gained and which lost?

One way of gaining an insight into these issues is to examine the manner in which, in light of revenue developments during the fiscal year, the Saudi government revised its allocation to the major budgetary categories. Did expenditure on certain categories vary systematically with unanticipated changes in revenue? If so which sectors gained and which lost? Do these patterns provide insights into the manner in which the government established budgetary priorities during this period?

While it did not look directly at linkages with defense expenditures, an analysis of the 1979–88 period found the following:

- Human resource development and health and social development allocations were the only budgetary categories to have their budgetary shares increase with expanded, unanticipated deficits. They were also the only sectors to have their budgetary shares increase during periods of increased actual (realized) budgetary deficits.
- Human resource development and health did not have their budgetary shares expanded with increases in expected revenue. This finding is consistent with the notion that, because of their high priority, their funding levels were assured. Given this, marginal increases in revenue could be safely used by the authorities to fund lower-priority projects.
- The deficit-related expansion in human capital seems to have come in part at the expense of longer-term investment in economic capacity. Specifically, transportation and communications, economic services, and infrastructure had their budgetary shares contracted during periods of increased unexpected and actual deficits.[10] This finding is consistent with that of Hicks and Kubisch, who document the vulnerability of capital formation during periods of austerity.[11]

In general, the main findings of this study confirm the high priority granted to human resource development by the Saudi authorities. Resources in this sector have been preserved relative to other sectors during the current period of austerity. Budgetary cuts have occurred in Saudi Arabia, but education has been relatively spared. The long-term nature of the commitment by the government to this sector is also evidenced by the fact that it appears to be relatively safe from budgetary cuts during periods of budgetary deficit. In fact, deficits may owe their size to the authorities' commitment to providing adequate funding for these programs. The same could be said of health and social expenditures.

From this analysis one can conclude that, while defense has retained its leading share of the budget during the recent period of relative fiscal austerity, Saudi Arabia does not appear to have fallen into the guns-versus-education syndrome. In fact, the two types of expenditure appear to complement each other in the minds of the Saudi budgetary authorities. The country appears firmly committed to its responsibility of providing educational and occupational opportunities to the majority of its citizens.

Methodology

To see whether these conclusions held up, defense was explicitly introduced into the analysis the interaction of defense with other budgetary shares, and this was assessed by use of cointegration analysis. Specifically, to shed light on these issues a vector error-correction model was used. If there is evidence of cointegration between two variables – i.e. they move in a similar pattern over time – then an error-correction representation of the dynamic relationship between the two variables allows for incorporation of the long-run (or low-frequency) movements contained in their cointegrating equation. More specifically, if two variables Xt and Yt are cointegrated, then the current change in Xt, for example, reflects not only lagged changes in Yt but also lagged levels of Yt. In other words, part of the short-run change in Xt reflects an adjustment that brings it into alignment with the trend value of Yt.

The Saudi Arabian Monetary Authority's Annual Report breaks down the government's main expenditure items into defense and security, human resource development, transport and communications, economic resource development, health and social development, infrastructure development, municipal services, government lending institutions, local subsidies, and administration.

To assess the manner in which defense expenditures interact with these budgetary items two sets of cointegration analysis were performed: in the first set the non-defense shares were set as the dependent variable, with defense the independent term; and in the second set defense and non-defense were reversed, with defense the dependent variable. Here cointegration is identified by the statistical significance of the error-correction coefficient.

Specifically, a statistically significant coefficient of an error-correction term indicates that part of the short-term change in the value of the left-hand side (dependent) variable reflects an adjustment toward the long-run relationship given by the cointegrating relation and thus provides an indirect test of cointegration. A related point to note is that when two variables are cointegrated Granger causality necessarily exists in at least one direction.[12]

Results

Through this analysis several interesting patterns emerge (see Table 8.2):

- Defense and human resources are not cointegrated. That is there is no long-run link between their budgetary shares. On the other hand, increases in either produce a short-run increase in the other. In this sense, defense expenditures do not come at the expense of human resource development.
- Somewhat surprisingly, no statistically significant patterns were found between defense and transport/communications.
- Health services and defense experience the most complex set of relationships. These budgetary shares are highly cointegrated. Because the error-correction term is significant for both defense on health and health on defense, it is appetent that the burden on adjustment to correct deviations from the cointegrating relation is borne by both variables. In other words, both variables respond to changes in the other. It should be noted, however, that the short-run adjustment of health to changes in defense is positive, while the defense share of the budget contracts upon increases in health expenditure. In long-run equilibrium however, each variable has a positive relationship with the other.
- Adjustments in economic services occur largely in response to movements in defense expenditures. While this short-run adjustment may be positive, with increased defense resulting in expanded economic services, the long-run pattern is clearly negative. The same pattern characterizes the relationship between infrastructure and defense. In addition, in both cases it is apparent that movements in economic services or infrastructure do not affect the share of the budget allocated to defense.
- The share of the budget allocated to municipal services is also negatively affected in the long term by expanded defense expenditures. The reverse is also the case. In the short run, however, these patterns are not predictable enough to be statistically significant.
- Government allocations to lending institutions suffer at the expense of defense expenditures, with negative adjustments to increased defense expenditures occurring in the short and long run.

Table 8.2 Saudi Arabia: cointegration test for long-run defense/budgetary expenditure equilibrium, 1979–95

Budget category	Error-correction coefficient		Long-term coefficient		Short-run impact	
	Dependent variable		Dependent variable		Dependent variable	
	non-defense (defense)		non-defense (defense)		non-defense (defense)	
	non-defense	(defense)	non-defense	(defense)	non-defense	(defense)
Human resources	−0.17 (−0.97)	−0.59 (−2.18)	2.61 (1.36)	0.37 (1.73)	+	+
Transport and communications	−0.13 (−1.97)	−0.34 (−1.48)	0.21 (0.32)	−0.10 (−0.14)	ins	ins
Health services	−1.05 (−4.60)	−1.52 (−6.07)	0.39 (6.40)	2.49 (13.11)	+	−
Economic services	−0.98 (3.37)	−0.80 (−1.45)	−0.29 (−3.69)	−1.14 (−0.88)	+	ins
Infrastructure	−0.21 (−3.81)	−0.28 (−1.71)	−0.71 (−4.34)	0.50 (0.27)	+	ins
Municipal services	−0.29 (−4.54)	−1.39 (−2.36)	−0.32 (−2.16)	−1.31 (−4.75)	ins	ins
Lending institutions	−0.31 (−4.69)	−0.11 (−0.73)	−1.73 (−5.41)	0.43 (0.23)	−	ins
Subsidies	−0.13 (−0.25)	−1.15 (−3.11)	−1.54 (−0.22)	4.00 (3.69)	ins	−
Administration	−1.09 (−1.98)	0.07 (−0.33)	0.81 (2.45)	4.47 (0.37)	−	−

Notes: Cointegration analysis using Pesaran's ADRL estimation method. See Pesaran and Pesaran (1997) for the specific computational methods used. Augmented Dickey-Fuller tests indicated that the budgetary shares all have unit root, i.e. they are non-stationary. Brackets indicate τ-statistics.

- Increased local subsidies are not affected by allocations to defense. However, increases in this budgetary category produce contractions in the defense share of the budget. This occurs in both the short and longer term.

- Finally, defense and public administration are weakly cointegrated, with increased defense producing short-run declines in administration. However, in the longer term expanded defense expenditures produce a corresponding increase in the share of the budget allocated to administration.

Several of these budgetary links with defense can best be illustrated by means of variance decomposition analysis. Here we are interested in the percent of the variance of one variable that is caused by movements in the other. Because the variables are cointegrated, we can again use the vector error-correction form of autoregression to assess the response of one variable to movements in the other.

The case of defense and allocations to the economy can be illustrated by applying this analysis to infrastructure. If we produce an increase in the share of the budget allocated to infrastructure, only marginal changes occur in defense. In fact, after ten periods, past values of defense still explain over 99 percent of the variance of that category's budgetary share (see the top of Table 8.3). On the other hand, after ten periods, increases in defense account for nearly 95 percent of the variance in the share of infrastructure in the government's budget (see the bottom of Table 8.3).

In the case of subsidies (see Table 8.4) it is clear that the government's program of local allocations has a great effect on the variance of defense expenditures. The reverse is not the case. Finally, and as has been noted, health and defense tend to affect each other over time, with the variance decomposition analysis suggesting (see Table 8.5) that this effect is slightly stronger from health to defense than vice versa.

The general pattern that emerges from these results is one whereby movements in defense largely control the adjustment of other major budgetary shares. This movement tends to be positive in the short run for both economic and human services. However, in the longer term increased defense expenditures largely come at the expense of allocations to the economy. Areas such as human resource development and health services do not suffer over time from expanded defense budgets. The effect of subsidies on defense is interesting in that it suggests that some groups in Saudi Arabia not only are powerful enough to preserve their payments, but can do so over long periods of time and at the expense of allocations to the defense sector.

As noted in Table 8.1, this conclusion must be tempered by the fact that defense still accounts for about one-third of the budget, while subsidies' share of the budget in 1995 was only 4.6 percent. Still, given the

217

Table 8.3 Variance decomposition tests: defense and infrastructure development

Period	Standard error	Defense	Infrastructure
Order of VAR: defense, infrastructure			
Variance decomposition of defense			
1	1.210373	100.0000	0.000000
2	1.592280	99.99451	0.005490
3	1.858997	99.97874	0.021263
4	1.991127	99.96981	0.030194
5	2.060697	99.92916	0.070839
6	2.104976	99.89574	0.104258
7	2.138600	99.85250	0.147495
8	2.166637	99.79643	0.203566
9	2.193102	99.74651	0.253488
10	2.219813	99.70274	0.297257

Period	Standard error	Infrastructure	Defense
Order of VAR: infrastructure, defense			
Variance decomposition of infrastructure			
1	0.095535	100.0000	0.000000
2	0.121083	85.44301	14.55699
3	0.211637	28.53682	71.46318
4	0.298819	15.92498	84.07502
5	0.366433	12.08405	87.91595
6	0.432114	9.186759	90.81324
7	0.493746	7.427277	92.57272
8	0.545832	6.533074	93.46693
9	0.592266	5.896355	94.10365
10	0.635879	5.385884	94.61412

Note: The method of computation is vector error-correction autoregression with response standard errors calculated through 100 Monte Carlo repetitions.

improvement in private investment productivity usually associated with infrastructure and other economic services, the negative impact that defense has had on allocations must bear some of the responsibility for the weakening of the link between private-sector investment and the non-oil economy.

Remittances

The outflow of private transfers, which includes workers' remittances, is a significant contributor to the kingdom's current payments imbalance. The number of overseas residents in the kingdom is estimated at 5–6 million,

Table 8.4 Variance decomposition tests: defense and subsidies

Period	Standard error	Defense	Subsidies
Order of VAR: defense, subsidies			
Variance decomposition of defense			
1	0.610945	100.0000	0.000000
2	0.615594	98.69332	1.306680
3	0.755057	74.79622	25.20378
4	1.202869	43.74147	56.25853
5	1.578888	39.56225	60.43775
6	1.860501	36.84978	63.15022
7	2.099617	35.04899	64.95101
8	2.303546	34.28269	65.71731
9	2.489484	33.58054	66.41946
10	2.665479	33.04865	66.95135

Period	Standard error	Subsidies	Defense
Order of VAR: subsidies, defense			
Variance decomposition of subsidies			
1	0.406278	100.0000	0.000000
2	0.644648	99.98496	0.015037
3	0.767561	99.93678	0.063218
4	0.835379	99.88671	0.113289
5	0.885087	99.84580	0.154199
6	0.931314	99.81339	0.186610
7	0.977380	99.78978	0.210221
8	1.022679	99.77119	0.228810
9	1.066380	99.75530	0.244700
10	1.108243	99.74172	0.258280

Notes: The method of computation is vector-error correction autoregression with response standard errors calculated through 100 Monte Carlo repetitions.

and in 1994 net private transfers were recorded at $15 billion, compared with a current-account deficit of $9.1 billion.[13]

Clearly the Saudi authorities are looking closely at ways to reduce the hard-currency outflows associated with the large expatriate community. The Riyadh Chamber of Commerce and Industry is conducting a study on opening up investment opportunities for expatriates so that some of the money now remitted would remain inside the kingdom. The study's recommendations include permitting non-Saudis to invest in the stock market – at present only GCC nationals can invest – and real estate. (Foreigners are able to invest in mutual funds offered by the local commercial banks.) Although other policies may push up remittances, it is not clear whether these changes would result in a sizable reduction in the outflow of expatriate

Table 8.5 Variance decomposition tests: defense and health

Period	Standard error	Defense	Health
Order of VAR: defense, health			
Variance decomposition of defense			
1	0.949598	100.0000	0.000000
2	1.118723	99.87266	0.127341
3	1.223944	89.48703	10.51297
4	1.280562	84.66337	15.33663
5	1.318006	85.19339	14.80661
6	1.348875	85.82303	14.17697
7	1.366369	85.53605	14.46395
8	1.378418	84.94050	15.05950
9	1.386237	84.85715	15.14285
10	1.392367	84.93275	15.06725
Period	*Standard error*	*Defense*	*Health*
Order of VAR: health, defense			
Variance decomposition of health			
1	0.360179	100.0000	0.000000
2	0.389988	97.95515	2.044851
3	0.426058	92.94083	7.059167
4	0.447312	92.60774	7.392260
5	0.460546	92.69930	7.300704
6	0.463896	91.50271	8.497292
7	0.466818	90.40560	9.594396
8	0.467884	90.17850	9.821503
9	0.468599	89.90679	10.09321
10	0.471018	89.32616	10.67384

Notes: The method of computation is vector-error correction autoregression with response standard errors calculated through 100 Monte Carlo repetitions.

earnings. Many workers would probably continue to remit a substantial proportion of their earnings home, as in many cases this is the principal source of income for their families and their sole reason for working in Saudi Arabia. Moreover, the tightening of some of the regulations on the expatriate community is likely to increase the outflow of workers' remittances. For example, the newly enforced order that embassy schools cannot enroll children beyond the age of 16 is expected to increase remittances, because the families of many workers will be forced to return home for their children's schooling, thereby requiring workers remaining in the kingdom to remit more money to their families.

The recent increase in remittances is even more striking when compared to the pattern of investment in the kingdom (see Table 8.6). As a share of GDP, remittances increased from 3.75 percent in 1971 to slightly over 15 percent by 1994. Starting out at a slightly higher figure of 4.56 percent in 1971, private investment increased to only 11.47 percent by 1994. While showing no discernible trend, government investment started the period (1971) at 5.10 percent of GDP, only to finish at 5.33 percent. These patterns are even more dramatic when viewed as shares of non-oil GDP. From a low of 4.87 percent in 1975, remittances had increased to nearly 24 percent by 1994. In contrast, government investment declined from a high of 45.75 percent in 1978 to 8.43 percent in 1994. The share of private investment was much more stable, falling from a high of 24.4 percent in 1977 to 18.19 percent in 1994.

To determine the extent to which remittances interact with investment in the kingdom an analysis was undertaken similar to that performed above on budgetary shares. Here we are especially interested in determining whether

Table 8.6 Private investment and remittances, 1971–94

Year	Share of GDP			Share of non-oil GDP		
	Remittances	Government investment	Private investment	Remittances	Government investment	Private investment
1971	3.75	5.10	4.56	11.53	17.71	14.05
1972	3.93	4.89	4.11	13.97	17.41	14.64
1973	3.86	3.43	2.36	24.84	22.14	15.23
1974	1.85	5.27	4.77	9.18	26.20	23.71
1975	1.40	10.63	6.45	4.87	36.96	22.72
1976	2.12	13.33	8.06	6.42	40.40	24.40
1977	2.57	17.96	8.14	6.44	45.04	20.41
1978	4.18	19.65	7.77	9.73	45.72	18.09
1979	5.08	15.97	6.02	14.97	47.06	17.30
1980	3.53	20.85	8.94	7.20	42.52	18.24
1981	3.51	14.08	6.82	9.99	40.09	19.44
1982	3.50	15.99	8.22	7.07	32.32	16.63
1983	4.41	13.45	11.10	7.79	23.77	19.64
1984	5.38	13.18	11.56	8.79	21.55	18.91
1985	6.04	10.44	11.22	8.90	15.38	16.54
1986	6.64	9.28	11.81	8.98	12.56	15.99
1987	6.71	9.95	11.27	9.17	13.59	15.40
1988	8.55	8.43	11.09	11.73	11.56	15.22
1989	10.29	8.46	10.48	14.99	12.32	15.27
1990	10.73	10.84	6.90	17.63	17.81	11.35
1991	11.65	10.22	8.32	19.25	16.89	13.75
1992	10.87	6.99	11.85	18.87	12.14	20.57
1993	13.26	6.76	13.61	21.30	10.87	21.87
1994	15.06	5.33	11.47	23.86	8.43	18.19

Sources: Investment: Thirty-Second Annual Report, Saudi Arabian Monetary Agency, Riyadh, 1996; Remittances: World Development Indicators, World Bank, Washington, 1997.

any long-run patterns exist between remittances and investment. Similarly, if these patterns exist, what is the nature of the short-run adjustment process that occurs to restore stability after a change in one of the variables. As with the budgetary analysis, several patterns emerged. Looking at the impact of remittances on investment (see Tables 8.7 and 8.8) and based on the statistical significance of the error-correction term (Ecmt-1), it is apparent[14] that private investment (both actual and anticipated) and remittances are cointegrated – that is, they form a close long-run association (Table 8.7). While the long-run pattern is one of increased remittances being associated with

Table 8.7 Impact of remittances on investment: full information estimate of error-correction model

Exogenous variables	Private investment	Anticipated private investment	Total public investment	Public infrastructure investment	Public non-infrastructure investment
Constant	1.92	1.36	4.22	3.00	0.56
	(2.74)	(2.18)	(5.01)	(4.03)	(1.08)
Ecmt-1	−0.49	−0.37	−0.38	−0.32	−0.51
	(−3.60)	(−2.74)	(−4.79)	(−3.98)	(−2.68)
D investment-1			0.24	0.38	
			(1.48)	(2.22)	
Dt-2			−0.04	0.02	
			(−0.22)	(0.10)	
Dt-3			0.57	0.50	
			(3.35)	(2.65)	
D remittances	−0.23	−0.11	0.44	−0.16	0.57
	(−1.05)	(−0.55)	(1.86)	(−0.61)	(1.71)
Dt-1	−0.50	−0.56	0.75	0.63	
	(−2.20)	(−2.55)	(2.28)	(2.50)	
Dt-2		−0.48	0.70		
		(−2.44)	(2.45)		
Dt-3			0.36		
			(1.43)		
Long-run coefficient	0.67	0.94	−1.66	−0.78	−0.42
	(3.37)	(2.92)	(−3.83)	(−2.22)	(−1.72)
R2	0.47	0.537	0.85	0.76	0.41
DW	1.66	2.05	2.31	2.02	2.10
F	4.52	4.06	7.65	6.41	5.67

Notes:
Dependent variable = measure of investment; ( ) = *t* statistic.
Error-correction parameters and long-run coefficients computed using Pesaran's ADRL estimation method. See Pesaran and Pesaran (1997) for the specific computational methods used.

higher levels of private investment, short-run increases in remittances have a dampening (the negative sign on the D remittances term) impact on private investment.

In contrast, private investment remittances and government investment (both for infrastructure and non-infrastructure) form a long-run negative relationship. That is, increases in remittances and public investment form a long-run pattern whereby government allocations to capital formation have contracted over time with expanded remittances.

While the pattern of remittances has influenced investment in the kingdom, the reverse is not true (see Table 8.8). Both private and public investments have had a negligible impact on the long-run pattern of shorter-run adjustments in the country's remittances. This result is surprising in that one might expect that both private and public investment would respond to increased domestic economic activity and would thus be associated with remittances which also reflect that activity.

A somewhat different pattern was found when both remittances and investment were expressed as shares of non-oil GDP (see Table 8.9). The

Table 8.8 Impact of investment on remittances: full information estimate of error-correction model

Exogenous variables	Private investment	Anticipated private investment	Total public investment	Public infrastructure investment	Public non-infrastructure investment
Constant	0.39	−0.11	0.49	0.85	−0.01
	(0.44)	(−0.13)	(0.62)	(1.24)	(−0.02)
Ecmt-1	0.09	0.04	0.04	0.03	0.11
	(0.74)	(0.34)	(0.48)	(0.44)	(1.32)
D investment	−0.04	0.07	−0.03	−0.07	0.19
	(−0.25)	(0.40)	(−0.43)	(−1.11)	(1.38)
Dt-1					
D remittances					
Dt-1					
Dt-2					
Long-run	0.56	−1.95	0.71	2.14	−1.66
coefficient	(0.31)	(−0.20)	(0.26)	(0.37)	(−1.25)
R2	0.04	0.04	0.05	0.10	0.13
DW	2.63	2.50	2.57	2.59	2.64
F	0.34	0.38	0.40	0.95	1.31

Notes:
Dependent variable = remittances.
Error-correction parameters and long run coefficients computed using Pesaran's ADRL estimation method. See Pesaran and Pesaran (1997) for the specific computational methods used.

share of remittances in non-oil GDP does not form a long-run equilibrium with private investment as a share of non-oil GDP. However, increased remittances do cause a fairly sharp fall in the private investment/non-oil GDP ratio. Again, changes in private investment do not have a corresponding effect on remittances. When expressed as shares of non-oil GDP, public investment and remittances move together and form a long-run relationship. This relationship is negative, with increased remittances reducing government investment. All of this adjustment occurs through the error-correction term.

Table 8.9 Remittances and investment shares of non-oil GDP: full information estimate of error-correction model (shares of non-oil GDP)

Exogenous variables	Remittances/private investment		Remittances/public investment	
	Dependent variable		*Dependent variable*	
	Private investment	*Remittances*	*Public Investment*	*Remittances*
Constant	−8.55	4.83	11.92	3.61
	(−1.15)	(1.02)	(2.60)	(1.20)
Ecmt-1	−0.08	−0.04	−0.29	−0.11
	(−0.31)	(−0.32)	(−2.93)	(−0.69)
D investment		−0.20		−0.06
		(−0.87)		(−1.06)
Dt-1	−0.79		0.27	
	(−2.28)		(1.29)	
Dt-2	−1.04		0.37	
	(−2.98)		(1.69)	
Dt-3	−0.67		0.46	
	(−2.44)		(1.77)	
D remittances	0.15		−0.41	
	(0.10)		(−2.13)	
Dt-1	−1.24			
	(−3.09)			
Dt-2	−0.88			
	(−3.54)			
Dt-3	−0.36			
	(−2.20)			
Long-run coefficient	0.66	−4.77	−1.43	−0.53
	(0.89)	(−0.32)	(−2.96)	(−0.81)

Notes:
Dependent variable = remittances.
Error-correction parameters and long-run coefficients computed using Pesaran's ADRL estimation method. See Pesaran and Pesaran (1997) for the specific computational methods used.

Conclusions

For Saudi Arabia, the syndrome of sudden affluence in the 1970s was made possible by an economic order based on unearnt income. Specifically, the economic link between production and consumption was severed, while the government assumed the role of provider, establishing an elaborate welfare state and thus securing its role. As long as money was available to lubricate the economy, the system worked smoothly for over a decade or so. Even into the 1980s, with the transformation of the physical landscape progressing at high speed – with the building of an industrial infrastructure, hospitals, and utilities – the social and political structures were fixed and secured. Clearly, without the constant flow of funds through the elaborate income distribution networks, most of the status quo is unsustainable. It is no longer possible to cover up structural weaknesses and policy inconsistencies.[15]

In sum, the old system has run into diminishing returns and is no longer capable of sustaining high rates of economic growth. In particular, the breaking of the link between private investment and non-oil GDP appears to be the critical structural change occurring in recent years. Clearly, identification of the precise mechanisms through which the break occurred should be a high priority for future research. As for the present, one can only speculate as to the causes of this development, although several patterns associated with defense expenditures and remittances may provide a partial explanation. In particular, both defense expenditures and remittances appear to have reduced the provision of government expenditures – economic services, infrastructure, public investment – that ordinarily enhance the productivity of private investment. One can conclude that this also carries over to the quality of those services. In addition, increased remittances appear to depress private-sector investment in the short term. The effects associated with remittances and defense expenditures are therefore consistent with the observed decline in the effectiveness of private-sector investment in expanding non-oil GDP.

Notes

1 See Robert E. Looney's works, "A post-Keynesian assessment of alternative Saudi Arabian austerity strategies," *Kuwait University Journal of the Social Sciences*, vol. 23, no. 3, autumn, 1995, pp. 251–73; "Real or illusory growth in an oil-based economy: government expenditures and private sector investment in Saudi Arabia," *World Development*, vol. 20, 1992, pp. 1367–76; "Oil revenues and viable development: impact of the Dutch disease on Saudi diversification efforts," *American Arab Affairs*, no. 27, 1989, pp. 29–36; "Saudi Arabia's development strategy: comparative advantage versus sustainable growth," *Orient*, vol. 30, 1989, pp. 75–96.
2 A.M.A. Ghamdi, "Economic development and revenue instability: the Saudi experience," *METU Studies in Development*, vol. 19, no. 1, 1992, pp. 67–80.

3 M.H. Nagi, "Development with unlimited supplies of capital: the case of OPEC," *Developing Economies*, vol. XX, 1982, pp. 1–19; H. Beblawi and G. Luciani, *The Rentier State*, Croom Helm, London, 1987; Vahan Zanoyan, "After the oil boom," *Foreign Affairs*, vol. 74, no. 6, November/December, 1995, pp. 2–7; and K.A. Chaudhry's related works, "The price of wealth: business and state in labor remittance and oil economies," *International Organization*, vol. 43, 1989, pp. 101–46, and *The Price of Wealth: Economies and Institutions in the Middle East*, Cornell University Press, Ithaca, New York, 1987.

4 C.W.J. Granger, "Some recent developments in a concept of causality," *Journal of Econometrics*, vol. 39, 1988, pp. 199–211; and "Investigating causal relations by econometric models and cross-spectral methods," *Econometrica*, vol. 37, 1969, pp. 424–38.

5 C. Hsiao, "Autoregressive modeling and money-income causality detection," *Journal of Monetary Economics*, 1981, pp. 85–106.

6 D.L. Thornton and D.S. Batten, "Lag-length selection and tests of Granger causality between money and income," *Journal of Money, Credit and Banking*, 1985, pp. 164–78.

7 W.W. Charemza and D.F. Deadman, *New Directions in Econometric Practice: General to Specific Modelling, Cointegration and Vector Autoregression*, Aldershot, Hants, Edward Elgar, England, 1992.

8 N. Caiden and A. Wildavsky, *Planning and Budgeting in Poor Countries*, John Wiley, New York, 1974.

9 N. Hicks and Ann Kubisch, *Finance and Development*, 1984, pp. 37–9.

10 Robert E. Looney, "Budgetary priorities in Saudi Arabia: the impact of relative austerity measures on human capital formation," *OPEC Review*, vol. 15, no. 2, summer, 1991, pp. 133–52.

11 Hicks and Kubisch, "Cutting government expenditures in LDCs."

12 See consistent argument by S.M. Miller and F.S. Russek in "Cointegration and error correction models: the temporal causality between government spending and taxes," *Southern Economic Journal*, June, 1990, pp. 221–9.

13 *Saudi Arabia Country Report*, Economist Intelligence Unit, London, 1996.

14 M.H. Pesaran and M. Pesaran, *Microfit 4.0: Interactive Econometric Analysis*, Camfit Dats, Cambridge, 1997.

15 Paul Aarts, "Saudi Arabia: from fiscal crisis to political crisis?," *JIME Review*, no. 29, summer, 1995, pp. 23–34; B. Beedham, "The cash-flow of God," *Economist*, vol. 332, August 6, 1994; J. Gerth, "Saudi stability hit by heavy spending over last decade," *New York Times*, August 22, 1993; G.F. Gause, *Oil Monarchies: Domestic Security Challenges in the Arab Gulf States*, Council on Foreign Relations, New York, 1994; Zanoyan, "After the oil boom."

EPILOGUE: FROM COLD WAR TO COLD PEACE

Thoughts on the future of the peace process and the political economy of Middle East trade

George Wilson

Introduction

At Professor Wright's request, I have written a summary chapter that links past events and theories to the current Middle East peace process. However, in doing so I have decided to confine my remarks to two concepts on its events schema: historical origins which made it possible, and linkages between politics and trade that have served as barriers to productive diplomatics in Arab–Israeli negotiations. I will also make reference to the preceding chapters of this volume, which help engage dialogue in the phenomena associated with what is loosely known as the "Middle East."

The peace process

The Middle East peace process would have been inconceivable without the demise of the USSR in December, 1991, and the earlier termination of the cold war, which coincided with Gorbachev's assertion that "we will deny you an enemy." With Soviet and ex-USSR assistance to the Middle East cut off, and with the new Commonwealth of Independent States (CIS) supporting the Allied effort against Iraq, along with Saudi Arabia, Egypt, Syria, and others, while Jordan and the Palestinian Liberation Organization (PLO) took the Iraqi side against Kuwait, relationships among the Arab states were more thoroughly mixed than ever. In retrospect, a triple set of events from 1989 through 1991 – the détente between the former USSR and the U.S. that ended the cold war, the collapse of the Soviet empire, and the Gulf war – paved the road for implementing alternative approaches to resolving the Arab–Israeli struggle. All sides were induced to take new initiatives and risks not hitherto deemed feasible. Indeed, the very direction of the new initiatives was formed by these events, along with a willingness by both the Rabin–Peres and Bush–Quayle governments to settle the differences between Arabs and Israelis. Today the Arab governments seem collective only in that they remain suspicious of the Israelis' real agendas, a point Drake made in Chapter 1 and Gabbay in Chapter 6. What persists is the commonality of anti-Israeli feelings. If nothing else, the Benjamin Netanyahu administration has refocused this suspicion and brought back a façade of unity to the Arab world that was lost during the Gulf war.

Soviet decline and the end of the cold war

The major result of the long-running containment polices of both the U.S. and the USSR between 1945 and 1991 was, of course, the great non-event: no atomic war occurred. Its likelihood in the near future is now negligible and the ability to prevent a worldwide nuclear conflagration is greater than ever, despite the possible spread of nuclear materials to rogue hands. The other critical result of the ending of the cold war was the overwhelming victory of political and economic liberalism over autocracy in its varied forms (fascism, communism à la Russe, feudalism, etc.), and over detailed central planning in its communist or socialist forms. Adam Smith doubtless smiles, while Karl Marx is thoroughly upset with the Russians, whom he hated anyway, for so completely mucking up his ideas. So complete was the collapse of communism in the USSR and its Warsaw Pact satellites that some were led to believe in such things as "the end of history," a time, according to Fukuyama, marked only "by economic calculation, the endless solving of technical problems ... and centuries of boredom"![1]

This nonsense was based on a misrepresentation of Hegelian dialectics which maintained that the two remaining opportunists were communism and capitalism, and that the victory of the latter led to the end of the dialectic process and hence of history as well. We need not dwell on this, but the truth is that the great events of 1989–91 represent a global upheaval, the significance of which may exceed anything that has happened in the last 500 years, at least in terms of impacts on so large a proportion of the world so suddenly. However, as opposition groups continue to rise against the Middle East peace process, it is clear that the number of opportunists have not decreased. They may well have become more brazen as a result of economic decline.

Why did the USSR collapse and so fast?

The political and economic strength of the former Soviet Union was regularly and widely overestimated. Politically, the Kremlin failed to understand the increasing restiveness of the Soviets in the so-called "Near Abroad," whose ethnic mixes and problems were so different from those of the largely Russian center.[2] Economically, although most observers had recognized the dilapidation of the physical infrastructure and the long lines of people waiting outside shops which regularly ran out of even the most basic necessities, Soviet officials seem to feel there was no real sense of any fundamental malaise. Indeed, massive Soviet architecture seemed to represent a sense of (ugly) solidity and permanence, and certainly served to hide the extent of the inefficiencies engendered in a worn-out planning apparatus that systematically ignored market demands. Such failures are perhaps not surprising, since a key tenet of Marxism was to ignore market functions in determining prices.[3]

With such a distorted view of microeconomics and market mechanisms, it is little wonder that Western-style efficiency got such short shrift, and that resource allocation was perforce left to a central planning body unconcerned with, and certainly unaware of, individual wants or needs. How could agencies which believed that the value of a commodity consists only of the amount of socially necessary labor time it embodies possibly allocate scarce resources except by whim? If every unit of the value-creating substance creates the same amount of value whether it makes bicycles, vodka, or tractors, how could it allocate labor among alternative production processes sensibly? But individuals were ignored by Russian collectivism, so much so that one is reminded of the statement that as "a communist I love humanity but I hate people."[4]

The early result was tragic: evidence suggests millions died in Stalin's attempt to create a "new Soviet man" economy administered from the center via a regime that ignored "civil rights" in its zeal for producing "stuff," regardless of its market or social value. This central administration ran roughshod not only over the people, but also over the environment. Accordingly, this system lasted only as long as its leaders ruled with determined ruthlessness. Gorbachev's refusal to employ the ruthlessness of Stalin, Krushchev, or Brezhnev contributed to the collapse of the polity and economy, neither of which was as strong and robust as the Western world had feared. They did not even get half of the supply–demand apparatus right. The result was that, as Russian workers put it, "They pretend to pay us. We pretend to work." When reality dawned on the Kremlin, the "long, long patience of the plundered poor" had given out.[5]

Is this situation so different from that found now in Iraq or Iran, for example, where dictators rule only through ruthlessness? Or in the camps in Jordan and Palestine – which, as Ziai points out in Chapter 5, house more refugees per capita than any other region in the world – where the poor have lost their patience? Or in Lebanon, where the people suffer persistent bombing?

Capitalism triumphant

The end of the cold war ushered in a more or less global capitalistic approach to economic matters. However, long before this, the ability of such an approach to engender rapid growth had been demonstrated by Japan from about the mid-1950s. This was followed about a decade later by high growth rates in the so-called Asian Tiger economies – Hong Kong, Singapore, South Korea, and Taiwan, all of whom raised their economic levels (gross national/domestic product (GNP or GDP) per capita) from among the very lowest in the world to the top twenty within two or three decades. Japan maintained twenty years of growth exceeding an average of 10 percent per year. The others achieved similar growth of real GNP in the 1970s. These are growth rates unparalleled in recorded economic history.[6]

The general strategy was a heavy reliance on private enterprises aided or pushed by governments wanting to push exports to the then rapidly growing economies of North America and Western Europe. Like Israel and its immediate Arab neighbors, these miracle growth economies had little and had to rely on human talent for growth. Still, it is wrong to characterize them as originally strictly capitalistic because the Asian Tigers had plenty of government subsidies and were often offered the protection of market cartels. However, in contrast to the situation described in Wright's second case study in Chapter 2 on the Palestinian Authority (PA) or in Looney's discussion of the budgetary failures in Saudi Arabia (Chapter 8), the Asian governments expected accountability and profitability. Imports were monitored to include mostly investment goods to stimulate even faster growth and education, and higher savings rates; entrepreneurship in small and medium-sized enterprises (SMEs) was strongly encouraged. And – not so dissimilarly to the situation Nitzan and Bichler describe in Chapter 3 concerning Israel's war economy – the post-war takeoff for Japan was also stimulated by the Korean war because, as the U.S. procurement center for the Korean war, Japan was enabled to hold the yen at unusually low levels. The U.S. also protected several Asian Tiger nations from both external aggression and internal conflict, giving them production flexibility.

The economic successes of the market-oriented capitalistic approaches taken in many Asian countries contrast sharply with the economic failures blatantly revealed by the collapse of communism and with the market malaise seen in the Arab countries, which continue to maintain centralized distribution systems and centralized controls. The process continues, invigorated by an explosion of new technologies that have rapidly been diffused around the world, thereby stimulating global markets in many goods and services. This has generated a plethora of new market and market-niche opportunities that transcend national boundaries. Malaysia, Thailand, and more recently Indonesia have become the second wave of new Asian Tigers. Fortunately, there are a few rapidly growing Arab states, such as those now being called the Trucial Tigers, i.e. Oman, Qatar, and the United Arab Emirates (UAE), which have recently taken monumental strides toward economic liberalism. Unfortunately, these are not the Arab states where poverty is rampant and which are breeding revolutionary movements. In

Egypt and Jordan, in particular, earlier movements toward liberalism have recently been reversed. This promotes neither democracy nor development.

Moreover, since the peace process began, trends toward market liberalism have increasingly reflected the wish of some Arab nations – and certainly of Israel – to remove barriers which impede their participation in the global economic sphere. The prerequisites for this are developing regional, as well as national, efficiencies and comparative advantages. Some tradeoffs will be necessary in order for this goal to be reached by nations whose conflicting trade agendas engender base levels of distrust in a regional system. As Gabbay pointed out in Chapter 6, the development of regional electricity and power infrastructures would likely produce cost efficiencies and would facilitate the development of regional comparative advantages. However, it is also true that the nation which controls the land on which these facilities are built will enhance its political influence in the region. That is implicit in any set of policies designed to stimulate growth. Neither side in the Middle East peace process is likely to let this latter factor pass its doors easily.

Still, global economic integration provides special opportunities at this time. Even without a peace process – which essentially seeks to strip away certain political and religious barriers to trade not only within the Middle East but also beyond – the Arab states and Israel need to set reforms in order to pursue these opportunities. Therefore the peace process, if viewed through economic lenses – as is proposed in the preface – should best be seen as a means for making the changes these nations have long needed to make. The opportunity presented now is that reforms can happen on a regional scale.

Admittedly, there is less unanimity in the political sphere concerning the necessity for democratic arrangements such as free and dual-party elections. But elections, while valuable, are not the only form of participation which can support a liberalized market system. Successful market economies in Asia did not begin with much in the way of electoral democracy. At the same time, proven electoral systems have not always led to successful capitalism, as India and the Philippines illustrate. Thus, while "Emirate capitalism" will continue to persist in the Middle East, it need not impede growth – that is, as long as leaders promote market expansion instead of industrial protectionism.

The same may be said with respect to religion, although some religions may be more compatible than others with the emergence of certain capitalistic institutions, the sanctioning of the profit motive, and private property, including instruments of production, as a means for enhancing community development and the just distribution of resources. Certainly, this has historically been the case with Islam and most Protestant denominations.[7] The point is that religion has not impaired economic development in countries supporting free markets. This is evident in the Asian Tigers, and in many Catholic and Muslim countries as well. For example, the list of the richest twenty-three nations in the world – those the World Bank refers to as "high-income economies" (from $12,210 (Ireland) to $36,080 (Switzerland) in terms of GNP per capita in 1992) contains one or more countries whose dominant religion is Protestantism, Catholicism, Islam, Judaism, Buddhism-Shinto, and Confucianism. Only Hinduism is missing among them. For nations exhibiting fairly rapid GNP or GDP growth per capita per year between 1980 and 1992 – say 3 percent or more – only three out of sixteen are Christian.[8] The implication of this is that a highly successful market system can develop and thrive more or less independently of the predominant religious belief in any given nation.

Thus in the present context it is a fair generalization that neither religion nor the political systems necessarily have a decisive influence on the creation of an effectively functioning market system unless the authorities in either sphere actively seek to stifle trade. Iran's theocracy and Iraq's dictatorship show the type of gratuitous costs that can be foisted upon citizens. But in reality it is selfish leaderships and not the predominant religion of Islam that constitutes serious obstacles to market development in these countries. After all, the Prophet was a merchant, and his views on usury do not prevent capital markets from functioning, as is evidenced by the rapid growth in Islamic banking. Nor is it necessary to embellish a full-blown democracy although, with its emphasis on individualism, democracy is more consistent with free markets than authoritarianism, and provides a more efficient way to change political leadership without bloodshed and revolution.

The issue of process

The economic dimension of the peace process is fairly straightforward. After Arab hostility toward Israel got beyond pretending that the state did not exist, or that the country could and would be driven into the sea, the Arabs and Israelis could discuss matters of peace, at least as a mere absence of war, and perhaps even agree to more or less permanent boundaries.[9] Since the end of the cold war, the fall of the USSR, the Gulf war, and at least into the Peres government, this seems to be well understood.

What is needed now is not only a ceasefire, but also a long-lasting peace. This requires a process to ensure its continuance and to attract long-term capital or even public capital from outside the region. In Chapter 1 there is an excellent discussion of what is meant by a "process" as distinguished from an "event," and Laura Drake defines the word "normalization" as used by Peres as being "achieved through the exchange of embassies, cultural, and interpersonal cooperation ... and, eventually, a unified security regime." I will simply highlight this from the economic perspective.

Economic ties between two or more nations are crucial in building regional cooperation and, indeed, peaceful collaboration. Once established on the basis of mutual profitability, they require movement, more or less free, of goods, people, capital, resources, and indirect communications across borders. If mutually beneficial, these movements will be difficult to break as long as they continue to hold out opportunities for entrepreneurs to function profitably. A good deal of private and public capital is available globally and is actively seeking opportunities for the kinds of investments that should prove viable in the Middle East if the region can effectively reduce the risks that now persist in the region. Once several large connections or joint operations are begun, the tenacity with which they will be sustained and expanded may be substantial. If more of these types of relationships come about, the vulnerability of any single state in the region to other non-economic types of friction (ethnic, religious, etc.) should be reduced. Strong economic ties and a bustling economy should act as a solution for many problems and a glue to help hold a country (or region) together. This is the basis of Keynes's quip many years ago:

> [D]angerous human proclivities can be canalized into comparatively harmless channels by the existence of opportunities for money-making and private wealth, which, if they cannot be satisfied in this way, may find their outlet in cruelty, the reckless pursuit of personal power and authority, and other forms of self-aggrandizement. It is better that a man should tyrannize over his bank balance than over his fellow-citizens.[10]

Of course, economic matters may themselves lead to conflict, but if there are many commercial arrangements in a multitude of areas or industries the broader incentive to keep the channels of trade open may forestall and even prevent a wider conflict. Many savants have viewed economic activity as an outlet for competitive and combative spirits, and even for promoting more rational behavior in the workforce. There is much ambiguity in these more or less benign side-effects of greater reliance on a free-market system. Certainly the view, often vaguely expressed, that the militancy of any state can be much reduced by simply strengthening economic ties, is more than a little far-fetched. It is, however, useful to remember that the beginnings of the post-Second World War European Economic Community (EEC) started with a distinctly and strictly economic arrangement, the European Coal and Steel Community (ECSC), in 1952. This arose from the Schuman Plan of 1950, which proposed a union of the French and German coal and steel industries, with the deliberate intention of making a future war between these two countries impossible. It was so successful that it became the proto-type for the now larger European Union (EU). Trade ties may or may not be used again for such purposes with such success, but one thing *is* certain about foreign trade: it is very much a positive-sum process. There are real net benefits for all participants. This will be true in Arabia, too, especially if the GCC states can reach policy planning parity.

The politics of trade

In the present context, "politics" refers to the terms and conditions under which goods and services, as well as people, are allowed to cross borders from one country to another. It also specifies which commodities, services, and people will be allowed to enter or leave. All such trade is inevitably "political," since it is the political process that initially sets the rules and then changes them as the political need is perceived differently. All politics is not about trade, but all regulations concerning trade are political. This does not mean that such rules are not often violated. Even the Arab embargo against Israel failed to prevent many products evading these trade edicts.

The reasons for this were revealed several hundred years ago. The political element of trade perhaps reached its apex when a system of government known as "mercantilism" or "Cameralism" was in vogue in France, England, Germany, Italy, and other countries. It was so entrenched that Adam Smith wrote *The Wealth of Nations* in 1776 largely to refute its pernicious doctrines, and in the process developed the rationale for the then emerging market system. In any event, for countries without gold mines or colonies from which gold and silver could be stolen, the only way to acquire bullion, deemed necessary to finance wars and the extravagances of rulers, was to stimulate domestic exports via subsidies or special incentives, and to restrict imports through the use of embargoes or high tariffs. Since other nations would be trying to do the same thing, the incentive to retaliate was very high and therefore induced conflict, and often war.

The mercantilist position was further self-defeating beyond the retaliation problem because, as David Hume later pointed out, it sought to impede a "naturally operative system" allocating the world supply of bullion between trading nations. What they failed to recognize was that cross-border trade competition is definitely not a zero-sum game. That means the total output of all commodities will be greater than if trade is not interfered with if the first country specializes in producing those goods in which its "comparative advantage" is greatest and the less efficient country produces those goods where its "comparative disadvantage" is least. Through free trade the gains will be distributed between the countries in proportion to their relative demands for each. Both sides are therefore better off than without international trade.

The essence of this theorem is apparently somewhat subtle and therefore is supported by virtually all economists, while most politicians, workers, and citizens disagree violently when arguments over tariffs, cheap foreign labor, and the like arise. In the Middle East most nations seem to fear fuller participation in free trade and the great, surging global market. But overcoming these fears will enable the region to address its most pressing problems. Huge differences in economic levels exist between most Arab countries and their citizenries, as has been discussed in earlier chapters; in

Jordan, Lebanon, Syria, Egypt, and the Palestinian "entity," GDP per head varies from a low of barely $550 in Egypt to a high of $1300 in Syria (1991 prices), while in Israel it is almost $12,000. The extreme poverty of Israel's neighbors gives them little scope for experimentation with free trade or much else without some fairly substantial assistance guarantees to tide them over perhaps for many years. Fear of the total economic dominance of Israel in a regime of fair trade is an impediment almost as large as the fundamental mistrust between the Arabs and Jews that has continued since Israel's creation. The free-trade route to a lasting peace will be hard to sell to the poorer Arab states, and will require numerous modifications before one can expect an outcome as benign as the theory implies. Even free trade between Canada and the U.S. – agreements between "good neighbors" with much in common – took years of negotiation, and the North American Free-Trade Agreement (NAFTA) was more difficult still. This highlights the magnitude of the task in the Middle East.

Yet, ultimately, this is the only way to improve the economies of the poorest countries and to achieve a permanent ceasefire. In the present context, I mean the general thrust toward market orientation across highly sensitive borders, such as Syria, Lebanon, Jordan, Egypt, and Israel, long-lasting peace is dependent on some tangible progress being made toward closer commercial and economic integration.

The opening of an air route between Israel and Jordan and the establishment of air transportation between the PA territories and the region are the sorts of developments that need to be extended to other industries or services. "Managed trade" or disguised protectionism has not worked well, even in large countries like India, and it continues to impede growth in the Arab states. Thus what is being tried in the Middle East, and is so ably discussed in the earlier chapters, is "the only way" to go; it has both theoretical and analytical basis, and it has been more successful than other paths.

But markets must be both free and fair. Most people are aware that a market-only approach will lead to inequalities within nations and among them. A market approach implies competition, and hence winners and losers. The results to be expected are a far higher output of higher-quality goods and services than people are willing to buy. It also implies the absence of monopoly, and of course the openness of free trade among nations and fair entry into domestic markets as well. Private property and a legal system that supports it and sanctions the profit motive are necessary too. Countries that find these features immoral or unworthy may of course opt out or seek modification in the implementation. Even countries that basically accept the requirements for the economic outcomes of competitive capitalism can and do provide safety nets for their citizens, as was pointed out by Adam Smith in 1776, Galbraith in 1971, and Wright et al. in this volume.[11]

The future of the peace process

The strategy proposed throughout this book is to use economic leverage via freer markets, more open borders, commercial cooperation, and trade inter-dependencies as means for creating an atmosphere in which peoples and nations – such as Arabs and Israelis – who have historically harbored enor-mous tension and extreme mistrust can live and work together in harmony. Since what is likely to develop along current lines is dominance by Israel, against whom most of the tension and hatred is directed, it is unlikely that new trade relationships alone will suffice to sustain "normalization." It is a most tenuous assumption to believe that growing economic integration of the bilateral kind involved here (i.e., Israel–Lebanon, Israel–Syria, Israel–Jordan, etc.) will suffice to change feelings of antipathy and prejudice on either side.

Furthermore, the basic problem is not one of trade expansion per se, but belongs to a broader set of problems with crucial economic impacts; it remains intimately related to the poverty level of Palestinian refugees, some living within camp walls where they at least receive aid, and others else-where in the region with little or no access to the most basic resources. These Palestinians are now, after almost fifty years, the descendants of those who were originally dispossessed of their lands and livelihoods after the creation of the state of Israel. From the *First Interim Report of the UN Economic Survey Mission for the Middle East* in December of 1949 to the present day, economic incentives – providing employment opportunities, educational and health assistance, dreaming about grandiose schemes to harness the River Jordan, stimulating economic growth, especially in areas of refugee concentration, creating special incentives (i.e. bribes) to convince refugees to resettle elsewhere in the region, and so on – have all been to no avail. The refugees, in particular, and Arabs, in general, feel this grave injustice should be met with "restitution". It is doubtless naive to believe that economic growth stimulated by agreements on intra-regional trade liberalization will be enough to achieve "normalization" in the Israelis' sense of the word. Laura Drake's statement that "Arab populations seem to want prosperity rather than confrontation ... but also without Israelis directly in their midst" is all too true and is likely to remain the case. Of course, the goals of absence of war and improved economic status for the poor Arab states should not be disparaged. But if the fate of the Palestinians was the original concern, and if this remains the central issue, then the failure remains as monumental as it was almost half a century ago.

Can we eschew such pessimism? Possibly. After all, some reasonably intelligent people believe that there exists or perhaps will shortly exist a "new world economic order" driven by global markets that will initially push many nations of the world to band together into common markets as a first step; these will then evolve into economic unions and finally into new political states. If this is a realistic scenario, then the existing peace process in the Middle East may work out if global markets keep growing and driving regional groupings, including the Middle East, along with them. This assumes, among other things, that the regional blocs do not behave like their former components and act like greedy mercantilists. Unfortunately, as the case studies presented earlier, greed may have taken root too deeply on all sides of the field. It also assumes, more importantly, that Israel will be accepted among its neighbors almost like any other state in the region, and that Israelis will resist the urge to implement discriminatory and protectionist policies and legal structures. As the degeneration of civil society in Palestine continues – as so aptly illustrated by Ziai in Chapter 5 – and as the peace process becomes bogged down as a result of Mr. Netanyahu's administration, this may be unrealistic. Still, there remain reasons to be hopeful.

The current world situation

In fact, as is proposed in this work, the world economic climate may not be supportive of efforts to reconcile the differences between Arabs and Israelis. The peace process and the end of the cold war coincided with a world economic slump. Even the U.S. suffers from what I choose to call twenty years of "high-level creeping stagnation."[12]

It was no accident that the U.S. "accepted" payments from other nations for its role in the Gulf war, that it is the biggest "deadbeat" in the United Nations, and that it otherwise uses the excuse of not being able to "afford" certain activities unless they can be shown to be especially attractive and do not cost much in the first place. Can the world afford such a "deadbeat" superpower? The answer is no: the world needs leadership.

And then there is the U.S. fiscal deficit – namely, the foreign trade deficit – which has also contributed to the overall sluggishness of the economy. U.S. exports of goods and services exceeded imports every year between 1946 and 1982. Net exports have been negative ever since, reaching record levels of well over $100 billion from 1984 through 1988, and again during 1994 and 1995. During this period the U.S. shifted from being the world's biggest creditor to become its largest debtor. Even the Social Security Trust Fund is mortgaged. The chronic net export deficit contributes to the overall sluggishness of the economy, since it subtracts directly from total spending for the other components of annual GDP. It also makes the U.S. an even less willing donor to countries that need foreign capital, unless it can see how those aid distributions either protect its domestic corporations from foreign competition or in some way create net positive returns for American firms. The U.S. will ultimately support sensible arrangements like those embodied in the EU, NAFTA, the Association of South-east Asian Nations (ASEAN), and in areas like the Middle East, but given its recent stagflation this is unlikely to become policy soon.

What this means specifically for the Middle East and the peace process is that a buoyant world economy cannot be counted on, since the U.S., the largest player in most global markets, remains bogged down in an economic and industrial policy quagmire. One must reluctantly conclude that neither the Middle East nor any other area seeking to develop economically can expect much special external stimulus or Marshall Plan-type help from the U.S. anywhere near the beginning of the new millennium. Israel may remain a special case, but as Nitzan and Bichler point out in Chapter 3, the fact is that U.S. firms and their partners in Israel gain much from American military assistance and development aid. As for the Arab side, the situation does not mean that international trade will not provide an engine for positive growth. However, they will have to assert their positions in the global markets by building successful corporate and economic structures and networks. To do less than this will result in their continuing to be absorbed by the economic and political manipulations of others, which makes setting and satisfying their own policy agendas impossible.

Notes

1 Francis Fukuyama, 'The end of history', *The National Interest* 18 (summer).
2 For a fascinating analysis of this, see Helene Carrere d'Encausse, *The End of the Soviet Empire*, Basic Books, Harper Collins, New York, 1993.
3 Karl Marx, *Capital*, Modern Library, New York, 1906, p. 44, part 1, ch. 1.
4 Edna St. Vincent Millay, *Aria de Capo*, 1920.
5 This is a phrase used to describe the socialist uprisings of the 1840s in Western Europe directed against the exploitative nature of the then evolving capitalist system and also the later 1848 uprisings. Ironically, it is more applicable to the Eastern European revolutions of 1989–91.
6 Even with the currency crashes seen throughout Asia in 1998, their economic successes are historically significant, as are the rates of recovery being seen in several of the Asian countries.
7 R. H. Tawney, *Religion and the Rise of Capitalism*, Harcourt Brace, New York, 1926; and Max Weber, *The Protestant Ethic and the Spirit of Capitalism*, translated by Talcott Parsons, George, Allen & Unwin, London, 1930.
8 World Bank, *World Development Report*, New York, Oxford University Press, Table 1, Basic Indicators, 1994, pp. 162–3.
9 "The PLO is believed to have removed any references from the Palestinian National Charter to the destruction of the State of Israel. However, there is some belief, not only in Israeli circles, that this never really happened. Although several weeks before the recent elections, Shimon Peres, while still Prime Minister, hailed the apparent move as 'the greatest revolution that the Middle East had known in the last hundred years,' there is some evidence in the above article that the PLO has not, in fact, yet removed such references and still proclaims the goal of liberating Palestine. This cannot be pursued further here but it remains an obstacle to the process I wish to take up now" (Y. Porath, "Antisocial text", *New Republic*, 8 July, 1996, p. 9).
10 John Maynard Keynes, *The General Theory of Employment, Interest and Money*, London, Macmillan, London, 1951, p. 374.

11 Adam Smith, *An Inquiry into the Nature and Causes of the Wealth of Nations*, 1776, Modern Library, New York, 1937, pp. 78–9; John Kenneth Galbraith, *A Contemporary Guide to Economics, Peace and Laughter*, Boston, Mass., Houghton Mifflin Company, 1971.

12 The following are a few of the results of this situation: the growth of family incomes has virtually stagnated since 1973 despite an increase in the number of workers per family; the national unemployment rate was an average of two percentage points higher during the 1970s and 1980s than it had been in the preceding two decades; and the poverty rate in the last several years is higher than it was in 1971. These phenomena went unnoticed until 1991, when Wallace Peterson wrote the article "The silent depression" (*Challenge*, July–August, 1991), on which Eric Hobsbawm then based his article "The crisis decades" (*The Age of Extremes*, Pantheon, New York, 1994, ch. 14), and which led to Jeffrey Madrick's *The End of Affluence* (Random House, New York, 1995)

SELECT BIBLIOGRAPHY

Aarts, P. (1995) "Saudi Arabia: from fiscal crisis to political crisis?," *JIME Review* 29, summer: 23–34.

Abed, G. T. (1988) *The Palestinian Economy: Studies in Development Under Prolonged Occupation*, London: Routledge.

Agreement on Gaza and the Jericho Area (1994) Cairo, Egypt, May 4.

Aharoni, Y. (1969) "Institutional rigidity and resource utilization," in Hebrew, *Economic Quarterly* 16(62), July: 157–68.

—— (1976) *Structure and Performance in the Israeli Economy*, in Hebrew, Tel Aviv: Cherikover.

—— (1991) *The Political Economy of Israel*, in Hebrew, Tel Aviv: Am Oved and the Levi Eshkol Institute.

American Academy of Arts and Sciences (1992) *Transition to Palestinian Self-government: Practical Steps Toward Israeli–Palestinian Peace*, report, Cambridge, MA, and Bloomington, IN: American Academy of Arts and Sciences (AAAS) and Indiana University Press.

'Aqiqi, A. (1959) *Lebanon in the Last Years of Feudalism: A Contemporary Account*, trans. M. Kerr, Beirut: American University of Beirut.

Arian, A. (1985) *Politics and Government in Israel*, in Hebrew, Tel Aviv: Zmora-Bitan.

—— (1989) *Politics in Israel: The Second Generation*, 2nd edition, Chatham, NJ: Chatham House.

Asadi, F. (1990) "How viable will the agricultural economy be in the new state of Palestine?," *GeoJournal* 21(4): 375–83.

Averitt, R. T. (1968) *The Dual Economy*, New York: W. W. Norton.

Balaj, B., Diwan, I. and Philippe, B. (1998) "External assistance to the Palestinians: what went wrong," in J. W. Wright, Jr. (ed.) *Economic and Political Impediments to Peace in the Middle East: Structural Flaws and Crucial Failures in the Process*, London: Macmillan.

Barakat, H. (ed.) (1988) *Toward a Viable Lebanon*, Washington, DC: Center for Contemporary Arab Studies, Georgetown University.

Barkey, H. (1995) "Can the Middle East compete?," in L. Diamond and M. Plattner (eds.) *Economic Reform and Democracy*, Baltimore, MD: Johns Hopkins University Press.

Barnet, R. J. (1972) *Roots of War: The Men and Institutions Behind U.S. Foreign Policy* New York: Atheneum.

240

Barnett, M. N. (1992) *Confronting the Costs of War: Military Power, State, and Society in Egypt and Israel*, Princeton, NJ: Princeton University Press.

Beblawi, H. and Luciani, G. (1987) *The Rentier State*, London: Croom Helm.

Becker, G. (1964) *Human Capital*, New York: National Bureau of Economics and Research, Columbia University Press.

—— (1971) *The Economics of Discrimination*, Chicago, IL: University of Chicago Press.

—— (1993) "An economic approach to behavior: the Nobel lecture," *Journal of Political Economy* 101(3), June: 385–409.

Becker, G. and Murphy, K. J. (1990) "Human capital, fertility and economic growth," *Journal of Political Economy* 98(5): 12–33.

Bejsky, M., Ziller, V., Hirsh, Z., Sarnat Z. and Friedman, D. (1986) *Report of the Commission of Inquiry into the Manipulation of Banking Shares*, in Hebrew, Jerusalem: Government Printer.

Ben-Basset, A. and Marom, A. (1988) "Is the demand for money in Israel stable? (1965–1983)," *Bank of Israeli Economic Review* 60, January: 52–71.

Ben Dor, G. (1977) "Politics and the military in Israel in the seventies," in Hebrew, in M. Lissak and E. Gutmann (eds.) *The Israeli Political System*, Tel Aviv: Am Oved.

Ben-Porath, Y. (ed.) (1986) *The Israeli Economy: Maturing Through Crises*, Cambridge, MA, and London: Harvard University Press.

Ben-Rafael, E. and Sharot, S. (1991) *Ethnicity, Religion and Class in Israeli Society*, Cambridge: Cambridge University Press.

Ben-Shahar, H., Fishelson, G. and Hirsch, S. (1989) *Economic Cooperation and Middle East Peace*, London: Weidenfeld & Nicolson.

Berglas, E. (1970) "Defense, standard of living, and foreign debt," in Hebrew, *Economic Quarterly* 17(67), September: 191–202.

—— (1983) "Defense and the Economy: The Israeli Experience," discussion paper no. 83.01, Jerusalem: Maurice Falk Institute of Economic Research.

Bichler, S. (1991) "The political economy of military spending in Israel," in Hebrew, unpublished doctoral dissertation, Jerusalem: Department of Political Science, Hebrew University.

—— (1994–5) "Political shifts in Israel, 1997 and 1992: unsuccessful electoral economics or long range realignment?," *Science and Society* 58: 415–39; revised as "Between capitalism and Jewish voters: electoral economics in Israel, 1977 to 1997," in J. W. Wright, Jr. (ed.) *Economic and Political Impediments to Middle East Peace: Structural Flaws and Crucial Failings in the Process*, London; Macmillan.

Bichler, S. and Nitzan, J. (1996) "Military spending and differential accumulation: a new approach to the political economy of armament – the case of Israel," *Review of Radical Political Economics* 28(1): 52–97.

—— (forthcoming) "Putting the state in its place: US foreign policy and differential capital accumulation in Middle-East 'energy conflicts,'" *Review of International Political Economy*.

Birks, J. S. and Sinclare, C. A. (1992) "Repatriation, remittances, and reunions: what is really at stake for Arab countries supplying labour to the Gulf Co-operation Council States?," C. E. Davies (ed.) *Global Interests in the Arab Gulf*, Exeter: University of Exeter Press.

241

Brand, L. A. (1993) "The economics of shifting alliances: Jordan's relations with Syria and Iraq, 1975–1981," *International Journal of Middle East Studies* 26(2), May: 301–26.

Caiden, N. and Wildavsky, A. (1974) *Planning and Budgeting in Poor Countries*, New York: John Wiley.

Chaudhry, K. A. (1977) *The Price of Wealth: Economies and Institutions in the Middle East*, Ithaca, NY: Cornell University Press.

—— (1989) "The price of wealth: business and state in labor remittance and oil economies," *International Organization* 43: 101–46.

Choueiri, Y. (ed.) (1993) *State and Society in Syria and Lebanon*, New York: St. Martin's Press.

Clawson, P. (1992) "The limited scope for economic cooperation in the contemporary Levant," in S. L. Spiegel (ed.) *The Arab–Israeli Search for Peace*, Boulder, CO: Lynne Reiner Publishers.

—— (1994) "Mideast economies after the Israel–PLO handshake," *Journal of International Affairs* 48(1), summer: 155–9.

Clawson, P. and Rosen, H. (1995) "The economic consequences of peace for Israel, the Palestinians and Jordan," policy paper no. 25, in *Report of the American Academy of Arts and Sciences*, Washington Institute for Near East Policy.

Cockburn, A. and Cockburn, L. (1991) *Dangerous Liaison: The Inside Story of the U.S.–Israeli Covert Relationship*, Toronto: Stoddart Publishing.

Cooley, J. K. (1992) "Middle East water: power for peace," *Middle East Policy* 1(2): 12.

Cotran, E. and Mallat, C. (eds.) (1996) *The Arab–Israeli Accords: Legal Perspectives*, London: Kluwer International Law.

Coulton, N. A. (1998) "Between supply shocked markets," in J. W. Wright, Jr. (ed.) *Economic and Political Impediments to Peace in the Middle East: Structural Flaws and Crucial Failures in the Process*, London: Macmillan.

Dahl, R. A. (1991) *A Preface to Economic Democracy*, Los Angeles, CA: University of California Press.

Declaration of Principles on Interim Self-government Arrangements (1993) Washington, DC, 13 September.

"Developing the Palestinian economy: an interview with George T. Abed" (1994) *Journal of Palestine Studies* 23(4): 41–51.

Drury, R. T. and Winn, R. C. (1992) *Plowshares and Swords: The Economics of Occupation in the West Bank*, Boston, MA: Beacon Press.

Eban, A. (1995) "The six days war," in W. Laqueur and B. Rubin (eds.) *The Israel–Arab Reader*, 5th edition, New York: Penguin.

Falk, R. A. and Weston, B. H. (1992) "The relevance of international law to Israeli and Palestinian rights in the West Bank and Gaza," in E. Playfair (ed.) *International Law and the Administration of Occupied Territories*, Oxford: Clarendon Press.

Farsoun, S. (1995) "The Arabs: preparing for the 21st century," *Mideast Monitor* 10(2), spring: 10.

Fawaz, L. (1994) *An Occasion for War: Civil Conflict in Lebanon and Damascus in 1860*, London: I. B. Tauris.

Feiler, G. (1993) *Labor Migration in the Middle East Following the Iraqi Invasion of Kuwait*, Jerusalem: Israel/Palestine Center for Research and Information.

Feisler, G. (1993) "Palestinian employment prospects," *Middle East Journal* 47(4), autumn: 633–51.

Field, M. (1996) *Modernizing the Arab Economies*, Stabsabteilung Friedrich-Ebert-Stiftung.

Fischbach, M. R. (1994) "The implications of Jordanian land policy for the West Bank," *Middle East Journal* 47(4), summer: 492–651.

Fishelson, G. (1992) "Regional economic cooperation in the Middle East," in S. L. Spiegel (ed.) *The Arab–Israeli Search for Peace*, Boulder, CO: Lynne Rienner Publishers.

Ford, K. and Peterson, D. (1996) "Conducting business in the West Bank and Gaza," *Developing Alternatives* 5(2), fall 1995/winter 1996: 1–6.

Fourth Geneva Convention, Arts. 6, 16, 17, 33, 47, 55, 59, 76.

Gabbay, S. M. (1997) *Social Capital in the Creation of Financial Capital*, Champaign, IL: Stipes.

Galbraith, J. K. (1958) *The Affluent Society*, Boston, MA: Houghton Mifflin Company.

—— (1959) *Economics and the Art of Controversy*, New York: Vintage Books.

—— (1971) *A Contemporary Guide to Economics, Peace, and Laughter*, ed. A. D. Williams, Boston, MA: Houghton Mifflin Company.

Gates, C. (1989) *The Historical Role of Political Economy in the Development of Modern Lebanon*, Oxford Centre for Lebanese Studies, Oxford.

Gause, G. F. (1994) *Oil Monarchies: Domestic Security Challenges in the Arab Gulf States*, New York: Council on Foreign Relations.

Gerges, F. A. (1995) "Egyptian–Israeli relations turn sour," *Foreign Affairs* 74(3), May/ June: 70.

Ghamdi, A. M. A. (1992) "Economic development and revenue instability: the Saudi experience," *METU Studies in Development* 19(1): 67–80.

Goldberg, G. (1992) *Political Parties in Israel: From Mass Parties to Electoral Parties*, Tel Aviv: Ramot, Tel Aviv University.

Government of Israel, the Ministries of Foreign Affairs and Finance (1994) *Development Options for Regional Cooperation*, proposals to the Middle East and North Africa Economic Summit, Casablanca, Morocco, October, IV-5–1, IV-5–2, IV-6–2, IV-6–10.

Gozansky, T. (1986) *Formation of Capitalism in Palestine*, Haifa: Miphalim Universitaim.

Greenwood, C. "The administration of the occupied territories in international law," in E. Playfair (ed.) *International Law and the Administration of Occupied Territories*, Oxford: Clarendon Press.

Gulati, R. (1995), "Does familiarity breed trust? The implications of repeated ties for contractual choices in alliances," *Academy of Management Journal* 38: 85–112.

HC 337/71 (1972) *The Christian Society for the Holy Places v. Minister of Defense et al.*, 26(1), Piskei Din 574.

Hague Regulations, Art. 50.

Hakeynee, R. (1994) "The political process and the elites: statements by the elites regarding the peace process from the mid-1980s until the Declaration of Principles (September 1993)," in Hebrew, mimeograph, Jerusalem: Hebrew University.

Halevi, N. and Klinov-Malul, R. (1968) *The Economic Development of Israel*, New York and Jerusalem: Praeger.

Haley, P. E. and Snider, L. (eds.) (1979) *Lebanon in Crisis: Participants and Issues*, Syracuse: Syracuse University Press.

Hasid, N. and Lesser, O. (1981) "Economic resources for Israel's security," in Hebrew, *Economic Quarterly* 28(109): 243–52.

Hass, A. (1995) "Gaza's workers and the Palestinian Authority," *Middle East Report*, May–June/July–August: 26, 27.

Hazboun, S. and Bahiri, S. (1994) "Palestinian industrial development and Israeli–Palestinian attitudes to cooperation," *Palestine–Israeli Journal of Politics, Economics, and Culture* 1(4), autumn: 74–81.

Horowitz, D. (1982) "The Israeli defense forces: a civilianized military in a partially militarized society," in R. Kolkowitz and Korbonski (eds.) *Soldiers, Peasants and Bureaucrats*, London: George Allen & Unwin.

—— (1989) *Trouble in Utopia: The Overburdened Polity of Israel*, Albany, NY: State University of New York Press.

Horowitz, D. and Lissak, M. (1988) "Democracy and national security in a continuous conflict," in Hebrew, *Yahadoot Zemanenu* 4: 27–65.

Hudson, M. (1968) *The Precarious Republic: Political Modernization in Lebanon*, New York: Random House.

Israeli Military Order No. 378 (Arts. 89 & 90) (1988) in *Al-Haq: Law in the Service of Man, Punishing a Nation: Human Rights Violations during the Palestinian Uprising, December 1987–1988*, Al-Haq, Ramallah, December: 260, 277.

Israeli–Palestinian Declaration of Principles, Annex IV: "Protocol on Israeli-Palestinian Cooperation Concerning Regional Development Programs," section B-4: "Regional Desalinization and other water development projects," 13 September.

Israeli–Palestinian Interim Agreement on the West Bank and Gaza Strip (1995) Washington, DC, September.

Jawhary, M. (1995) *The Palestinian–Israeli Trade Agreements: Searching for Fair Revenue-sharing*, Jerusalem: Palestine Economic Research Institute (MAS).

Johnson, M. (1986) *Class and Client in Beirut: The Sunni Muslim Community and the Lebanese State, 1840–1985*, London: Ithaca Press.

Keohane, R. O. and Nye, J. S. (1989) *Power and Interdependence: World Politics in Transition*, 2nd edition, London: Scott, Foresman & Company.

Khalaf, S. (1979) *Persistence and Change in 19th-century Lebanon: A Sociological Essay*, Beirut: American University of Beirut.

—— (1987) *Lebanon's Predicament*, New York: Columbia University Press.

Khalidi, A. S. (1988) *The Arab Economy in Israel: The Dynamics of a Region's Development*, London: Croom Helm.

—— (1988) "The economy of the Palestinian Arabs in Israel," in G. Abed (ed.) *The Palestinian Economy*, London: Routledge.

—— (1995) "Security in a final Middle East settlement: some components of Palestinian national security," *International Affairs* 71(1): 1–18.

Klieman, A. (1992) *Double-edged Sword: Israeli Defense Exports as an Instrument of Foreign Policy*, in Hebrew, Tel Aviv: Am Oved.

Kretzmer, D. (1987) *The Legal Status of Arabs in Israel*, Tel Aviv: International Center for Peace in the Middle East.

Kubursi, A. (1995) "The economics of peace: the Arab response," *Regional Economic Development in the Middle East: Opportunities and Risks*, symposium by Center for Policy Analysis on Palestine, Washington, DC, 6 October.

Kuttab, D. (1994) "The peace process and the Palestinian interest: an interview with Sari Nusseibeh," *Palestine–Israeli Journal of Politics, Economics, and Culture* 1(4), autumn: 69–73.

Land and Water Establishment (1996) *Update on the Human Rights Situation in the West Bank*, Jerusalem, 13 March.

Levi, H. (1979) "Capital structure, inflation and the price of capital in Israeli industry, 1964–1978," in Hebrew, discussion paper no. 795, Jerusalem: Maurice Falk Institute of Economic Research.

—— (1981) "Capital structure, inflation and the price of capital in Israeli industry from 1964 to 1978," in Hebrew, research paper no. 122, Jerusalem: Maurice Falk Institute of Economic Research.

Lewin-Epstein, N. (1989) "Labor market position and antagonism toward Arabs in Israel," *Research in Inequality and Social Conflict* 1: 165–91.

Lewin-Epstein, N. and Semoyanov, M. (1994) "Sheltered labor markets, public sector employment, and socioeconomic returns to education of Arabs in Israel," *American Journal of Sociology* 100: 622–5.

Looney, R. E. (1989) "Oil revenues and viable development: impact of the Dutch disease on Saudi diversification efforts," *American Arab Affairs* 27: 29–36.

—— (1989) "Saudi Arabia's development strategy: comparative advantage versus sustainable growth," *Orient* 30: 75–96.

—— (1991) "Budgetary priorities in Saudi Arabia: the impact of relative austerity measures on human capital formation," *OPEC Review* 15(2), summer: 133–52.

—— (1992) "Real or illusory growth in an oil-based economy: government expenditures and private sector investment in Saudi Arabia," *World Development* 20: 1367–76.

—— (1995) "A post-Keynesian assessment of alternative Saudi Arabian austerity strategies," *Kuwait University Journal of the Social Sciences* 23(3), autumn: 251–73.

Looney, R. E. and Frederiksen, P. C. (1985) "The evolution and evaluation of Saudi Arabian economic planning," *Journal of South Asian and Middle Eastern Studies* 9: 3–19.

Mackie, A. (1995) *Electricity in the Middle East: Plugging in the Power Gap*, London: Financial Times Press.

Masoud, S. (1984) *Directory of Arab Joint Ventures*, Kuwait: International Center for Public Enterprises in Developing Countries.

Melman, S. (1985) *The Permanent War Economy: American Capitalism in Decline*, New York: Simon & Schuster.

Melnick, R. (1988) "Two aspects of the demand for money in Israel, 1970–1981," *Bank of Israel Economic Review* 60, January: 36–51.

—— (1995) "Financial services, co-integration, and the demand for money in Israel," *Journal of Money, Credit, and Banking* 27(1), February: 140–53.

Meltzer, J. (1992) "The Arab economies in mandatory Palestine and in the administered territories," *Economic Development and Cultural Change*: 844–65.

Merhav, M. (1989) *Economic Cooperation and Middle East Peace*, London: Weidenfeld & Nicolson.

Migdal, J. S. (1989) "The crystallization of the state and the struggles over rule-making: Israel in comparative perspective," in B. Kimmerling (ed.) *The Israeli State and Society. Boundaries and Frontiers*, New York: State University of New York Press.

Mintz, A. (1984) "The military-industrial complex: the Israeli case," in M. Lissak (ed.) *Israeli Society and its Defense Establishment*, London: Frank Cass.

Mishal, S., Semoyanov, M. and Gabbay, S. M. (1997) *Economic Entrepreneurship in an Era of Peace*, Israel: Chaim Herzog Center for Middle East Studies and Diplomacy, Ben Gurion University.

Nagi, M. H. (1982) "Development with unlimited supplies of capital: the case of OPEC," *Developing Economies* xx: 1–19.

Nakhjavani, M. and Nitzan, J. (1994) "From flywheel to fanbelt: the growing importance of emerging markets," *Emerging Markets Analyst* 3(8), December: 6–12.

Nitzan, J. (1992) "Inflation as restructuring: a theoretical and empirical account of the US experience," unpublished doctoral dissertation, Montreal: Department of Economics, McGill University.

—— (1994) "The Israeli defense industry: a peace dividend for stock pickers?" *Emerging Markets Analyst* 3(1): 8–9.

—— (1996) "Israel and South Africa: prospects for their transitions," *Emerging Markets Analyst* 4(10): 12–18.

Nitzan, J. and Bichler, S. (1995) "Bringing capital accumulation back in: the weapondollar–petrodollar coalition – military contractors, oil companies and Middle-East 'energy conflicts,'" *Review of International Political Economy* 2(3): 446–515.

Odeh, B. J. (1985) *Lebanon: Dynamics of Conflict*, London: Zed Books.

Oslo II, Art. XIII, para 2(a), and Art. XII, para 1.

Owen, R. (ed.) (1976) *Essays on the Crisis in Lebanon*, London: Ithaca Press.

—— (1992) *Power and Politics in the Making of the Modern Middle East*, New York: Routledge.

Palestinian Bureau of Statistics (1996) *Demographic Survey 1995*, June 2.

Palestinian Central Bureau of Statistics (1995) *Labor Force Survey*, September/October 1995 round.

Peres, S. (1993) *The New Middle East*, New York: Henry Holt & Company.

Peri, Y. (1983) *Between Battles and Ballots: Israeli Military in Politics*, Cambridge University Press, Cambridge.

Robinson, G. E. (1993) "The role of the professional middle class in the mobilization of Palestinian society: the medical and agricultural communities," *International Journal of Middle East Studies* 25(2), May: 301–26.

Robinson, J. (1962) *Economic Philosophy*, Harmondsworth: Penguin.

Rowley, R., Bichler, S. and Nitzan, J. (1988) "Some aspects of aggregate concentration in the Israeli economy, 1964–1986," working paper, Montreal: Department of Economics, McGill University.

Roy, S. (1991) "The political economy of despair: changing political and economic realities in the Gaza Strip," *Journal of Palestine Studies* 20(3), spring: 58–69.

—— (1994) "Separation or integration: closure and the economic future of the Gaza Strip revisited," *Middle East Journal* 48(1), winter: 11–30.

246

—— (1995) *The Gaza Strip: The Political Economy of De-development*, Washington, DC: Institute for Palestine Studies.

—— (1995) "Beyond Hamas: Islamic activism in the Gaza Strip," *Harvard Middle Eastern and Islamic Review*, 2: 1–39.

Sadan, E. (1985) "National security and national economy," in Hebrew, in Z. Lanir (ed.) *Israeli Security Planning in the 1980s: Its Politics and Economics*, Tel Aviv: Tel Aviv University, The Jaffee Centre for Strategic Studies, Ministry of Defense.

Sadowski, Y. (1988) *Egypt's Islamic Movement: A New Political and Economic Force*, Washington, DC: Brookings Institution

Sagi, E. and Sheinin, Y. (1994) "Opportunities for trade with Arab countries," in Hebrew, *Economic Quarterly* 41(1), April: 15–27.

Salibi, K. (1988) *A House of Many Mansions: The History of Lebanon Reconsidered*, Berkeley, CA: University of California Press.

—— (1993) *The Modern History of Jordan*, New York: I. B. Tauris.

Sampson, A. (1977) *The Arms Bazaar. From Lebanon to Lockheed*, New York: Viking Press.

Scherer, F. M. and Ross, D. (1990) *Industrial Market Structure and Economic Performance*, 3rd edition, Boston, MA: Houghton Mifflin.

Schofield, R. (ed.) (1994) *Territorial Foundation in the Gulf States*, London: UCL Press for the University of London School of Oriental and African Studies.

Shaban, R. A. and Al-Botmeh, S. M. (1995) *Poverty in the West Bank and Gaza*, Jerusalem: Palestine Research and Economic Policy Research Institute (MAS), Jerusalem.

Shahar, B., Fishelson, H. G. and Hirsch, S. (1989) *Economic Cooperation and Middle East Peace*, London: Weidenfeld & Nicolson.

Shami, 'A. (1981) *tatawwur at-tabaqah al-'amilah fi al-ra'smaliyyah al-Lubnaniyyah al-mu'asirah* [The development of the working class within contemporary Lebanese capitalism], Beirut: dar al-Farabi.

Shapiro, Y. (1977) *The Democracy in Israel*, in Hebrew, Ramat Gan: Massada.

—— (1984) *An Elite Without Successors: Generations of Political Leaders in Israel*, in Hebrew, Tel Aviv: Sifriat Poalim.

Sharkansky, I. (1987) *The Political Economy of Israel*, New Brunswick, NJ: Transaction Books.

Shehadi, N. and Harney, B. (eds.) (1989) *Politics and the Economy in Lebanon*, Oxford: Centre for Lebanese Studies.

Smith, A. (1937) *An Inquiry into the Nature and Causes of the Wealth of Nations*, New York: Modern Library.

Smith, R. P. (1977) "Military expenditure and capitalism," *Cambridge Journal of Economics* 1(1), March: pp. 61–7.

Smooha, S. (1980) "Existing and alternative policy towards the Arabs in Israel," *Megamot* 36(7): 169–206.

"Special Supplement to Annex V: Protocol on Economic Relations, Israeli–Palestinian Interim Agreement" (1995) *Palestine Report*, December: 15–25.

Sullivan, D. (1998) "International aid and the peace process: the Palestinian Authority vs. civil society," J. W. Wright, Jr. (ed.) *Economic and Political Impediments to Middle East Peace: Structural Flaws and Crucial Failures in the Process*, London: Macmillan.

Sweezy, P. M. (1972) *Modern Capitalism and Other Essays*, New York: Monthly Review Press.

Tawney, R. H. (1926) *Religion and the Rise of Capitalism*, New York: Harcourt Brace.

Tibi, B. and Tschirgi, D. (1991) "Perspectives on the Gulf crisis," *Cairo Papers in Social Science* 14: 1–95.

United Nations Security Council, Resolution 425, March 19, 1978.

Usher, G. (1995) "Palestinian trade unions and the struggle for independence," *Middle East Report*, May–June/July–August: 20–1.

Wilson, R. (1994) "The economic relations of the Middle East: toward Europe or within the region?," *Middle East Journal* 48: 268–87.

—— (1998) "Will the peace process bring portfolio investment flows into the Middle East?," in J. W. Wright, Jr. and L. Drake (eds.) *Economic and Political Impediments to Middle East Peace: Critical Questions and Alternative Scenarios*, London: Macmillan.

Wolkinson, B. W. (1989) "Equal employment opportunities for Israeli Arab citizens," discussion paper no. 48, Tel Aviv: Golda Meir Institute for Social and Labor Research, Tel Aviv University

World Bank (1994) *World Development Report*, New York: Oxford University Press.

—— (1995) *Will Arab Workers Prosper or Be Left Out in the Twenty-first Century? Regional Perspectives on World Development Report*, Washington, DC: World Bank.

Wright, A. (1995) "Are Middle Eastern banks safe?," *International Journal of Commerce and Management* 5(3): 90–105.

Wright, J. W., Jr. (1995) *Islamic Banking in Practice: Problems in Jordan and Saudi Arabia*, University of Durham Centre for Middle Eastern and Islamic Studies Occasional Papers Series, no. 48, May.

—— (1995) "American trade and Islamic banking in the Israeli occupied territories," *International Journal of Commerce and Management* 5(4): 71–94.

—— (ed.) (1996) *Business and Economic Development in Saudi Arabia*, London: Macmillan.

—— (ed.) (1999) *Economic and Political Impediments to Middle East Peace: Structural Flaws and Crucial Failures in the Process*, London: Macmillan.

Wright, J. W., Jr. and Drake, L. (eds.) (1999) *Economic and Political Impediments to Middle East Peace: Critical Questions and Alternative Scenarios*, London: Macmillan.

Yatziv, G. (1979) *The Class Basis for Party Association: The Example of Israel*, in Hebrew, Jerusalem: Department of Sociology, Hebrew University.

Zanoyan, V. (1995) "After the oil boom," *Foreign Affairs* 74(6), November/December: 2–7.

Zaucker, J., Griffel, A. and Gubser, P. (1995) "Toward Middle East peace and development," InterAction occasional paper, December.

Zureik, E., Mougrabi, F. and Sacco, V. F. (1993) "Perceptions of legal inequalities in deeply divided societies: the case of Israel," *International Journal of Middle East Studies* 25(3): 423–42.

INDEX

111, 231, 238; *see also* economic cooperation

economic services: Saudi expenditure 210, *212*, 213, 214, 215, *216*, 217, 225

economic structures: Arab countries and global markets 238; Israel 5, 44, 48, 77–8, 80–93, 110

economics: crime and welfare 42; diplomacy 41, 45, 65; disaggregate route of political economy 73; impediments to peace process; incentives and the peace process 64, 233; inequalities 3–4, 6, 42, 43, 45, 47, 48, 87, 109–25, 124, 237; and morality 7, 42; and the nation-state 75–6; relationship with politics 1, 4, 19, 23, 42, 64; separation from politics 48–9, 73, 77, 82; *see also* aggregate approach; macroeconomic approach; microeconomic approach

Economics, Peace and Laughter (Galbraith) 3, 42

economies: Arab countries 25, 238; Arab fears of Israeli domination 14–15, 17, 22, 27, 155, 235; Israel's transformation since end of 1980s 73–5, 91–3, 96–101; Lebanon 183–7, 188, 194, 198; militarization of Israel 5, 6, 59–60, 73, 74–5, 78, 79, 80, 82, 88–9, 90, 92–3, 97, 98, 100, 196; Palestinian 136–7, 138, 140–1; parallels between Israel and U.S. 74, 75, 79–80; Saudi Arabia 5, 6, 104, 203–25; Soviet Union 228, 229; Syria 194; U.S. decline 79, 237–8

Ecuador: Israeli export of arms to 88

education: benefits of military service to Israel 116; competition between Arabs and Israelis for access 125; differences in achievement of Jews and Arabs 111, 114, 115; discrimination against Arabs in resource allocation 116, 119, 135; Gulf States 53; impact of Israeli closure policies 145–7; Israeli superiority 22; Lebanese–Syrian regional cooperation 199; Palestinian NGOs 61; Saudi expenditure 214

Egypt, Egyptians: benefits of USAID funds 59; borders with Palestinian self-rule areas 130; concepts of new Middle East 16; conflict between government and people regarding peace 28, 33; decline in economic growth 56, 235; decline in wages 53; and electricity grid project 21, 160–1, 162; importance of economic integration for peace 235; infrastructure development projects 155; labor force growth rate 52; natural gas resources 157, 166; and normalization of relations with Israel 11, 29, 33; Palestinian imports from 50; peace agreements with Israel 25, 27–8, 33, 155, 166, 169, 183; and Peace Pipeline Project 166–7, 174; potential markets for Israel 23; as pro-Western 96; public opinion on water supply proposals 19; relationship with Israel 17, 28, 102n, 172; restriction of citizens visiting Israel 30; reversal of moves toward liberalism 231; role in Hebron agreement 172; support of Allied effort against Iraq 227; trade alliances 2; and U.S. defense firms 60

Eilat (Israel) 161, 174

Eisenstadt, S. N.: *Israeli Society* 113

El Al 21

elections: Israel (1996) 45, 169, 172

electoral systems: Israel 125; and market economies 231

electricity: grid project 21, 160, 160–3, 169, 170, 171, 174, 231; Lebanese–Syrian regional cooperation 199; rehabilitation of utilities in Lebanon 189, 191

Electrode Factory (Gaza) 144

elites: Arab 75, 113, 116; benefits of aid funds 64, 124; inequitable concentration of wealth 47, 87; intellectuals' resistance to Arab–Israeli normalization 26; Israeli 6, 44, 46, 75, 77, 81, 82, 87, 92, 93, 100, 108n, 109, 114, 124; Lebanon 192–3, 199; Saudi Arabia 204; successes of Arab–Israeli cooperation 25; U.S. support of 46

Elmusa, Sharif 49

Elron 90, 107n

employment: Arabs' dependence on Jewish-owned concerns 117; benefits of military service to Israel 116; creation through economic cooperation 49, 65; PA patronage in Gaza 63; Palestinian transfers outside territories 51; and promotion of peace 48; restrictions on

Oxford Institute for Energy Studies 164

Palestine Liberation Organization (PLO)
60, 148n, 197, 238n; in Beirut 197;
support of Iraq against Kuwait 227;
talks with Israel 131, 183
Palestine, Palestinians: air transportation
235; banks in 1920s 106n; boycott on
Israeli goods 49, 98; British mandate
rule 185; Chamber of Commerce 144;
clashes between youths and Israeli
forces 51; community in Lebanon 192,
196–8; decline of banking system 54;
decline of business and investment 60,
139, 141–2, 144, 147; degeneration of
civil society 237; dependence on aid
56, 148; detentions 46, 47, 63, 132,
137; Diaspora 50, 51; dispossession of
after creation of Israel 236; economic
booms 80, 84; economic effects of
Israeli occupation 50–1, 64, 98, 106n,
133, 134, 136, 147–8; economic
inequalities 46, 47, 48, 82, 237;
economic subordination to Israel 44,
49, 50–1, 106n, 136–40, 141–2, 144;
effect of competing trade agendas 64;
effect of Israeli human rights violations
6; effect of Israeli occupation on
agriculture 51, 136; effects of closures
by Israel 44, 64, 110, 128, 129–30,
133, 134–5, 137, 138, 139, 140, 141,
142–3, 145–8; effects of defeat by
Israel in 1948 war 115; experience
with Israeli peace 33; expulsion of
resistance movements from Jordan
197; failure of development of capital
markets 56, 60; geographic centrality
and functions 20; geographical
replacement by Israel 27;
implementation of self-rule (1994)
128, 130, 131, 132, 135; importance
of economic integration for peace 235;
income via employment transfers
outside 51; inequality and poverty 46,
47, 48, 51, 82, 98, 140, 147–8;
investment from Gulf entrepreneurs
52; Israeli exploitation of water
reserves 18, 51, 106n; Israeli
occupation of territories 49, 61, 82,
98, 128, 130–2, 147, 169; Israeli
restrictions on movement 30, 128,
129, 133, 134, 142–4; Israeli

withdrawals from territory 169; Jewish
investment 110; labor force and
markets 6, 24, 45, 49, 52, 55, 61, 64,
82, 84–5, 97–8, 115, 133, 138, 147,
156; likely effect of repatriation 53–4,
54–5; mistaken idea of peace as
alleviating poverty 27; monetary
control problems 57, 58–9; National
Charter 238n; negotiations with Peres
12; non-compliance regarding Oslo
Accords 170; opposition to peace
treaty with Israel 28; and Peace
Pipeline project 166, 167, 174; pre-
1948 Arab majority 115; problems of
social services provision 61–2, 63–4,
65; proletarianization 82, 84; refugees
6, 31, 48, 184, 196–8, 229, 236; and
regional cooperation with Lebanon
192; relations with Jews in Israel 114,
124; relationship with Israel 24, 33,
65, 97, 169, 169–71; residency
restrictions and land-ownership
prohibitions 31, 106n; scenario of
genuinely independent state 48–9;
security concerns 167; statelessness 22;
trade regulations imposed on 50,
136–7; unemployment 55, 62–3, 98,
134, 138, 139–40, 141, 147
Palestinian Authority (PA) 4, 230;
agreements with Israel 196; Civil
Affairs Coordination Committee 135;
conflict and corruption in organization
of funds 48, 57–8, 60–4, 65, 128;
crackdown on Islamic groups 63–4;
failure to solve refugee problem in
Lebanon 197, 199; human-rights
violations by 6, 51, 128; inability to
assist needy population 140–1, 148;
inability to prevent Hamas attacks 32;
increased powers for setting trade
agendas 49–50; insufficient
international assistance to 128, 139,
140, 141; and Peace Pipeline project
167; powerlessness to end Israeli
control 130; theoretical powers in self-
rule areas 130, 131; vested interests in
resisting peace settlement 41
Palestinian Businessmen's Association
137, 144
Palestinian Council 131–2, 148n
Palestinian Council for Higher Education
146

INDEX

wars 78, 79; large companies and corporations 74, 79; as major market for Israeli exports 24, 73; merger waves 96; Middle East interests and policies 43, 169, 173; military bias of economy 79–80, 88, 92; military exports to Middle East 43, 59–60, 79–80, 91, 97; military Keynesianism 74, 79; Palestinian efforts to compete with for investment 59; presence in UN 237; promotion of Turkish solution to Israeli–Syrian water problem 19; recent referenda 44; relations with Arab countries 45; role in Gulf war 237; technology for exploitation of gas 165; war economy 78–9
universities: Gulf States 53; Israeli restrictions on Palestinian access 132, 133, 145–7
Urdan 90
USAID (U.S. Agency for International Development) 40–1, 59, 60
Uzzi, B.D. 159–60

variance decomposition analysis: Saudi defence expenditure 217, *218, 219, 220*
Veblen, T. 78
Vebudplan (company) 161
Vietnam: American involvement in war 78, 79, 80
violence: clashes in occupied territories 129
Volkswagen (company) 99
voters: influence of perceptions and prejudices 44, 45, 64

wages: decline in Levant 53; erosion in Israel 92, 115; inequality between Jews and Arabs in Israel 110, 114, 115, 118–19, 120–1, 122–3, 138; Palestinian losses and the economy 140, 147; Palestinian workers 82, 138
Wall Street 27
Wallerstein, Immanuel 22
Walton, Michael 53–4
war: atomic 228; and economic cooperation in Europe 175, 233; following creation of Israel (1948) 115, 197; involvement of populace 25; long

history of in Middle East 156; state of 11; *see also* civil war; cold war; Gulf war; Second World War
war economy: Israel 40, 73, 74–5, 80, 90, 93, 94, 96, 97, 98, 230; U.S.A. 78–9, 80
Warsaw Pact countries: collapse of communism 228
water: Israeli diversion of supplies and restrictions on occupied areas 18, 51, 65, 106n, 136, 195; Lebanese–Syrian regional cooperation 199; proposals for economic cooperation 18–19, 22–3; rehabilitation of supplies in Lebanon 189, 199
The Wealth of Nations (Smith) 234
welfare: and crime 42; Israeli obligations toward Palestinians 132–3, 147, 148; recent U.S. referendum on reform 44; Saudi Arabia 225; and sustainable peace 4
Wertheimer, Stephen 107n
West Bank 35n, 115; curfew periods 134; effect of import regulations 50; effect of permit system on trade 136, 137, 142; effects of border closures by Israel 110, 142; effects of occupation on economic development 3–4, 128–48; governing authority of PA 61; impacts of closures on education 145–7; introduction of self-rule 130; Islamic groups 63; Israeli citizens in 110; Israeli control of financial markets 60, 97; Israeli diversion of water from 18, 51; Israeli expropriation of land 51, 98; Israeli failure to withdraw military forces from self-rule areas 130; Israeli obligations toward residents under humanitarian law 132–3, 147; Israeli occupation 49, 50, 61, 82, 84, 124–8, 130–2, 134, 142–3, 147; Palestinian cheap labor 24, 97; Palestinians and intermarriage 31; poverty 47, 140, 147–8; proposals for water supply 19; refugees in 47, 196; restrictions on movement of goods 142–4; restrictions on movement of residents 128, 129–30; settlements 12; unemployment 55, 62, 139–40, 141; workers in Israel 138, 142
Western Desert: natural gas 166
Wilson, George 7

271